CW01426338

First Edition 2012

Edited by George Stimson

Cover art by Dietrich Maerz

B&D Publishing, LLC
PO Box 652
Richmond, MI 48062
www.ironcross1939.com

Printed in China
ISBN: 978-0-9823146-6-1

The AWARDS of the HEER

Volume I

by
Dietrich Maerz/Bernd Hartmann

Contrary to his counterpart of August 1914, the German soldier entered Hitler's war in September 1939 with less patriotic feelings. The early successes of the *Blitzkrieg* era, however, soon instilled a great deal of confidence in him, as this famous photograph shows.

TABLE OF CONTENTS

VOLUME I

FOREWORD

This book documents all of the decorations which could be awarded to soldiers of the German Army during the Second World War.

In order to revise the 1945-instituted prohibition of wearing war decorations, and also in the face of the pending creation of the new German Bundeswehr with former soldiers of the Wehrmacht, the West German government appointed an expert committee in 1953. In a report released in the autumn of that year, the committee recommended the allowance of the wearing of the awards of the Second World War, but with removed swastikas. The board reasoned the proposal as follows:

> *"The deeds of the awarded soldiers cannot be connected to the political goals the NS regime pursued with the war."*

This reasoning led to the "Law About Titles and Awards" of 26. July 1957 which included permission to wear war decorations. One of the inherent goals of this law was to legitimize the honorable roll of the common, non-political soldiers during World War Two.

In performing their military duties, the regular German soldiers (like all soldiers on all sides of the conflict) were convinced that they were fighting for the life of their Fatherland and therefore fought for a good and just cause. And because of that fact their awards (to use the title of a period source) were indeed *Der Lohn der Tat* ("The Award of the Deed").

Universal human decency requires us to regard these awards, which were earned with much effort and pain, with respect. And the great interest in these awards today by collectors from all over the world supports this position.

Therefore, we are proud to present the expanded and updated English version of this heretofore German language-only book. We hope the readers will enjoy it as much as it was our pleasure to put it together.

June 2012

Bernd Hartmann — Dietrich Maerz

ACKNOWLEDGMENTS

No book in this hobby can be done without the help of fellow collectors. In the age of the Internet and e-mail, this circle of friends becomes ever larger which has a positive influence on the contents of the book projects. It is always amazing to experience the willingness to help and to contribute to the effort. The authors extend their deepest gratitude to the collectors and dealers listed below, as well as all the unnamed supporters and friends.

Arndt, Oliver
Brücker, Bastian
Bernecker, Manfred
Brüggemann, Kay Max
Burmeister, Jason
Durante, Thomas
Distelhorst, Dr. Ron
Eiffler, Markus
Falk, Michael
Garlasco, Marc E.
Gaspar, COL Michael
Gminder, Prof. Dr. Rolf
Grünbaum, Daniel
Hardin, Neil
Hatton, Marcus
Hermann Historica OHG
Heukemes, Frank
Hritz, Bob
Huckfield, Kevin
Jablonskis, Tony
Jordt, Alex
Kiuss, Thomas
Lobbe, Michael
Lozancic, George
Miller, Mark
Niewiarowicz, Ken
Orchard, Simon
Peters, Mike & Lisa
Pilch, Allan
Rackete, Hans-Dieter
Romani, Carlo
Saul, Arran
Schneider, Dirk
Sierra, Ramon
Stimson, George
Takiguchi, Akira
Thies, Andreas
von Renz, Alexander
Weber, Sascha
Weitze, Helmut
Winkler, Kai
Wolfe, Steve
Wöschler, Sascha
Zahn, Willi

INTRODUCTION

This book sees itself in the long tradition of the series of publications started by Dr. Heinrich Doehle with his fourth edition of the title *Die Auszeichnungen des Grossdeutschen Reichs*. While Dr. Doehle presented all orders and medals of the Third Reich, this book limits itself to the decorations a soldier of the German *Heer* could be awarded in the time frame between 1. September 1939 and 8. May 1945.

Apart from "The Doehle," which was most likely in the hands of early post-war collectors in Germany, and the periodicals *Uniformen-Mark*t and *Schwert und Spaten*, there were not many reliable sources of information on German awards available immediately after the war. Allied soldiers who had fought in Germany brought home many souvenirs, including all kinds of orders and medals. It was easy for occupation soldiers to trade cigarettes for such "Nazi memorabilia." In the awards manufacturing town of Lüdenscheid, for example, special cardboards with medals were put together and supplied to occupation forces as so-called "salesman sample boards" (below).

Clearly, the leftover stocks of awards makers' wares were still quite ample. And this applied not only to orders and medals, but also to a lot of other materials such as swords, daggers, caps, uniforms, insignia, weapons - indeed everything that had been needed to supply the German armed forces in which about 17 million soldiers had served during the war.

But the stocks were not always filled with finished products. Sometimes only parts were left over, but these could be easily assembled to a final product. Sometimes, as was the case with the late post-war B-type Steinhauer & Lück Knights Crosses, new parts were made and used, either with original dies or newly made ones.

And nobody thought bad of it! The Germans supplied Allied soldiers with what they wanted to have, and there was no difference for anybody between an "old" or "new" Infantry Assault Badge. It was a German badge, it had a swastika, and it was a desired souvenir.

Certainly the majority of the medals, daggers, pistols, and such of this period were genuine and made before 8. May 1945. This was due to the huge quantity of material produced during the war which was now no longer of any immediate use and thus available. But it is important to realize that there was a transition process from genuine objects over to partially genuine objects and finally to completely newly made ones. For certain memorabilia the transition time might have been longer, reaching up into the 1970s, but for some rarer items (such as the Knights Cross), it was clearly shorter. This process was always demand-driven, and that demand came from the occupation forces, especially from the US soldiers.

Above: A Soviet soldier cleans the steps of the *Reichskanzlei* of hundreds of cased *Treuedienst-Ehrenzeichen*, remnants of the *Präsidialkanzlei*.

It is also useful to know that most of the early collectors of German militaria were located in the United States and that they built up much of their collections out of the souvenir trunks of the WW2 soldiers. The so-called "hotel buys," where dealer/collectors rented hotel rooms and advertised in the local newspapers that they were buying all kinds of war relics for cash, brought in a multitude of material from both the European and Pacific Theaters of Operations.

In the early days, this only source for collectors - "bought directly from a Vet" - was a sure guarantee of originality. It was flat out inconceivable that anything remotely fake or post-war could end up in the hands of a veteran, who brought it back personally.

There was no scientific method employed (or even necessary) to verify anything. The material was available in huge quantities and it was also relatively cheap.

The first serious attempts to categorize the awards and medals of the Third Reich were made in the early 1960s. Before that time, the only references listing the range of available decorations were the price lists of early German dealers such as Mrs. Paetzold, wife of Dr. Kurt-Gerhard Klietmann, with their operation *Ordens-Sammlung* in Berlin, Eduard Schiffer in Bielefeld, who used Steinhauer & Lück as a supplier and Friedrich Sedlatzek, who marketed old and new material, mainly from Rudolf Souval/Wien.

The book *Deutsche Auszeichnungen* by Dr. Kurt-Gerhard Klietmann (1971) was the first book in Germany in a series of publications which tried to categorize the orders and medals of the Third Reich together with some information regarding award criteria and regulations.

First steps in the UK and the USA were made by Ailsby, Littlejohn, Angolia, Pia and others. Bender Publishing in California was a true pioneer in publishing outstanding references and still today publishes highly educational books.

However, most of these books (if not all) omitted the fact of multiple makers and variations and only gave a genuine representation of the order, medal or badge in question. This left the collector with a lot of unanswered questions ("Why does my Panzer Assault Badge look different?", "Why has my badge a stamped number?"). The only early exception was Vern E. Bowen's book *The Prussian and German Iron Cross*, self-published in 1986. Bowen was the first one who really tried to write a coherent history of the order and the medals themselves. Apart from some omissions, misinterpretations and partially false informations, the work itself stands as a monumental undertaking during that pre-Internet time, full with high value and indispensable information.

When the Internet became more and more a medium for collectors worldwide to exchange informations not only in written form via e-mail but also in the form of discussions with detail photographs and previously unpublished documents, the flow of information increased exponentially. The collectors became aware of the fact that there is more than just one maker for a specific order or badge and that the earlier rules, like "the swastika has to be rim high," are neither sufficient nor correct to describe a genuine piece.

Some authors, like Gordon Williamson, realized that the need for a kind of categorizing or detailed description of variations was needed and his book *The Iron Cross of 1939* was a start in this direction. In Germany, Jörg Nimmergut produced his series *Deutsche Orden und Ehrenzeichen* between 1997 and 2004. The decisive step to monographs, meaning the realization that it is necessary to cover one specific badge or order within only one book

was taken by Sascha Weber, Germany, in 2004 and more thoroughly by Frank Heukemes, Germany, in 2005, followed by equally dedicated authors producing equally important books, covering only one badge or order, but in depth and with the goal to possibly list all variations.

This concentration on monographs has reinvigorated the hobby and has created a new

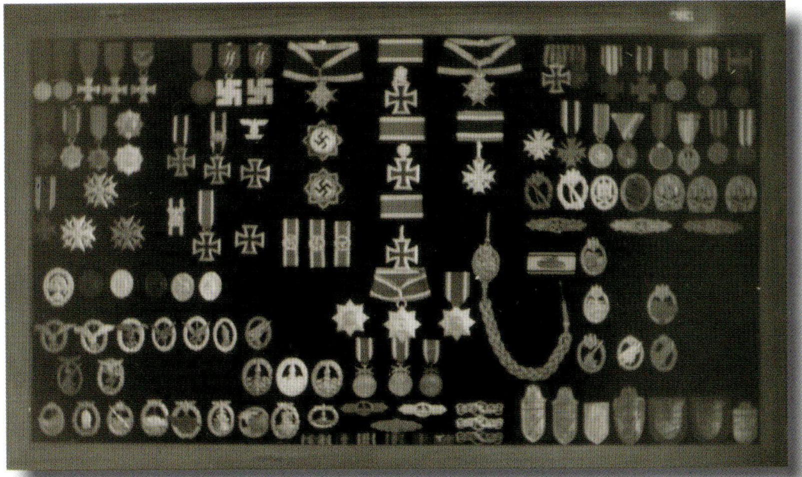

Above: Photograph of a "one each" US-collection of the mid 1960s.

breed of collector. The very first collector generation wanted to have "one each" in order to display the whole range of Third Reich orders and badges. Now the collecting world concentrates more and more on one badge with the goal to collect all makers and sub-variations of this particular award. The picture below shows such a collection.

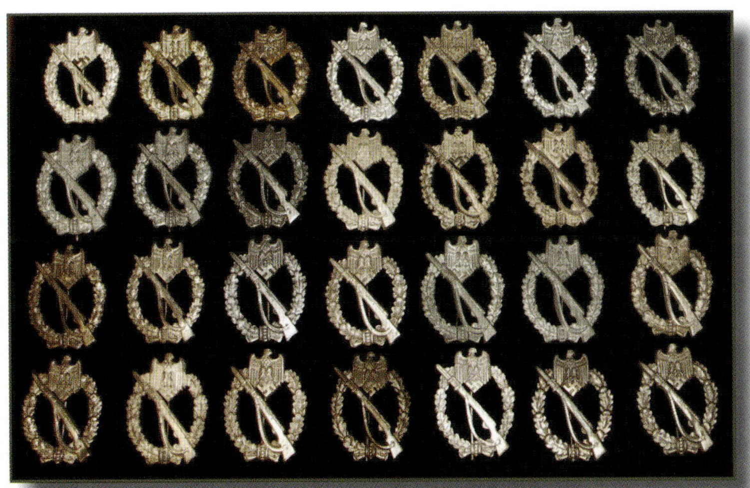

Since the first of these serious monographs were authored in 2004 a great deal of such books have been published ranging from the orders of the Knights Cross and German Cross over the popular war badges like the Panzer Assault Badge, Flak Badge and Close Combat Badge up to the War Merit Cross 2. Class and Wound Badges.

This has left a gap between the earlier introductory books and the very specific ones.

Any new collector sees himself confronted with these highly detailed and scientific works and is possibly deterred by the sheer magnitude of knowledge seemingly necessary to even grasp a starting understanding of collecting awards of the Third Reich. He might browse through such a book and might come to the false conclusion that he never ever will be able to sort this all out and then might fall pray to one of the numerous fakes which have infested the market in the last 60 years.

He needs to have a starting point and such a starting point should be a book which presents all the orders and medals which were awarded during the Third Reich. He certainly can fall back to one of the earlier works mentioned, but the information included is no longer up to the standards of the 21st century.

That is why the authors here came to the conclusion that a set of books is needed which give the starting collector a good overview over each award and provides a survey of the amount of variations in order to make a decision, and will also have a fairly comprehensive bibliography to deepen the knowledge. If such a set can even provide the experienced collector with a quick and comprehensive overview about each award, it might be even useful for every collector.

That is why we came up with this two-volume set and that is why we followed a strict framework for each award discussed: history, regulation, design, and so on..., with the goal to cover nearly all aspects of each award, including the 1957 versions. The amount of orders and medals which could possibly be awarded to a member of the German field army (*Heer*) was quite large, which is understandable. Future books covering the awards of the *Luftwaffe* and the *Kriegsmarine* will be less voluminous.

We hope that this first volume in a series of introductory books will be of help to the starting as well as the advanced collector.

German national eagle from the cover of the Oakleaves to the Knights Cross of the Iron Cross award document.

MARKINGS

There are two types of markings that one can find on German orders and medals of the Third Reich. One is a numerical or alpha-numerical stamp indicating the material used. In most of the cases this is in regards to the silver content of a given medal. The known numbers are "800", "900" and "935" and indicate an 80%, 90% and 93.5% minimum content of silver, the balance of material is in most cases copper. The other known marking is "950PT" which stands for 95% platinum content and is found on the reverse of the A-Type of the Oakleaves with Swords and Diamonds to the Knights Cross of the Iron Cross.

Left: Silver content stamp "800" on a Juncker-made Knights Cross.

Right: "900" stamp on the reverse of a 2nd Type set of Oakleaves made by Gebr. Godet.

Left: The silver stamp "935" on a Steinhauer & Lück B-Type Knights Cross.

Right: Platinum content stamp "950PT" on the reverse of a "Diamonds" set, made by Otto Klein, Hanau. The "K in a circle" is the trade mark of the company.

The Golden Oakleaves with Swords and Diamonds were marked with the gold-content stamp "750" (18 karat) for the A-Piece and "585" (14 karat) for the B-Piece (see page 50-51).

The other type of marking indicates the maker of the award, medal or badge. There are two types of maker marks that can be encountered: LDO or PKZ. Before we explain the difference between the two, it should be noted that the lack of any marking is no indication of anything bad. Most of the earlier (approximately pre-spring 1942) orders and medals do not have any stamps at all because the rules and regulations regarding manufacturing quality and traceability of the makers were not yet installed. War badges and proficiency badges also do not have maker marks in most cases since they were not ordered by and distributed via the *Präsidialkanzlei*. For the decorations discussed in this book, this office was only responsible for the Order of the Iron Cross, the Order of the War Merit Cross, the Order of the German Cross and the East Medal. The other war badges fell under the auspices of the OKH.

The introduction of the orders and badges shortly after the beginning of the war was not accompanied by strict regulations regarding the manufacturing quality and the materials to be used during the production process. This, as an example, resulted in the production (and awarding) of Knights Crosses and Iron Crosses with non-iron cores.

On 15. July 1940 the most prominent manufacturers of orders and medals of Germany met at the *Hotel Russischer Hof* in Berlin and under the guidance of Dr. Doehle of the *Präsidialkanzlei* the *Leistungsgemeinschaft Deutscher Ordenshersteller* (LDO) was founded with the task to supervise the manufacturing, packaging and distribution of orders and medals of the Third Reich for the retail market. On 15. March 1941 LDO numbers were assigned to the members of the association and it was required to put the individual marking on any decoration supplied to the retail market. The decorations supplied directly to the *Präsidialkanzlei* or offices of the *Heer, Luftwaffe* and *Kriegsmarine* were not marked with the LDO code.

However, there are quite a few Knights Crosses and Oakleaves with the LDO code "L/12" for C.E. Juncker and "L/50" for Gebr. Godet. They were marked for the retail market after March 1941 and were - based on an order from the *Präsidialkanzlei* forbidding the private sale of these orders - removed from the market and sent to the *Präsidialkanzlei* for subsequent awarding. Due to the evidently large number of Knights Crosses recalled from the market end of 1941 there was no immediate need for restocking at the *Präsidialkanzlei* and only in early to mid 1944 PKZ-marked and awarded Knights Crosses and Oakleaves ("2", "20", "65" and "21") started to appear, followed by the last marked Knights Crosses with a "4" for Steinhauer & Lück. This observation led to the false assumption, which is still held true in some uninformed circles, that the *Präsidialkanzlei* numbers were introduced in mid 1944. As always in science and research one has to take a broader view and look at other orders and medals for additional evidence. The investigation into the German Cross and the East Medal shows that the *Präsidialkanzlei* numbers were introduced and used most likely from late 1942/early 1943 onwards. This is also in accordance with state-

ments from a contemporary witness, Mr. Preiss, who was the Vice-President of Steinhauer & Lück during the war.[1]

As a general rule (outside of the German Cross and Knights Cross of the Iron Cross and higher grades) any decoration with a PKZ number was either awarded or was in storage to be awarded. Any badge with an LDO number was a privately bought example or a piece intended to be sold within the private retail sector.

It is also important to note that there is no difference in parts used, manufacturing itself or finish between any orders and medals shipped to the *Präsidialkanzlei* or to any army offices and those to be sold in shops for private retail. The same dies and materials and finishes had to be used and were actually used in both cases.

The *Präsidialkanzlei* under the direction of *Unterstaatssekretär* und *SS-Oberführer* Dr. Doehle had to approve every order, badge and medal before the production could start and that office was also in charge of giving permission to manufacture and sell orders and medals for the private retail market. The information about such a permission was given to the LDO and this organization issued the LDO number for the previously approved company.[2] It would be a misconception to see the LDO as a separate institution - it was only in charge of the enforcement of the manufacturing rules and quality requirements for the

Right and below: A Deumer EK1 and two reverses below. They are identical save the marking. One is the PKZ number "3", the other one the LDO "L/11".

private market. The actual rules and requirements always came from the PKZ, the LDO was a subordinate institution.

It is therefore wrong to speak of "issue types" in connection with PKZ-numbered examples and of "Deluxe type" for those with an LDO-number. It is also wrong to say that LDO-marked examples would be "jeweller's copies." It might very well be that there was the occasional hand-made example (like Knights Crosses or Oakleaves made on board of a submarine or the Japanese-made Iron Crosses First Class), but to use this description for pieces which are not in accordance to the regulated and controlled examples of the Third Reich is wrong and is - in most cases - a synonym for fake or reproduction. Furthermore, the unauthorized fabrication of any orders and awards was punishable under the law "Title, Orders and Decorations" of 1. July 1937. This law was later extended on 3. May 1942 to include all war badges of the *Wehrmacht*.[3]

The majority of the war and proficiency Badges are not marked with a PKZ- or LDO-number. A great many, however, bear the logo or name of the manufacturer. A list of prominent manufacturer's logos can be found in the Infantry Assault Badge chapter. The badges which do not show any manufacturers's logo were for very long times categorized as "unknown" and sometimes even as fake (and some surely are fakes).

The immensely increased information flow via the Internet coupled with exchange of pictures and observations has allowed researchers to determine the maker of previously unassigned badges by means of comparing die features, production methods and hardware used. Some maker assignments are still provisional, some are heavily disputed, but the majority has been accepted as correct based on reasonable evidence and sound reasoning.

Unfortunately the fact, that a "badge with a maker name" can be sold with higher profits (since it is assumed that the assignment to a possible maker is a sure sign of originality), has led to a new trend in the hobby: a sometimes seemingly pathological fear of not having a maker assigned to an unknown maker badge with the result, that a maker will be assigned with the sometimes hair-raising and far-fetched argumentation.

The important feature of an order or a war or proficiency badge is not the maker but its undoubted originality. The past of the hobby has shown that time and research will produce the correct and resilient results. Patience is one of the virtues required when one indulges in this fascinating hobby.

1: *Orden und Militaria Journal* No. 26, 3. Jahrgang, September 1977, page 740.
2: Dietrich Maerz, *The Knights Cross of the Iron Cross*, page 55
3: *Reichsgesetzblatt Nr. 49/1942*

A *Feldwebel* of the infantry in a ditch on the Eastern Front. He wears the Iron Cross 1. Class 1939, the Infantry Assault Badge in Bronze and the Wound Badge in Black. The ribbon bar shows the Iron Cross 2. Class, the 4 Year Long Service Award and the West Wall Medal.

Chapter 1

The Order of the Iron Cross

Leutnant Willi Heinrich of *1/PzAbt Führer-Grenadier-Brigade* received the Knights Cross on 9. December, 1944.

Table of Contents

THE ORDER OF THE IRON CROSS

HISTORY

The Iron Cross of 1813

On March 10, 1813 the Prussian King Friedrich Wilhelm II founded the Iron Cross for the duration of the Liberation War against the occupation of the French Emperor Napoleon. The decoration of the Iron Cross was a bravery and merit award (*Ehrenzeichen*) in the grades Iron Cross Second Class, Iron Cross First Class, Grand Cross, and the so-called Iron Cross with Golden Rays. The King himself designed the cross and the final artistic design was done by the famous architect Karl Friedrich Schinkel.

According to the official regulations the obverse of the silver-framed cross was to be blackened and without any inscription. However, even during the Liberation War this regulation was ignored and the reverse of the cross was worn as the front. That original reverse side showed three centrally arranged oak leaves with the king's initials "FW" and the Prussian crown above it. Below the oak leaves the year of the foundation "1813" was cast into the iron core. From the year 1838 on it was left to the awardees which side they preferred as the obverse.

Contrary to the common award practice of that time, the Iron Cross was awarded without any consideration regarding rank or social standing. This principle of equality (remarkably a product of the French revolution) was not without lasting effect on the comradeship between all ranks of the front soldier. Each recipient received an award document.

The Iron Cross Second Class of 1813 was worn on a black ribbon with white stripes. The total number of this class of the order awarded was approximately 16,100. Since about 271,000 soldiers fought for Prussia, roughly every seventeenth soldier received this award. The Second Class Cross with a white ribbon and black stripes was the version for non-fighting participants and was awarded 373 times.

The Iron Cross First Class was to be worn on the left breast side of the uniform. It was awarded 668[1] times, and only two awards of the First Class were made to non-fighting participants. Precondition for the awarding of the First Class was the prior award of the Second Class.

The Grand Cross was larger in size than the First and Second Class and was worn on a ribbon around the neck. It was awarded only five times for outstanding merit in commanding the troops.

The Iron Cross with Golden Rays, as it was called, and which is better known as the

"Blücher Star," was not stipulated in the statutes but was nevertheless created and awarded to the sole recipient *Feldmarschall* Gebhard Leberecht Blücher, Fürst von Wahlstatt for the victory against Napoleon at Waterloo 1815.

Below: The Iron Cross First Class 1813. The obverse is devoid of any inscription, design, or date.

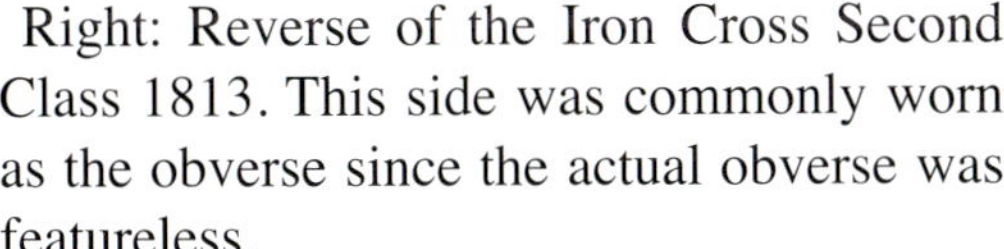

Right: Reverse of the Iron Cross Second Class 1813. This side was commonly worn as the obverse since the actual obverse was featureless.

The Iron Cross of 1870

On July 19, 1870, the day France declared war on Prussia, the Prussian King Wilhelm I reinstituted the Iron Cross, now being an order instead of a decoration (called *Ordenszeichen*, or order emblem). To the up-to-then blank obverse of the 1813 design a "W" with crown and the date "1870" were added. The reverse remained unchanged.

As was the case with the initial version, the Iron Cross of 1870 could be (and was) awarded without any consideration of rank and status to any soldier who had distinguished himself in action, or to those who had achieved other war merits as non-combatants. (However, other awards existed for merit so that the Iron Cross remained mainly a bravery decoration with a high value due to relatively low award numbers.)

King Wilhelm I allowed for the first time the awarding of the Iron Cross to non-Prussian soldiers of other German states. Thus the Iron Cross combined the multiple German states around a higher symbol and gained after the unification of Germany the status of the supreme and undisputable war decoration.

The Iron Cross of 1870 was, contrary to the 1813 version, available in sufficient quantity and in better manufacturing quality due to progress made in production. The recipient also received (like those of the cross of 1813) additional benefits in the form of honorary pay.

The Second Class of the Iron Cross of 1870 on the black ribbon with white stripes was awarded to 43,242 soldiers for bravery. With a total of approximately 600,000 German soldiers, about every fourteenth received the Second Class. The non-combatant version on the white ribbon with black stripes was awarded 4,002 times. The Iron Cross First Class, also with the "W", crown, and date, was awarded to 1,319 soldiers. Prerequisite for the award of the Iron Cross First Class was the earlier awarding of the Second Class of the order.[2]

A total of nine Grand Crosses were awarded, eight to Generals as a sign of appreciation and gratitude and one to the (now German) Emperor Wilhelm I.

Kaiser Wilhelm II, the grandson of *Kaiser* Wilhelm I, awarded on 26. August 1895 to all recipients of the Iron Cross second Class 1870 a silver oak leaf device with the jubilee number "25" which was to be affixed to the black-white ribbon.

Below: The Iron Cross First Class 1870 with the "W" for Wilhelm and the date of institution.

Above: Obverse of the Iron Cross Second Class 1870 which has the same design as the obverse of the First Class.

Right: The proclamation of King Wilhelm of Prussia as German Emperor Wilhelm I on January 18, 1871 in Versailles not only started the Second *Reich* but also elevated the Prussian decoration of the Iron Cross to the future bravery order of the German Empire and subsequently of the Third *Reich*.

The Iron Cross of 1914

After the outbreak of the Great War, *Kaiser* Wilhem II renewed the Order of the Iron Cross again on August 5, 1914. The grades were as before in 1870: the Iron Cross Second Class, the Iron Cross First Class, and the Grand Cross. The design was identical to the previous version, only the date was changed from 1870 to 1914. The reverse remained the same as before.

The Order of the Iron Cross of 1914 was awarded to all members of the German Army, despite its origin as a purely Prussian decoration. From March 16, 1915 on it was also possible to award the order to members of allied forces. The typical cross form also became a national recognition sign on air planes, balloons, and tanks.

Starting in 1915 the prestige of the order began to slide due to the very high award numbers, especially those of the Second Class. Later in the war it became evident that outstanding heroic deeds could no longer be rewarded sufficiently with the Iron Cross. This led to the awarding of the Prussian order *Pour le Mérite* for officers and the *Goldene Militärverdienstmedaille* (Golden Military Merit Medal) to NCOs and regular ranks.

Out of 13.4 million German soldiers who fought during the Great War, approximately 5,196,000 received the Second Class on the black ribbon with white stripes. The non-combatant version was awarded approximately 13,000 times. For former awardees of the Iron Cross of 1870 a repetition clasp in the form of a miniature Iron Cross on a silver bar was created when they earned the Second Class again in the Great War.

The Iron Cross First Class of 1914 was awarded to approximately 218,000 soldiers[3] and a total of five Grand Crosses were given to Generals and to Kaiser Wilhelm II. On March 24, 1918 *Generallfeldmarschall* von Hindenburg received the Iron Cross 1914 with golden rays, also called the *Blücherstern* (and later on the *Hindenburgstern*).

Above: A patriotic print honoring the soldiers of the Franco-Prussian War of 1970 with the newly crowned Kaiser Wilhelm I in the top center and the future Kaiser Wilhelm II to his right and the "99-days Kaiser" Friedrich III to his left.

REGULATIONS

On September 1, 1939, *Reichskanzler* and *Führer* Adolf Hitler renewed the Order of the Iron Cross for the third and last time. This ended the transition from the purely Prussian Order of 1813 and 1970, to the still Prussian but more pan-German Order of 1914, to the highest military decoration of the Greater German Empire, also called the Third *Reich*.

In the very first sentence Hitler makes reference to the initial reason for the 1813 foundation inasmuch as he refers to the attack on Poland as a defense against the threatening attacks of the enemies of the German people and invokes the heroic deeds of the former struggles to protect the Fatherland.

Verordnung über die Erneuerung des Eisernen Kreuzes

Vom 1.September 1939

Nachdem ich mich entschlossen habe, das Deutsche Volk zur Abwehr gegen die ihm drohenden Angriffe zu den Waffen zu rufen, erneuere ich eingedenk der heldenmütigen Kämpfe, die Deutschlands Söhne in den früheren großen Kriegen zum Schutze der Heimat bestanden haben, den Orden des Eisernen Kreuzes.

Artikel 1

Das Eiserne Kreuz wird in folgender Abstufung und Reihenfolge verliehen:

Eisernes Kreuz 2.Klasse,
Eisernes Kreuz 1.Klasse,
Ritterkreuz des Eisernen Kreuzes,
Großkreuz des Eisernen Kreuzes.

Artikel 2

Das Eiserne Kreuz wird ausschließlich für besondere Tapferkeit vor dem Feinde und für hervorragende Verdienste in der Truppenführung verliehen.

Die Verleihung einer höheren Klasse setzt den Besitz der vorangehenden Klasse voraus.

Artikel 3

Die Verleihung des Großkreuzes behalte ich mir vor für überragende Taten, die den Verlauf des Krieges entscheidend beeinflussen.

Artikel 4

Die 2.Klasse und die 1.Klasse des Eisernen Kreuzes gleichen in Größe und Ausführung den bisherigen mit der Maßgabe, daß auf der Vorderseite das Hakenkreuz und die Jahreszahl 1939 angebracht sind.

Die 2.Klasse wird an einem schwarz-weiß-roten Bande im Knopfloch oder an der Schnalle, die 1.Klasse ohne Band auf der linken Brustseite getragen.

Das Ritterkreuz ist ~~xxxxxxxxxxxxx~~ größer als das Eiserne Kreuz 1.Klasse und wird am Halse mit schwarz-weiß-rotem Bande getragen.

Das Großkreuz ist etwa doppelt so groß wie das Eiserne Kreuz 1.Klasse, hat anstelle der silbernen eine goldene Einfassung und wird am Halse an einem breiteren schwarz-weiß-roten Bande getragen.

Artikel 5

Ist der Beliehene schon im Besitz einer oder beider Klassen des Eisernen Kreuzes des Weltkrieges, so erhält er anstelle eines zweiten Kreuzes eine silberne Spange mit dem Hoheitszeichen und der Jahreszahl 1939 zu dem Eisernen Kreuz des Weltkrieges verliehen; die Spange wird beim Eisernen Kreuz 2.Klasse auf dem Bande getragen, beim Eisernen Kreuz 1.Klasse über dem Kreuz angesteckt.

Artikel 6

Der Beliehene erhält eine Besitzurkunde.

Artikel 7

Das Eiserne Kreuz verbleibt nach Ableben des Beliehenen als Erinnerungsstück den Hinterbliebenen.

Artikel 8

Die Durchführungsbestimmungen erläßt der Chef des Oberkommandos der Wehrmacht im Einverständnis mit dem Staatsminister und Chef der Präsidialkanzlei.

Berlin, den 1.September 1939

Der Führer

Der Chef des Oberkommandos der Wehrmacht

Der Reichsminister des Innern

Der Staatsminister und Chef der Präsidialkanzlei des Führers und Reichskanzlers

From the very beginning of the war the leadership was anxious to restrict the award of the Iron Cross to bravery deeds alone in order to give and maintain a high regard to the decoration. The impression that numerous awards went to the "ones in the rear" was to be avoided. With the subsequent institution of the Order of the War Merit Cross the possible bestowing of the Iron Cross for other merits instead of bravery was dispensed with.

The Order of the Iron Cross could not only be awarded to members of the *Wehrmacht,* but also to members of other organizations which had distinguished themselves with bravery during the conduct of the war. Such organizations were police, labor service RAD (*Reichsarbeitsdienst*), Organization Todt, Teno (*Technische Nothilfe*) and civil defense (*Luftschutz*). Also, soldiers of allied forces, volunteer soldiers of other nations, "volunteers of foreign tribes from the Bolshevik liberated areas," and also women (Red Cross or *Flakhelferinnen*) could be awarded with the Iron Cross. Priests could not receive the cross, unless "they had decided to switch from a pastor to a fighting soldier."[4]

On August 7, 1940 it was decreed:

"Soldiers, who can be awarded with the Wound Badge in Silver or Gold without consideration of the amount of wounds (author's note: loss of extremities or eye sight), have fulfilled the requirements for the Iron Cross Second Class, provided worthiness is existent. These soldiers must receive the Iron Cross within shortest time."[5]

Furthermore it was decreed on September 24, 1940 that a posthumous award of the Iron Cross was possible. Proposals needed to be submitted to the Supreme Command of the Army (OKH), Personnel Department (HPA). The medal and the award document were to be presented to the members of the family in a worthy style via an officer of the military district. An award to soldiers missing in action or to soldiers captured by the enemy was allowed regarding the initial regulations but was later forbidden by an order of the *Führer* on September 27, 1944.

DESIGN

The Order of the Iron Cross of 1939 has the same design as previous versions of the award and it is very simple. A metallic core (earlier pieces made of zinc or brass and later ones made of iron) is enclosed by a silver frame in the case of the Knights Cross and Grand Cross or by one made of *Neusilber* for the First and Second Class grades.

The awards for the repetition of a class of an earlier version, such as the clasps to the Iron Cross First or Second Class of 1914, show the national eagle in two different sizes.

The repetition indicators for the Knights Cross of the Iron Cross of 1939 are an oak leaf device as a stand-alone clasp or with the addition of swords. The higher classes are made in platinum or gold and with precious stones.

The Star to the Grand Cross of the Iron Cross was never officially founded nor awarded. It shows the same design as the previous *Blücherstern* of 1813 and *Hindenburgstern* of 1914, only the central motif is now the prominent swastika.

THE ORDER

Initially founded in just four classes, the order of the Iron Cross was expanded to a total of ten different awards. However, not all ten awards were grades on their own.

Two, namely the *Spange* First Class and *Spange* Second Class, were basically the same as the Iron Cross First Class, respectively Second Class, just in another form. Four awards, namely the Oakleaves, Oakleaves with Swords, Oakleaves with Swords and Diamonds and the Golden Diamonds, were a visual sign for a repeated award of the Knights Cross of the Iron Cross. Thus, the holder of the "Diamonds" could be considered as having been awarded the Knights Cross four times. One grade, the Star to the Grand Cross of the Iron Cross, was never founded and also never awarded. However, one approved example does exist and was basically ready to be awarded.

Above: A period overview of the Order of the Iron Cross of 1939 without the Grand Cross, the Golden Diamonds, and the Star. The medal in the top center is the Order of the German Cross in Gold (see next chapter).

The Iron Cross Second Class

Despite the high esteem that the Order of the Iron Cross had, the Iron Cross Second Class is one of the awards which can be readily found today due to the extremely high award numbers. It is estimated that a total of over 4.5 million crosses were awarded between September 1939 and May 1945.[6] The actual number is most likely never to be known, but as of February 1942 more than 1.6 million Second Class Crosses were shipped from the *Präsidialkanzlei* to the troops.[7]

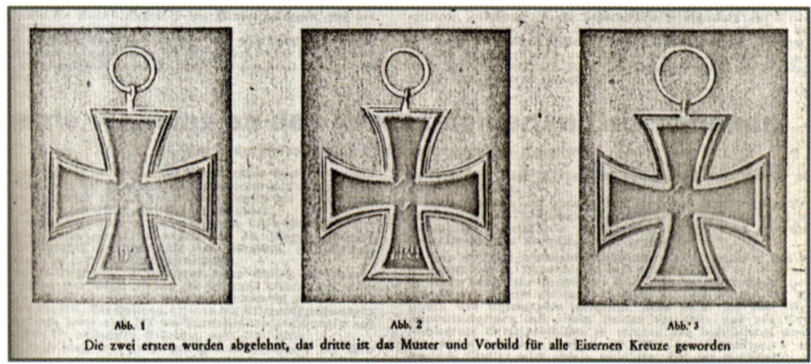

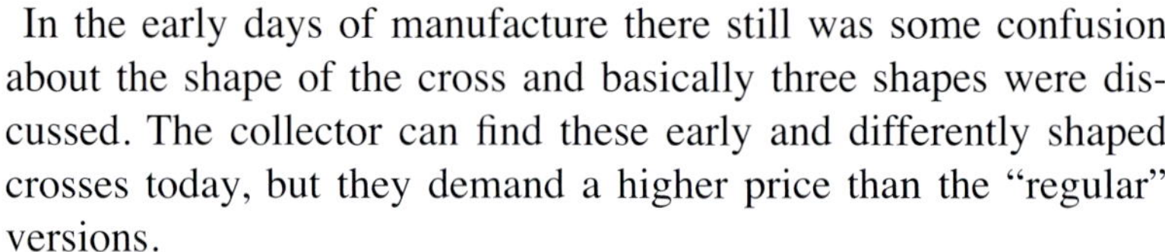

In the early days of manufacture there still was some confusion about the shape of the cross and basically three shapes were discussed. The collector can find these early and differently shaped crosses today, but they demand a higher price than the "regular" versions.

The regular dimensions of a "normal" Iron Cross Second Class (*Eisernes Kreuz 2. Klasse* or EK 2) are 44 mm x 44 mm, but that dimension can easily deviate by +/- 0.5 mm, depending on the maker.

Apart from the two so-called "Schinkel" versions, Schinkel A and Schinkel B, there are some other variations collectors have identified. The "wide frame" Iron Cross Second Class has its name from the slightly wider frame. The size of the cross is around 45 mm +/- 0.2 mm. Finally, the collector can seek the so-called *Übergrösse* or "over-sized" EK 2. Any cross - and there are not too many - which is over 46.5 mm falls into this category.

There are more sub-variations but they are based on minor variations and would be outside the framework of this book.

The EK 2 was not an order which was worn; only the red/white/black ribbon (which was changed from the traditional black/white/black to now show the national colors of Germany) was worn in the upper button hole of the uniform and/or as a small ribbon bar above the left breast pocket.

Left: The so-called "Schinkel B" type, a very rare variation.

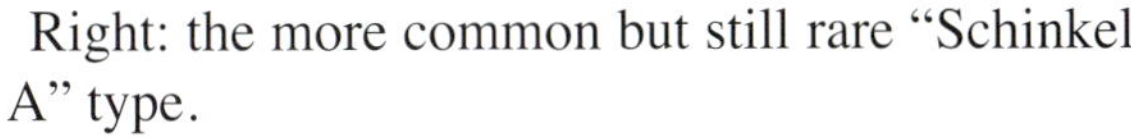

Right: the more common but still rare "Schinkel A" type.

Left: A so-called "wide frame" EK 2. Most of these crosses are marked "24" for *Arbeitsgemeinschaft Hanauer Plakettenhersteller.*

Left: The *Übergrösse (*oversize) variation is only distinguishable from the normal size by comparison. This example measures 46.9 mm across.

Right: This is the so-called "Round 3" variation. It got its name from the unusually shaped "3" in the obverse and reverse dates.

Left: This is the normal and approved version of the typical Iron Cross Second Class 1939 and it is this shape that most examples have. The typical size is around 44 x 44 mm.

THE KNOWN MAKERS OF THE IRON CROSS SECOND CLASS

MANUFACTURER	LDO #	PKZ #
Deschler & Sohn, München	L/10*	1
C.E. Juncker, Berlin	L/12	2
Wilhelm Deumer, Lüdenscheid	L/11	3
Steinhauer & Lück, Lüdenscheid	L/16	4
Fritz Zimmermann, Stuttgart	L/24	6
Paul Meybauer, Berlin	L/13	7
Otto Schickle, Pforzheim	L/15	-
Grossmann & Co., Wien		11
Gustav Brehmer, Marktneukirchen		13
Friedrich Orth, Wien	L/14	15
Alois Rettenmaier, Schwäbisch Gmünd		16
E. Ferd. Wiedmann, Frankfurt		19
Gebrüder Godet, Berlin	L/50	21
Boerger & Co., Berlin		22
Arbeitsgemeinschaft Graveure, Berlin		23
Arbeitsgemeinschaft Plakettenhersteller, Hanau		24
Arbeitsgemeinschaft Goldschmiedeinnung, Hanau		25
B.H. Mayer, Pforzheim	L/18	26
Anton Schenkl, Wien		27
Berg & Nolte, Lüdenscheid		40
Jakob Bengel, Idar-Oberstein		44
Karl Geschiermeister, Wien		50
Gottlieb & Wagner, Idar-Oberstein		52
J.E. Hammer & Söhne, Geringswald		55
Robert Hauschild, Pforzheim		56
Klein & Quenzer, Idar-Oberstein	L/26	65
Friedrich Keller, Oberstein		66
unknown		75
Ernst L. Müller, Pforzheim		76
Richard Simm & Söhne, Gablonz		93

MANUFACTURER	LDO #	PKZ #
Rudolf Souval, Wien	L/58	98
Rudolf Wächtler & Lange, Mittweida	L/55	100
Gebrüder Schneider, Wien	-	106
Hermann Aurich, Dresden	-	113
Franz Petzl, Wien	-	120
J.J. Stahl, Straßburg	-	122
Beck, Hassinger & Co., Straßburg	-	123
Eugen Gauss, Pforzheim	-	125
Eduard Hann, Oberstein	-	126
S. Jablonski GmbH, Posen	-	128
Franz Reischauer, Idar-Oberstein	-	132
J. H. Werner, Berlin	-	137
Julius Maurer, Oberstein	-	138
Schauerte & Hohfeld, Lüdenscheid	L/54	140
Funke & Brünninghaus, Lüdenscheid	L/56	-
Several unknown makers		

* LDO numbers with light orange back ground have not yet been found on genuine pre-May 1945 EK 2s.

It must be understood that this list cannot be complete; it represents the state of the research as of 2012.[8] One also has to realize that a very great number of Iron Crosses Second Class come without any stamping. The identification of unmarked makers is made by comparing frame and core characteristics with known examples.

Second Class crosses with an LDO stamp are far rarer than the ones with the *Präsidialkanzlei* numbers. Early crosses (meaning at least pre March 1941, when the LDO numbers were introduced) are unmarked and one can even find such early crosses with non-iron cores (zinc or brass). The collecting of Iron Crosses Second Class is a very wide and satisfying topic, the more so since it is very much affordable.

The *Wiederholungsspange* for the Iron Cross Second Class 1914

Any soldier who already had won the Iron Cross Second Class of 1914 and was awarded the Second Class of 1939 received a so-called *Wiederholungsspange* (repetition clasp). The clasp was in the form of a national eagle with short wings and was to be worn on the black and white ribbon of the EK 2 of 1914.

There are only two basic types but of course far more manufacturers. The early type is identified by the scalloped shape of the date bar; the later type has straight edges of the date bar.

Early type with the scalloped date bar.

Later type with the straight edges of the date bar.

The internal list of the *Präsidialkanzlei* shows a total of 81,115 *Wiederholungsspangen* EK2 sent out to the branches of the *Wehrmacht*. Apart from a very small shipment of 200 pieces to the *Heer* in February 1942, no shipments were made past July 1941. It can be assumed with a high degree of certainty that no more than the mentioned 81,000 *Spangen* were awarded.[9]

Of course, more awards were produced, but the majority of those were made for the private retail market and are marked with an LDO designation. The example to the right shows the marking for Paul Meybauer, Berlin L/13.

THE KNOWN MAKERS OF THE *SPANGE* FOR THE IRON CROSS SECOND CLASS 1914

Type	MANUFACTURER	LDO #
Early	possibly C. E. Juncker, Berlin	unmarked
	possibly Boerger & Co., Berlin	unmarked
	possibly Paul Meybauer, Berlin	unmarked
Later	Wilhelm Deumer, Lüdenscheid	L/11
	C.E. Juncker, Berlin	L/12
	Paul Meybauer, Berlin	L/13
	Otto Schickle, Pforzheim	L/15
	Steinhauer & Lück, Lüdenscheid	L/16
	Hermann Wernstein, Jena-Lobstedt	L/17
	B.H. Mayer, Pforzheim	L/18
	Hymmen & Co., Lüdenscheid	L/53
	Funcke & Brünninghaus, Lüdenscheid	L/56
	Boerger & Co., Berlin	L/57
	Several unmarked makers	

The early type *Spangen* are always unmarked and any possible identification of the maker was done by comparison to later, marked models. It is not known when the transition between the earlier and later types happened, but the most likely time is mid-1941 between the Polish campaign and the Campaign in the West. All awarded *Spangen* are unmarked since the *Präsidialkanzlei* numbers were introduced after the official distribution ceased in August of 1941.[10]

This fact can also be seen in that all of the later type *Spangen* are either unmarked or bear an LDO number which indicates a private purchase. Apart from the big exception of the L/12 Knights Cross, no LDO-marked orders or medals were ever awarded.

The Iron Cross First Class

The Iron Cross First Class was to be awarded to soldiers who distinguished themselves repeatedly with extraordinary bravery or to troop leaders who showed several outstanding merits in leading the troops. The prior award of the Second Class was mandatory and it was recommended that a certain time should have passed between the two awards. The simultaneous awarding of both classes needed the permission of the Supreme Command of the Army (*Oberkommando des Heeres*, OKH). Regular awards were approved at the divisional level.

The award numbers of the Iron Cross First Class are substantially lower than those for the Second Class. The literature shows a spread between 300,000 to 834,000 (both numbers including the *Wiederholungsspange* for the First Class 1914). Most likely a number around 700,000 for the Iron Cross First Class of 1939 is realistic, based on the fact that by February 1942 already over 200,000 First Class crosses were shipped out from the *Präsidialkanzlei*.[11]

The core of the Iron Cross First Class is normally made of iron, but earlier examples have cores stamped from sheets of brass, zinc, or even *Tombak* (a high grade brass). The frame and the back plate are made of *Neusilber*, a copper-nickel-zinc alloy. The back plate also holds the pin system, consisting of the pin, the hinge, and the catch. Some privately purchased example have a screw device instead of the pin system.

Above: An early and very rare Schinkel-type Iron Cross First Class.

Below: Regular type and shape of Iron Cross First Class of 1939.

Above: The typical reverse of a standard Iron Cross First Class.

Above: The more unusual and privately purchased screw back set up.

Early Iron Crosses First Class show no marking at all. With the introduction of the LDO-numbers in March 1941 at least the privately purchased items were stamped with the LDO-number of the manufacturer. Later, most likely around the end of 1942, the crosses delivered to the *Präsidialkanzlei* for subsequent distribution to the divisions were marked with the PKZ-number of the manufacturer. The markings can be found on the pin (inside or outside) or on the back plate.

Above: The PKZ-number on this example is stamped into the outside of the pin.

Above: The LDO number of this example is stamped below the catch.

THE KNOWN MAKERS OF THE IRON CROSS FIRST CLASS

MANUFACTURER	LDO #	PKZ #
Deschler & Sohn, München	L/10	1
C.E. Juncker, Berlin	L/12	2
Wilhelm Deumer, Lüdenscheid	L/11	3
Steinhauer & Lück, Lüdenscheid	L/16	4
Fritz Zimmermann, Stuttgart	L/24	6
Paul Meybauer, Berlin	L/13	7
Otto Schickle, Pforzheim	L/15	-
Ferdinand Hoffstätter, Bonn	L/19	8
Friedrich Orth, Wien	L/14	15
Alois Rettenmaier, Schwäbisch Gmünd	-	16
E. Ferd. Wiedmann, Frankfurt	-	19
C. F. Zimmermann, Pforzheim	L/52	20
Gebrüder Godet, Berlin	L/50	21
Boerger & Co., Berlin	-	22
Arbeitsgemeinschaft Plakettenhersteller, Hanau	-	24
B.H. Mayer, Pforzheim	L/18	26
Klein & Quenzer, Idar-Oberstein	L/26*	65
Rudolf Souval, Wien	L/58	98
Hymmen & Co,, Lüdenscheid	L/53	139*
Schauerte & Höhfeld, Lüdenscheid	L/54	140*
Wächtler & Lange, Mittweida	L/55	100
Carl Wild, Hamburg	-	107
Funcke & Brünninghaus, Lüdenscheid	L/56	116*
Petz & Lorenz, Unterreichenbach	unmarked	
Unknown maker	unmarked	

* these PKZ numbers have not yet been found on genuine pre-May 1945 EK 1.

Nearly every maker can be found with several different pin set-ups and sometimes even with different core types. Some maker, like Meybauer and Deschler & Sohn, even produced Iron Crosses First Class of 1914 in the style and with the frames of the 1939 style. The theme of the Iron Crosses First and Second Class of 1939 gives the collector a nearly limitless field of collecting.

The *Wiederholungsspange* for the First Class 1914 Iron Cross

Just as was the case with the holder of a 1914 Second Class Iron Cross who received a 1939 *Wiederholungsspange* for a subsequent award of a 1939 cross, the same procedure applied for subsequent winners of the Iron Cross First Class during the Second World War. This clasp was larger than the one of the Second Class and was worn on the tunic above the Iron Cross First Class of 1914.

There are also only two basic types but also far more manufacturers. The early type is again identified by the scalloped shape of the date bar, the later type has straight edges of the date bar.

Early type with the scalloped date bar most likely by C. E. Juncker, Berlin.

Later type with the straight edges of the date bar, made by Deumer, Lüdenscheid.

The internal list of the *Präsidialkanzlei* shows a total of 23,056 *Wiederholungsspangen* EK1 sent out to the branches of the *Wehrmacht*. Apart from a very small shipment of only 100 pieces to the *Heer* in February 1942, no shipments were made past August 1941. Just as is the case with the *Wiederholungsspange* for the EK2 it can be assumed with a high degree of certainty that no more than the mentioned 23.000 *Spangen* for the EK1 of 1914 were awarded.[12]

All of the early types are unmarked; all of the later types are either unmarked or have an LDO-number. No genuine *Wiederholungsspange* to the Iron Cross 1914 bears a PKZ-number. The majority of the *Spangen* have a pin system; some rare examples have a screw back fastening device.

THE KNOWN MAKERS OF THE *SPANGE* FOR THE IRON CROSS FIRST CLASS 1914

Type	MANUFACTURER	LDO #
Early	possibly C. E. Juncker, Berlin	unmarked
	possibly Boerger & Co., Berlin	unmarked
	Paul Meybauer, Berlin	unmarked
Later	Wilhelm Deumer, Lüdenscheid	L/11
	C.E. Juncker, Berlin	L/12
	Paul Meybauer, Berlin	L/13
	Otto Schickle, Pforzheim	L/15
	Steinhauer & Lück, Lüdenscheid	L/16
	Hermann Wernstein, Jena-Lobstedt	L/17
	B.H. Mayer, Pforzheim	unmarked
	C.F. Zimmermann, Pforzheim	L/52
	Hymmen & Co., Lüdenscheid	unmarked
	Funcke & Brünninghaus, Lüdenscheid	L/56
	Petz & Lorenz, Unterreichenbach	unmarked
	Unknown maker	unmarked

Most of the types with LDO-marking can also be found unmarked.

Since the *Wiederholungsspange* was to be worn above the Iron Cross of 1914, some companies sold both orders as a fixed combination (B.H. Mayer for example) or some soldiers had their awarded *Spange* attached to the original Iron Cross of 1914 by a jeweler. Such combinations, if genuine, demand premium prices and should be scrutinized regarding a modern fabrication using post-war fakes.

The jeweler-made combination to the right is a genuine example which belonged to *Feldmarschall* Erhard Milch. The *Spange* is an early Juncker type.

The Knights Cross of the Iron Cross 1939

The grade of the Knights Cross was a complete new addition to the Order of the Iron Cross and can be seen as the Third *Reich* equivalent to the *Pour Le Mérite* of the Great War. It was a neck order which could be and was awarded to the common soldier as well as to the highest ranking general.

The Knights Cross consists of a blackened iron core with a silver rim. The obverse shows the swastika with the date 1939 below; the reverse shows the initial foundation date of 1813 on the lower arm. Early awarded crosses have a *Neusilber* frame and cores made of zinc or brass. The size is 48 mm x 48 mm with minor variations. The weights vary a great deal from 26 to 34 grams (always with the suspension loop).

Above: Obverse and reverse of a Steinhauer & Lück Knights Cross, marked "800".

Below: The Knights Cross was awarded with a typically 72 cm long and 45 mm wide ribbon.

The award numbers of the Knights Cross are known and each recipient name is recorded and documented. The number of awarded crosses is around 7,200.[13]

From September 1939 until October 1941 each recipient could buy one or even more replacement crosses on the private retail market. After October 1941 this was forbidden and any Knights Crosses in the possession of the retail market were sent to the *Präsidialkanzlei* - one example could be kept for display purposes. As of October 1944 a total of 599 Knights Crosses were purchased as replacements from the *Präsidialkanzlei*, now the only source.[14] Based on these facts it can be assumed that only about 8,000 Knights Crosses were made and in circulation before May 1945. Today this number is considerably lower.

The PKZ-approved manufacturers are known and well documented. The above procedure makes clear that there might have been some not yet known manufacturers who privately sold some Knights Crosses in the early days of the Order to the roughly 1,000 eligible recipients up to October 1941. They are not identified yet and might never be. There are no jeweler-made private purchase Knights Crosses.

THE KNOWN MAKERS OF THE KNIGHTS CROSS OF THE IRON CROSS 1939

MANUFACTURER	LDO #	PKZ #	Variations
C. E. Juncker, Berlin	L/12	2	9
Otto Schickle, Pforzheim	L/15	-	2
Steinhauer & Lück	-	4	4
Gebrüder Godet, Berlin	-	-	1
C. F. Zimmermann	L/52	20	3
Klein & Quenzer, Idar-Oberstein	-	65	2
3/4 Ring, unknown	-	-	1

Most of the variations are in the area of the markings, meaning either none, the silver stamp only, or an LDO or PKZ-stamp. Only the early Juncker Crosses and the 3/4 Ring Knights Cross have non-magnetic cores. Most makers used the same frame and the same core over the full production time frame, a fact which makes identification of a real cross, intense study assumed, relatively easy. Only the company of Steinhauer & Lück had two core types and also two different frames, the A- and B-Type.

The Oakleaves to the Knights Cross of the Iron Cross 1939

The length and intensity of the war led naturally to situations where a previous recipient of the Knights Cross of the Iron Cross distinguished himself in a way which necessitated another award of the Knights Cross.

Consequently, the first addition to the Order of the Iron Cross after the initial September 1, 1939 institution date was made on June 3, 1940 and the first recipient was *Generalleutnant* Eduard Dietl on July 19, 1940.

The oak leaf device replaces the original loop of the Knights Cross and was designed in the tradition of the *Pour Le Mérite* and other Imperial Orders which were complimented with such a devices. A cluster of three individual oak leaves forms the shape. The size is 19 mm high by 20 mm wide, the weight is around 6.8 gr. Only two types were officially awarded and both were made by Gebrüder Godet, Berlin.

Type 1

Type 2

The most visual difference between the two types on the obverse is the distance of the right side of the center leaf to the center vein of the right most underlying leaf. This distance is smaller with the Type 1.

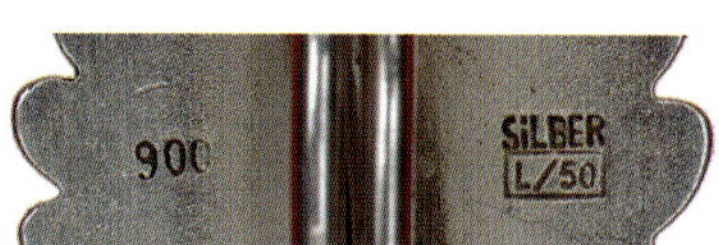

The above picture on the left shows the Type 1 which is normally marked “900” on the left reverse and “SiLBER” and below “L/50” in a box on the right. This type was awarded until approximately mid-1943. The right picture shows the Type 2 which is always marked “900” on the left side and “21” on the right side.

Between June 1941 and May 1945 a total of around 870 Oakleaves were awarded. Nearly all known recipients received either the Type 1 or the Type 2. Since the private sale of the Knights Cross and higher was prohibited from October 1941 on, any possible other makers must have produced between June and October and for a market which was only 39 possible buyers strong. However, it is known that at least two "900" "L/12" Juncker-made Oakleaves were worn by legitimate awardees. One was *General der Panzertruppe* Walter Kurt Nehring (# 383, February 2, 1944)[15] and the other one was *Leutnant* Adolf Dickfeld of *Jagdgeschwader 52* (# 94, May 18, 1942).[16] It is certainly possible that more are legitimate and that other companies (Steinhauer & Lück [17], Meybauer "L/13") produced in the short time frame where it was possible. But definitive proof has not yet been established.

THE KNOWN MAKERS OF OAKLEAVES TO THE KNIGHTS CROSS OF THE IRON CROSS 1939

Type	MANUFACTURER	Marking
Type 1	Gebrüder Godet, Berlin	900 - L/50
Type 2	Gebrüder Godet, Berlin	900- 21

Obersturmbannführer Michael Wittmann was one of the most successful tank commanders of World War II. The above picture was taken on January 30, 1944 on the occasion of the awarding of the Oakleaves at the *Berghof*. This specific copy with Hitler's signature dated February 2, 1944 was sent to Wittmann as a personal token of remembrance.

The Oakleaves with Swords to the Knights Cross of the Iron Cross 1939

Fifteen months after the institution of the Oakleaves it became necessary to create another grade to the Knights Cross of the Iron Cross. The addition of the "Swords" was also in the tradition of some Imperial Orders. The official date of the institution, on September 28, 1941, came nearly three months after the first awards were made to the *Oberstleutnante* Galland and Mölders on July 1, 1941.

A set of crossed swords were attached to the existing Oakleaves. Due to the time frame of the production of the Type 1 and the Type 2 of the Oakleaves, this also led to the creation of two types of the "Swords."

The weight is around 9.0 gr., the dimensions of the Oakleaves are of course the same as before. The swords are 24.2 mm long. The two swords are identical and made with the same die. The obverse of the left sword is the reverse of the right sword. They are soldered together in the middle.

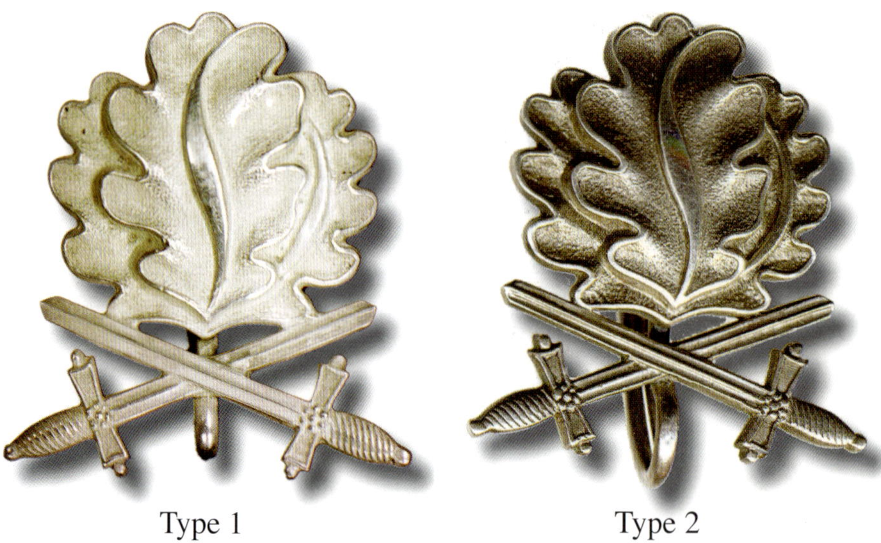

Type 1 Type 2

The reverse marking of each type is identical to the reverses of the Oakleaves of the corresponding type.

Only 150 "Swords" were awarded during the course of the Second World War, which makes this decoration one of the rarest. Unissued examples were found in the safe of the Castle Klessheim near Salzburg/Austria, the last place where the *Präsidialkanzlei* supply was stored. However, the total amount of genuine examples still in existence is most likely well under the number of original issued examples.

Since the Swords were introduced well after the prohibition of private sale of all grades of the Knights Cross of the Iron Cross there are no non-Godet pieces nor any so-called jeweler copies or private made examples. All such pieces can be assumed very safely as post war creations, including the "800" "L 12" (sic)[18], and the multiple Steinhauer & Lück types which are presented as real.[19]

THE KNOWN MAKER OF OAKLEAVES WITH SWORDS TO THE KNIGHTS CROSS OF THE IRON CROSS 1939

Type	MANUFACTURER	Marking
Type 1	Gebrüder Godet, Berlin	900 - L/50
Type 2	Gebrüder Godet, Berlin	900- 21

Obersturmbannführer Michael Wittmann met Hitler again on June 22, 1944 when he was awarded the Swords (# 71). He again received a personalized photograph with Hitler's signature and the date June 29, 1944.

Forty days later he and his crew were killed in Normandy near Caen.

The photo was sent from the Headquarters of the *Führer* by his personal adjutant *Hauptsturmführer* Günsche.

FÜHRERHAUPTQUARTIER, DEN 14.7.44

DER FÜHRER UND KANZLER DES DEUTSCHEN REICHES
ADJUTANTUR
SS-Hauptsturmführer Günsche

An
SS-Hauptsturmführer
W i t t m a n n
L ü n e b u r g

Lieber Kamerad Wittmann!

Beiliegend das versprochene Bild! Ich wünsche Ihnen alles Gute und weiterhin bestes Soldatenglück.

Mit besten Grüssen und
Heil Hitler!

Anlage.

The Oakleaves with Swords and Diamonds to the Knights Cross of the Iron Cross 1939

The official date of the institution is September 28, 1941 since the "Diamonds" were instituted with the same decree. Just as was the case with the Swords, the first award of the Diamonds was made earlier. The first recipient was *Oberst* Werner Mölders on July 16, 1941.

Only 27 soldiers of the *Wehrmacht* received the Diamonds. Each recipient was presented with two pieces: one so-called "A-Piece" which was made of Platinum and Diamonds and a so-called "B-Piece" for the daily wear. This piece was made of silver and studded with rhinestones.

The first two recipients, Mölders and Galland, received a different style of Diamonds. Some recipients never received the actual set (Marseille, Dr. Maus and von Saucken).

A-Piece *General der Panzertruppen* Hasso von Manteuffel, awarded on February 18, 1945 (# 24)

B-Piece *Oberleutnant* Erich Hartmann, awarded on August 25, 1944 (# 18)

Both A- and B-Pieces were manufactured by the company of Otto Klein, Hanau, and are stamped accordingly.

The Golden Oakleaves with Swords and Diamonds to the Knights Cross of the Iron Cross 1939

The last addition to the Knights Cross of the Iron Cross, representing the fifth award of the Knights Cross, was the Golden Oakleaves with Swords and Diamonds. Hitler instituted this grade on December 29, 1944 and the single award occurred on January 1, 1945 to *Oberstleutnant* Rudel.

The design is identical to the Oakleaves with Swords and Diamonds. The A-Piece is made of 750 grade gold and studded with diamonds. The B-Piece is made of 585 grade gold and the stones are sapphires. The manufacturer was also Otto Klein, Hanau and both A- and B-Pieces bear the typical Klein markings.

Right: *Oberst* Rudel with the Golden Oakleaves with Swords and Diamonds.

Erlaß des Führers
über die Stiftung des Ritterkreuzes des Eisernen Kreuzes
mit dem Goldenen Eichenlaub mit Schwertern und Brillanten.
Vom 29. Dezember 1944.

Als höchste Tapferkeitsauszeichnung stifte ich das

Ritterkreuz des Eisernen Kreuzes
mit dem Goldenen Eichenlaub mit Schwertern und Brillanten.

Diese Auszeichnung wird nur zwölfmal verliehen, um höchstbewährte Einzelkämpfer, die mit allen Stufen des Ritterkreuzes des Eisernen Kreuzes ausgezeichnet sind, vor dem Deutschen Volke besonders zu ehren.

Meine Verordnung vom 1. September 1939 über die Erneuerung des Eisernen Kreuzes ist entsprechend zu ergänzen.

Führer-Hauptquartier, den 29. Dezember 1944.

Der Führer
Adolf Hitler

Above: The text of the institution mentions that only twelve "well-tried single fighters" which already have received all the other grades of the Knights Cross of the Iron Cross will ever receive this "highest bravery award."

The Grand Cross of the Iron Cross 1939

The Grand Cross of the Iron Cross was already part of the initial institution of each version of the Order of the Iron Cross, so it was only normal that it would also be instituted as part of the 1939 version.

However, contrary to the previous versions where some kind of stipulation for the awarding was formulated, such as winning a decisive battle or conquering a great fortress, the 1939 regulation only stated that it was the *Führer's* personal decision to award the Grand Cross for "outstanding deeds which influence the course of the war in a decisive way."

The only recipient of this high order was *Generalfeldmarschall* Göring, who received the Grand Cross on July 17, 1940. He was also promoted to the newly created title of *Reichsmarschall* on the same day.

The Grand Cross has the same design as the Knights Cross but is considerably larger. The size is 63 x 63 mm, the weight is around 54 gr., and the ribbon is identical to the one of the Knights Cross, but is 60 mm wide.

Above: Obverse and reverse of the Juncker-made Grand Cross, marked "800" and "L/12" on the reverse.

All original Grand Crosses in existence were manufactured by the company C.E. Juncker, Berlin. The actual award piece was marked "800" only; later examples were marked "800" and "L/12". They were made in low numbers between the introduction of the LDO-numbers in March 1941 and the prohibition of the private sale and were collected by the *Präsidialkanzlei*. Cased examples were found in *Schloss* Klessheim by soldiers of the Third U.S. Infantry Division.

Above: *Reichsmarschall* Hermann Göring with both the Knights Cross and the Grand Cross of the Iron Cross. The picture demonstrates clearly the size difference between these two high orders.

The Star to the Grand Cross of the Iron Cross 1939

This grade of the order was never instituted nor awarded. It is not mentioned in any contemporary publications, most notably not even in the "*Die Auszeichnungen des Gross-deutschen Reichs*" by Dr. Doehle.

Nevertheless there exists an undisputed original which was ready to be awarded, most likely after a successful conclusion of the war. The Star was taken by soldiers from the Third US Infantry Division from *Schloss* Klessheim and rests now in the storage area of the West Point Museum in upstate New York as inventory number D-6574, complete with its case.

The size is 87 mm x 87 mm, the weight is around 61 gr. There are no maker marks but the Iron Cross First Class is a Godet product and it can be assumed that the maker of the Star was also Gebrüder Godet, Berlin.

Above and right: Obverse and reverse of the prototype of the Star to the Grand Cross of the Iron Cross

AWARD DOCUMENTS

Each grade of the order was accompanied by an award document. In the case of the Knights Cross and higher, two versions exist: the so-called preliminary document in the style of regular award documents of the Second and First Class, and the so-called formal document or "*Mappe*."

It is not possible to show all variations of the lower grades so one example each should suffice. The regular award documents for the Iron Cross Second Class, First Class and the preliminary documents are in the format A4 (150 x 210 mm). The formal documents and the *Mappen* are considerably larger.

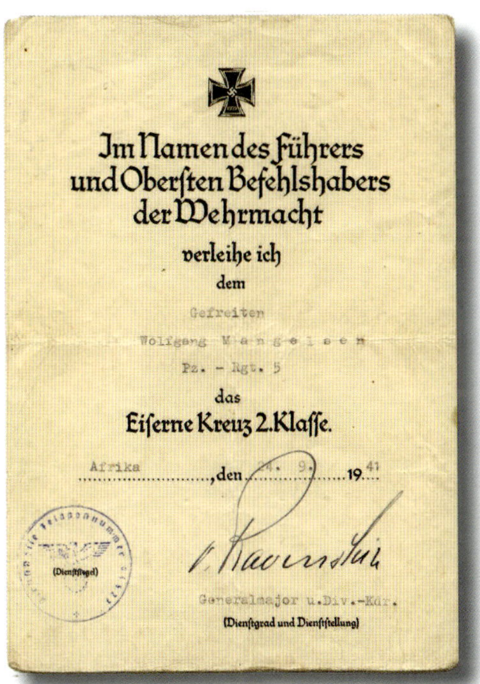

Im Namen des Führers
und Obersten Befehlshabers
der Wehrmacht
verleihe ich
dem
Gefreiten
Wolfgang M a n g e l s e n
Pz. - Rgt. 5
das
Eiserne Kreuz 2. Klasse.

Afrika, den 24. 9. 1941

(Dienstsiegel)

Generalmajor u.Div.-Kdr.
(Dienstgrad und Dienststellung)

Left: Standard award document for the Iron Cross Second Class to *Gefreiter* Wolfgang Mangelsen, issued in "Afrika" and signed by *Generalmajor* Hans von Ravenstein (captured November 29, 1941 near Tobruk).[20]

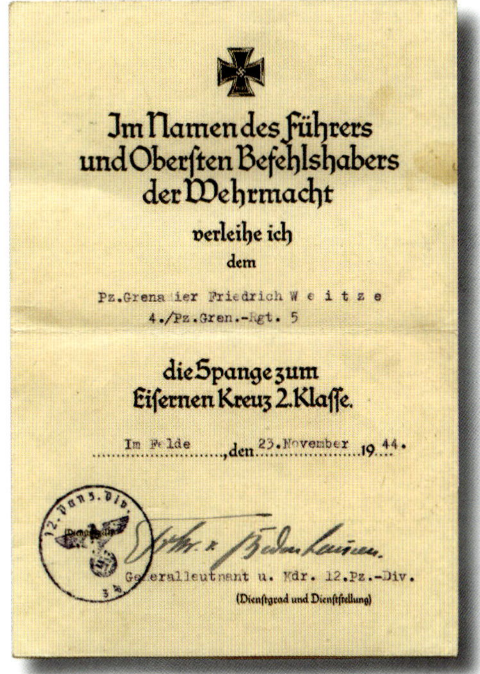

Im Namen des Führers
und Obersten Befehlshabers
der Wehrmacht
verleihe ich
dem
Pz.Grenadier Friedrich W e i t z e
4./Pz.Gren.-Rgt. 5
die Spange zum
Eisernen Kreuz 2. Klasse.

Im Felde, den 23. November 1944.

(Dienstsiegel)

Generalleutnant u. Kdr. 12.Pz.-Div.
(Dienstgrad und Dienststellung)

Right: Award document for the *Spange* Second Class to *Panzergrenadier* Friedrich Weitze, who was at that late date in the war (November 25, 1944) already over 40 years old. The document is signed by *Generalleutnant* Erpo *Freiherr* von Bodenhausen, Commander of the *12. Panzer-division*.

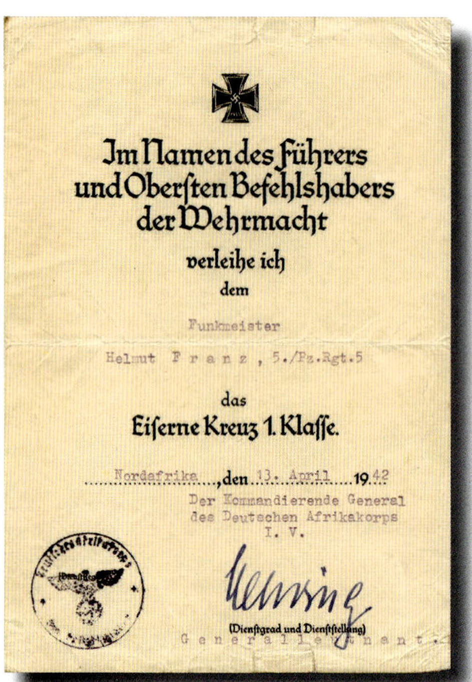

Im Namen des Führers
und Obersten Befehlshabers
der Wehrmacht
verleihe ich
dem
Funkmeister
Helmut Franz, 5./Pz.Rgt.5
das
Eiserne Kreuz 1. Klasse.

Nordafrika, den 13. April 1942

Der Kommandierende General
des Deutschen Afrikakorps
I. V.

(Dienstgrad und Dienststellung)
Generalleutnant.

Left: Award document for the Iron Cross First Class to *Funkmeister* Helmut Franz, signed by *Generalleutnant* Walther Kurt Nehring, Commander of the *Deutsches Afrikakorps* from March - August 1942.

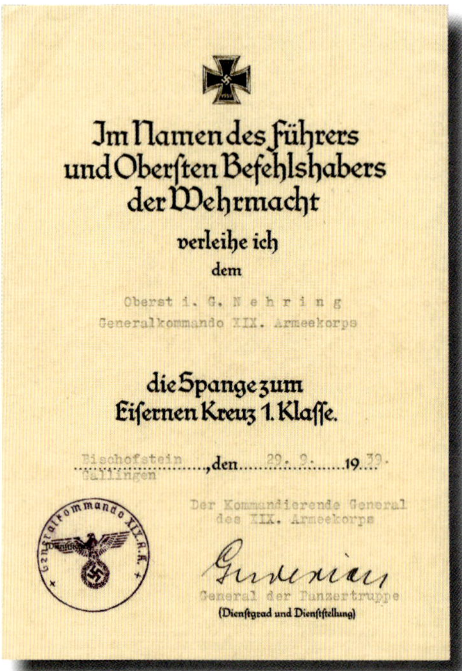

Im Namen des Führers
und Obersten Befehlshabers
der Wehrmacht
verleihe ich
dem
Oberst i. G. Nehring
Generalkommando XIX. Armeekorps
die Spange zum
Eisernen Kreuz 1. Klasse.

Bischofstein
Gallingen, den 29. 9. 1939.

Der Kommandierende General
des XIX. Armeekorps

General der Panzertruppe
(Dienstgrad und Dienststellung)

Above: Very early award document for the *Spange* First Class to then *Oberst* Walther Kurt Nehring, dated September 29, 1939 and signed by *General der Panzertruppe* Heinz Guderian.

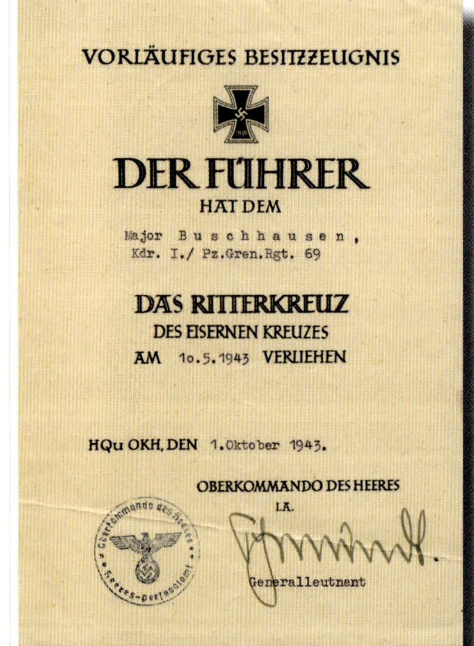

VORLÄUFIGES BESITZZEUGNIS

DER FÜHRER
HAT DEM
Major Buschhausen,
Kdr. I./ Pz.Gren.Rgt. 69
DAS RITTERKREUZ
DES EISERNEN KREUZES
AM 10.5.1943 VERLIEHEN

HQu OKH, DEN 1.Oktober 1943.

OBERKOMMANDO DES HEERES
I.A.

Generalleutnant

Left: Preliminary award document for the Knights Cross of the Iron Cross to *Major* Buschhausen and signed by *Generalleutnant* Rudolf Schmundt, who died from the injuries inflicted during the assassination attempt on Hitler.

Note that the wording is now "The *Führer* has awarded..." instead of "In the name of the *Führer*.."

Right: Preliminary award document for the Oakleaves to *General der Panzertruppen* W.K. Nehring, dated February 8, 1944. It is signed by *Generalleutnant* Wilhelm Burgdorf.

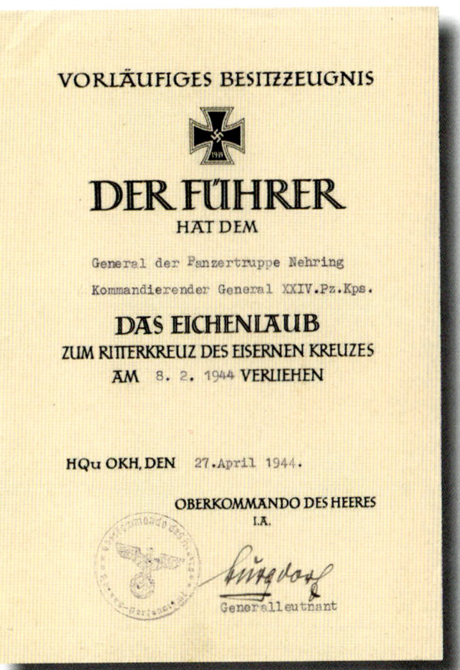

VORLÄUFIGES BESITZZEUGNIS

DER FÜHRER
HAT DEM

General der Panzertruppe Nehring
Kommandierender General XXIV.Pz.Kps.

DAS EICHENLAUB
ZUM RITTERKREUZ DES EISERNEN KREUZES
AM 8. 2. 1944 VERLIEHEN

HQu OKH, DEN 27.April 1944.

OBERKOMMANDO DES HEERES
I.A.

Generalleutnant

Below: Preliminary award document for the Oakleaves with Swords to *General der Panzertruppen* W.K. Nehring, dated January 22, 1945. It is signed by *Generalleutnant* Ernst Maisel.

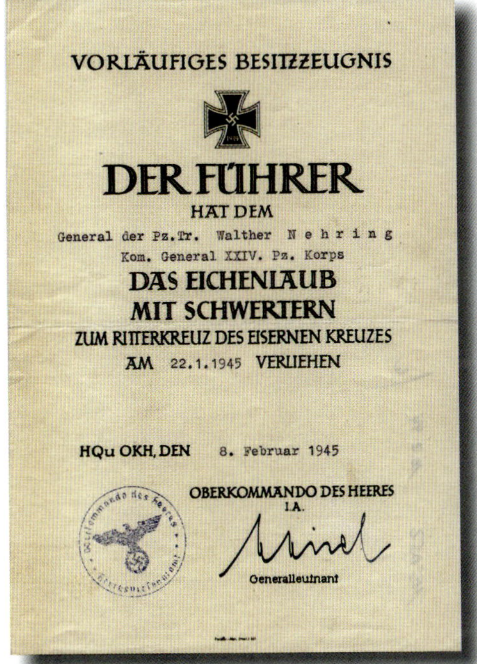

VORLÄUFIGES BESITZZEUGNIS

DER FÜHRER
HAT DEM

General der Pz.Tr. Walther N e h r i n g
Kom. General XXIV. Pz. Korps

DAS EICHENLAUB
MIT SCHWERTERN
ZUM RITTERKREUZ DES EISERNEN KREUZES
AM 22.1.1945 VERLIEHEN

HQu OKH, DEN 8. Februar 1945

OBERKOMMANDO DES HEERES
I.A.

Generalleutnant

Right: Extremely rare preliminary award document for the Oakleaves with Swords and Diamonds, issued to *Oberleutnant* Erich Hartmann and dated August 25, 1944. The document is issued by the *Luftwaffe* and signed by *Generaloberst* Bruno Loerzer.

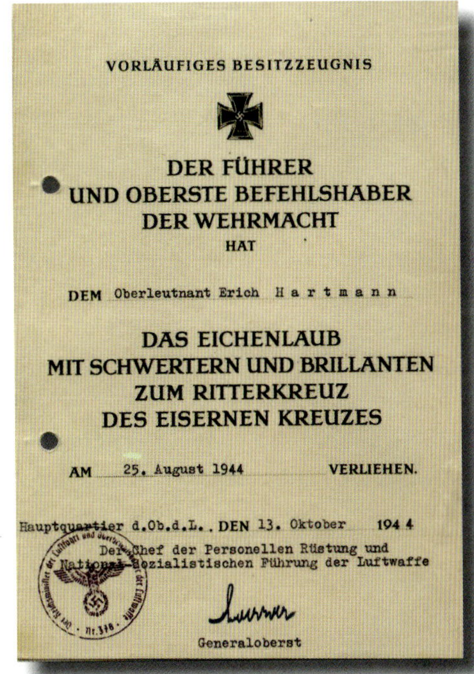

VORLÄUFIGES BESITZZEUGNIS

DER FÜHRER
UND OBERSTE BEFEHLSHABER
DER WEHRMACHT
HAT

DEM Oberleutnant Erich H a r t m a n n

DAS EICHENLAUB
MIT SCHWERTERN UND BRILLANTEN
ZUM RITTERKREUZ
DES EISERNEN KREUZES

AM 25. August 1944 VERLIEHEN.

Hauptquartier d.Ob.d.L., DEN 13. Oktober 1944
Der Chef der Personellen Rüstung und
Nationalsozialistischen Führung der Luftwaffe

Generaloberst

Left: Up until approximately January 1943 official award documents were presented in a hand-made, red *saffian*-covered leather *Mappe*, made in the bookbinder shop of Frida Thiersch.

The cover shows the national eagle.

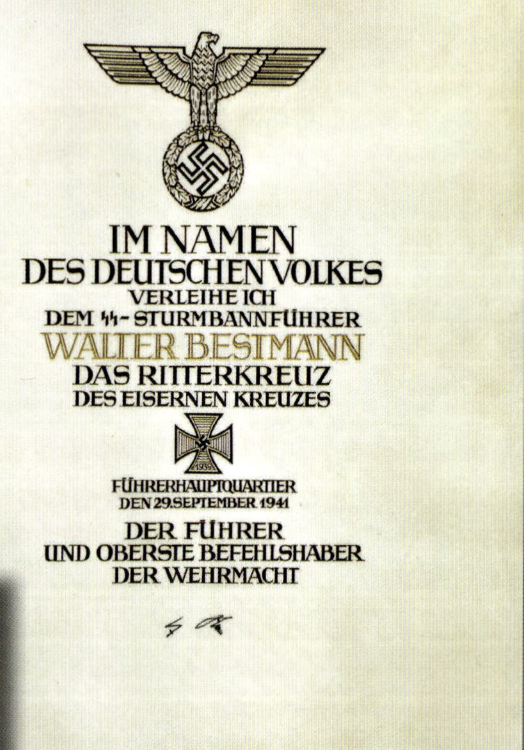

IM NAMEN
DES DEUTSCHEN VOLKES
VERLEIHE ICH
DEM SS-STURMBANNFÜHRER
WALTER BESTMANN
DAS RITTERKREUZ
DES EISERNEN KREUZES

1939

FÜHRERHAUPTQUARTIER
DEN 29.SEPTEMBER 1941
DER FÜHRER
UND OBERSTE BEFEHLSHABER
DER WEHRMACHT

Right: Inside the *Mappe* is the actual document. Eagle, text, and name are hand-made by highly skilled calligraphers.

The name of the awardee is always in gold in a clearly three-dimensional style.

Right: The *Mappe* for the Oakleaves is made of antique parchment and features a three-dimensional fire-gilded national eagle on the obverse.

IM NAMEN
DES DEUTSCHEN VOLKES
VERLEIHE ICH
DEM OBERSTLEUTNANT
PAUL-WERNER HOZZEL
DAS EICHENLAUB
ZUM RITTERKREUZ
DES EISERNEN KREUZES

FÜHRERHAUPTQUARTIER
DEN 14. APRIL 1943

DER FÜHRER
UND OBERSTE BEFEHLSHABER
DER WEHRMACHT

Left: The actual document is similar to the one of the Knights Cross award, but the national eagle is now executed in gold.

Not all recipients of the Oakleaves received a *Grosse Urkunde* (as is the case with the regular Knights Cross *Mappen*). At this state of the war the workload for F. Thiersch was too great for her to complete them all.

Left: The document for the Swords was presented in a very elaborate casette of considerable thickness.

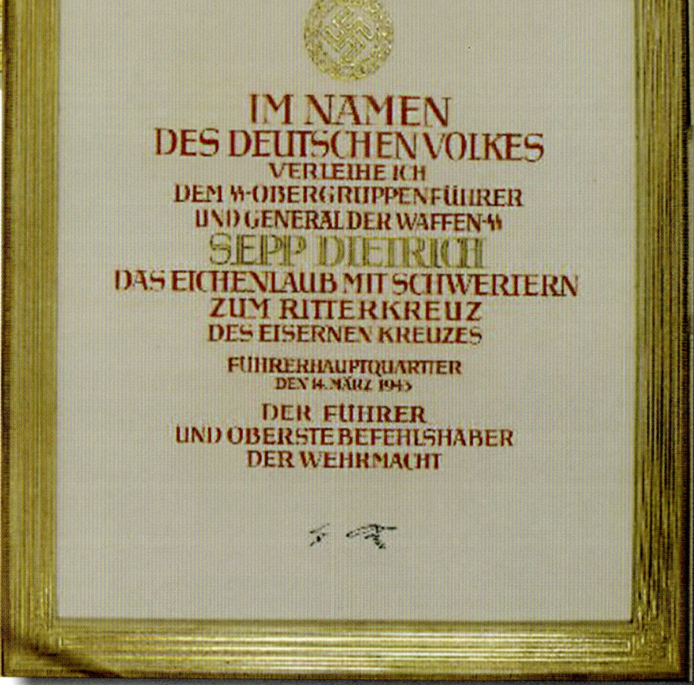

IM NAMEN
DES DEUTSCHEN VOLKES
VERLEIHE ICH
DEM SS-OBERGRUPPENFÜHRER
UND GENERAL DER WAFFEN-SS
SEPP DIETRICH
DAS EICHENLAUB MIT SCHWERTERN
ZUM RITTERKREUZ
DES EISERNEN KREUZES
FÜHRERHAUPTQUARTIER
DEN 14. MÄRZ 1945
DER FÜHRER
UND OBERSTE BEFEHLSHABER
DER WEHRMACHT

Right: The document itself is also framed. The lettering is now in red ink.

Not all recipients of the Swords received the *Grosse Urkunde* in the cassette.

Above: *Grosse Urkunde* for the Oakleaves with Swords and Diamonds for *Oberstleutnant* Werner Mölders. The document is not yet signed. The picture is taken from the magazine *Die Kunst im Deutschen Reich*, October 1942

Left: The cassette for the award document of the Grand Cross of the Iron Cross is even more elaborate. Golden Topaz, gilded frame work, the golden national eagle, and a diamond studded swastika are the ornaments of the lid.

IM NAMEN
DES DEUTSCHEN VOLKES
VERLEIHE ICH
DEM REICHSMARSCHALL
HERMANN GÖRING
DAS GROSSKREUZ
DES EISERNEN KREUZES
FÜHRERHAUPTQUARTIER
DEN 19. JULI 1940
DER FÜHRER
UND OBERSTE BEFEHLSHABER
DER WEHRMACHT

Right: The document is done in the same elaborate style.

Both pictures are from the magazine *Die Kunst im Deutschen Reich*. The document is not yet signed by Hitler.

PACKETS AND CASES

Each of the grades of the Order of the Iron Cross came with a package or a case. The lower grade of the Iron Cross Second Class and the Spange to the Second Class of 1914 were normally distributed to the divisions in paper packages. However, the privately purchased items were often packed in more elaborate cases or boxes which are quite rare and demand a far higher price than the actual award.

The following is only a very brief overview with some typical samples. It must be noted that there exists a great many variations in cases.

For very special occasions special red presentation cases were provided which had the required combination of awards all in one case.

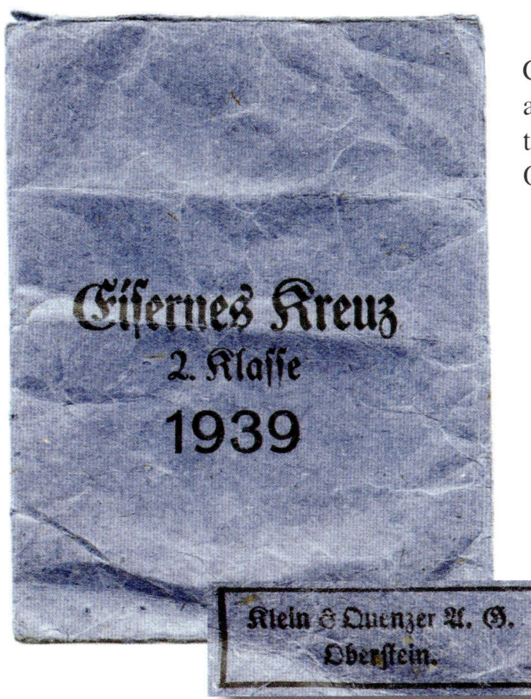

Left: Packet for the Iron Cross Second Class. The content was always one cross and a piece of ribbon. This packet is stamped on the reverse with "Klein & Quenzer A.G. Oberstein." The size is 104 mm x 130 mm.

Right: A typical paper package for the *Spange* Second Class. The reverse of the bag bears the name of Ziemer & Söhne, Oberstein.

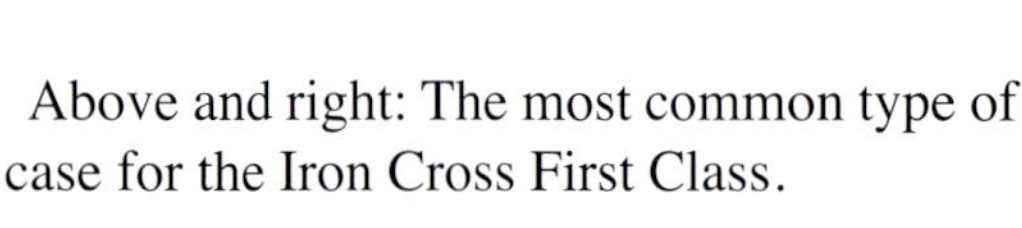

Above and right: The most common type of case for the Iron Cross First Class.

Left and below: Later type case for the First Class *Spange*.

Left: A screwback Iron Cross First Class in a special LDO-marked case. LDO cases are rarer than the regular cases.

Right: A Knights Cross in the typical elongated case. The ribbon is around 72 cm long.

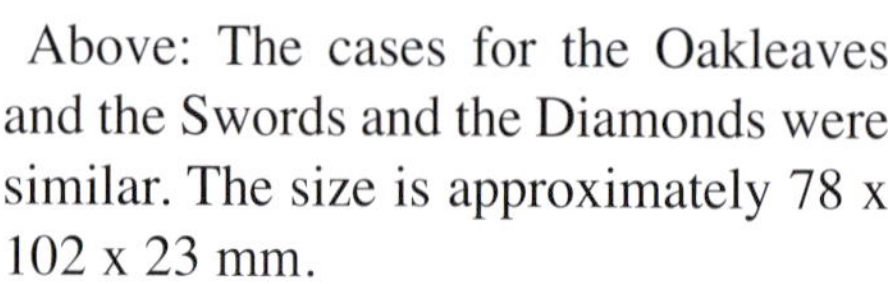

Above: The cases for the Oakleaves and the Swords and the Diamonds were similar. The size is approximately 78 x 102 x 23 mm.

Right: The case for the Diamonds has an additional gold line around the upper lid.

The Grand Cross sits in a red presentation case with the national eagle in gold imprint on the lid.

The Star to the Grand Cross rests in a red presentation case with black satin insert. The outside lid has a real metal Iron Cross First Class attached to the top.

For very special occasions special red presentation cases were provided which had the required combination of awards all in one case. These cases are extremely rare and extremely expensive.

Right: *Generaloberst* von Brauchitsch received the Knights Cross and the two *Spangen* in the special presentation case on October 27, 1939.

THE ORDER IN WEAR

All but one grade of the Order of the Iron Cross could be worn on the uniform for daily wear. The Iron Cross Second Class was only worn on the medal bar with the parade uniform; for daily wear only the ribbon was attached through the second button hole of the tunic. On the day of the award, however, pictures were taken with the medal attached to the uniform with a pin or such. This is why so many loose Iron Crosses in nearly mint condition can be found; they were stored away since they could not be worn.

Left: A *Panzermann* wears his Iron cross Second Class on the day of the awarding for the obligatory picture.

Right: Only on the medal bar was the Iron Cross Second Class worn, always in the first place.

Left: *Oberleutnant* Ferdinand Schröder, *KpChef 5./GrenRgt 1124* (*558 Volksgrenadierdivision*) wears the ribbon of the Iron Cross Second Class per regulations in the button hole. He was awarded with the Knights Cross on March 17, 1945.

Right: *Oberst* W. Daser, commander *InfRgt 388* (*214. InfDiv*) wears both *Spangen* per regulations.

Wachtmeister Wilhelm Pardon, *Zugführer 1./AufklAbt 15*, was awarded with the Knights Cross of the Iron Cross on December 9, 1944. Here he also wears the Iron Cross First Class, the General Assault Badge, and the Wound Badge in Silver on the breast pocket. Above the pocket he wears his Close Combat Bar. And he wears two Tank Destruction Badges on the upper right arm. He did not survive the war.

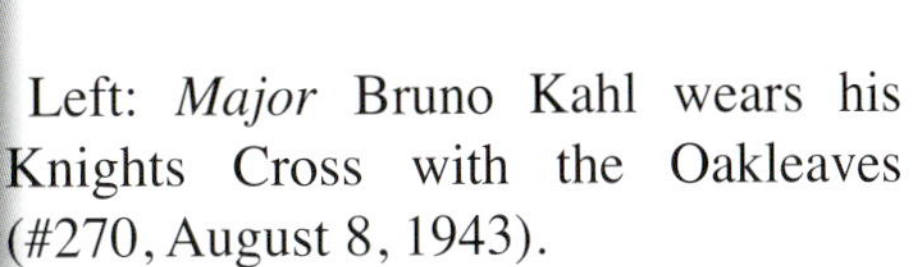

Left: *Major* Bruno Kahl wears his Knights Cross with the Oakleaves (#270, August 8, 1943).

Left: *Dr. med. dent. Major* Franz Bäke was the 49th recipient of the very high award of the Swords on February 21, 1944. He was commander of the *PzRgt 11* of the *6. PzDiv.* Note the three Tank Destruction Badges on his right upper arm. He survived the war and died in 1978.

Right: *General der Panzertruppen* Hermann Balck was the 19th recipient of the "Diamonds" on August 31, 1944 while he was commander of the *4. Panzer-Armee*.

Above: Iron Crosses Second Class are awarded to two soldiers in front of the troops. This must have been early in the war.

Below: Award ceremony of the Knights Cross in front of the troops.

MINIATURES AND STICKPINS

For the private evening dress or the private outfit the wear of miniatures or stick pins was authorized. All grades up to the Swords are known to have existed as miniatures. The typical size was either 16 mm or 9 mm. Collecting miniatures is still fairly inexpensive and rewarding. However, the higher grades of the Order of the Iron Cross already demand high prices.

Left: A 16 mm miniature with ribbon of the Iron Cross Second Class.

Right: Stickpins in 16 mm size of the *Spange* to the Iron Cross Second Class, early and late patterns.

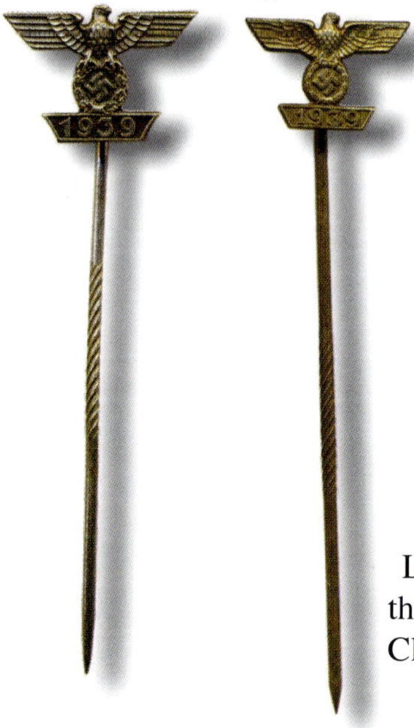

Left: Stickpins in 16 mm size of the *Spange* to the Iron Cross First Class, early and late patterns.

Left: 16 mm stickpin with the Iron Cross First and Second Class and a Wound Badge in Silver.

Above: One single 9 mm-sized Knights Cross with Oakleaves stickpin and one in combination with the Iron Crosses First and Second Class.

Left: 9 mm Stickpin of the Knights Cross with Oakleaves and Swords.

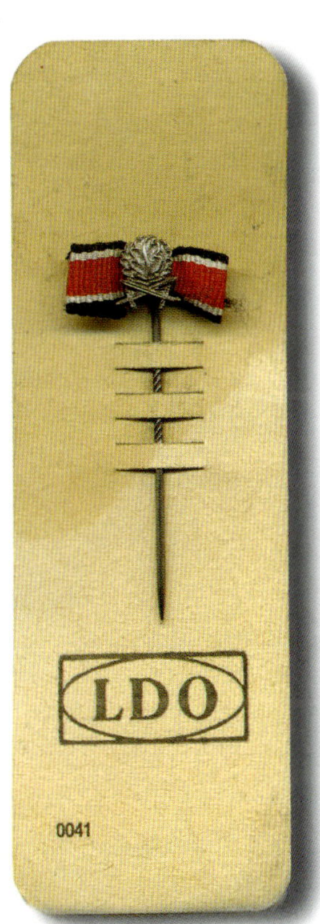

Right: Single 9 mm Oakleaves with Sword stickpin on the LDO card.

One can find all kinds of types, shapes, and combinations. Despite the regulations put in place by the *Präsidialkanzlei* and the LDO it seems that they were not obeyed closely by every company. No miniatures or stickpins were ever awarded together with the full size version. They were all private purchases.

FAKES AND REPRODUCTIONS

Every grade of the Order of the Iron Cross has been reproduced - including the miniatures! (Collecting orders and medals of the Third *Reich* in general is nothing for the faint hearted and gullible.)

However, the fakes are relatively easy to recognize and are for the greater part very well documented. Since the era of the Third *Reich* is over and the collector field is complete, it should be clear that it is very unlikely that previously unknown Knights Cross types or new Oakleaves variations will be discovered.

But the Iron Cross Second Class most likely still has some undiscovered makers and dedicated researchers are even finding new variations of the Iron Cross First Class.

The logical conclusion for the average collector out of this should be very easy and straightforward: study the originals and everything that does not compare to the documented originals is a reproduction! A lot of collectors try to keep up with the ever growing amount of fakes and want to see pictures of them and record their weights and technical data. It is a waste of time and energy since one will never keep up. The study of the real thing, however, is a closed subject with a limited number of genuine objects.

There are, however, two types of fakes: the first types are of unique styles with characteristics unlike those of known originals. These types can be excluded as genuine because they share nothing (except the basic award design) in common with genuine wartime pieces.

The other group encompasses the fakes which are modelled after an accepted original. This could be a very bad cast copy of an Iron Cross or *Spange* or the very good microcast of an Oakleaves set. Or the fake could be a die-struck Knights Cross which tries to mimic some of the original features but doesn't get it quite right. Some of these copies are dangerous and some of them are only detectable under a microscope and with a great deal of experience.

In the case of the higher priced grades of the Order of the Iron Cross it is advisable either to buy from a respected dealer or auction house with unconditional return guarantee or from a private person who has no objections if the medal can be shown to other collectors before buying.

THE 1957 VERSION OF THE ORDER

On July 26, 1957, a law was passed by the West German government which allowed the wearing of the former awards of the German Army. However, the original forms of the awards were not allowed to be worn, but rather so-called "denazified" versions which no longer exhibited the banned swastika.

The new design of the Order of the Iron Cross was actually again the old one. The swastika was replaced by the same three oakleaves which were already used by the earlier versions. Naturally, no "1957-version" of the Oakleaves, the Oakleaves with Swords and the Oakleaves with Diamonds exist, since theses awards never showed a swastika. Very often one can find examples on the market, presented as early 1957 products of these awards, but they are only fakes.

Former members of the *Wehrmacht* who were now members of the newly founded *Bundeswehr* and had been awarded the Iron Cross First Class or higher were only allowed to wear the award with the uniform on special occasions. For daily wear the decorations were worn as miniatures on a ribbon bar which was worn above the left breast pocket.

Right: The *Spange* for the EK1 and EK2 of 1939 in the 1957 versions.

Left and below: The EK1 and EK2 of 1939 in the 1957 versions.

Above: The Knights Cross of the Iron Cross in the 1957 version. This cross was made by the manufacturer Otto Schickle and is considered very rare. The other well known manufacturer of the 1957 version, Steinhauer & Lück, was also a former producer during the Third *Reich*. Early-made versions of the 1957 series are already demanding relatively high prices.

Above: A typical *Bundeswehr* ribbon bar (*Bandspange*) of a former recipient of the Knights Cross and other awards of the Second World War. The last medal is a post-war Sports Badge of the Federal Republic of Germany.

The early *Bundeswehr* took in quite a number of former *Wehrmacht* soldiers, which was actually a very normal and rational thing to do, especially in the light of the developing Cold War.

ODDITIES OF THE ORDERS OF THE IRON CROSS

It is very rarely the case that examples of high German military awards were also made by other countries. But in the case of the Order of the Iron Cross there are such awards due to the connection with some allies.

The most interesting subject (which would need a full study of its own) are the Spanish -made Iron Crosses. They were produced in Spain and were worn (and still are) by the awardees of the Spanish Legion which fought in Russia alongside German troops.

Right: Spanish-made Iron Cross First Class.

Left: The Iron Cross Second Class, made in Spain, with the typical ribbon clasp.

Right: The Japanese-made Iron Crosses First Class are very rare. They were made in Japan on order of the German military attache and approximately 25 were awarded to crew members of the raider *Michael*. [21]

Left: One can also find cloth versions of the Iron Cross First Class (and only of this class). Each example is more or less a unique item and must be judged individually by the material used and the type of construction. Original examples can be considered as rare.

FOOTNOTES

1 Reichel, Arthur, *127 Jahre Eisernes Kreuz* (2nd Eidtion, Dresden 1942). Stephen Previtera mentions a total of 16,938, including 869 for non-combatant. (*The Iron Time*, page 43). Regarding the First Class, Previtera shows a number of 638 (incl. non-combatants). Jörg Nimmergut shows a copy of an original document in his book *Das Eiserne Kreuz 1813 - 1939* (Edition Deutsches Ordensmuseum, 1990, München, page 52) which adds up to 16,321 awarded Second Class and 636 awarded of the First Class.

2 Reichel, Arthur, *127 Jahre Eisernes Kreuz* (2nd Edition, Dresden 1942). Stephen Previtera shows a total number of 47,244 for the Second Class and a total of 1,304 for the First Class (*The Iron Time*, page 126).

3 Reichel, Arthur, *127 Jahre Eisernes Kreuz* (2nd Edition, Dresden 1942). Stephen Previtera shows a total number of 3,803,384 for the Second Class and a total of 145,024 for the First Class (*The Iron Time*, page 206/230). G. Williamson (*The Iron Cross of 1939*, Bender Publishing) states "over 5 million for the Second Class and 250,000 for the First Class.

4 Merkblatt 15/5, *Orden und Ehrenzeichen,* July 1, 1943, page 21-22

5 Merkblatt 15/5, *Orden und Ehrenzeichen,* July 1, 1943, page 28

6 Stephen Previtera, *The Iron Time*, page 320

7 Maerz/Stimson, *The Iron Cross First Class*, page 33

8 Williamson lists in his book *The Iron Cross of 1939* a total of 51 makers. Fourteen have not been proven and can be considered listed in error. He missed two proven ones (132 and 140).

9 Stephen Previtera mentions a total number of 450,000 which seems far too high and does not agree with the official numbers of *Spangen* supplied to the *Wehrmacht*.

10 Williamson lists in his book *The Iron Cross of 1939* a total of nine manufacturers, among them three with *Präsidialkanzlei* numbers (21, 44, 111). This could not be confirmed. Nimmergut lists eight manufacturers (*Deutsche Orden und Ehrenzeichen*, Vol.IV, page 2171, among them one with a PKZ number (111).

11 Maerz/Stimson, *The Iron Cross First Class*, page 34

12 Stephen Previtera shows a total of 150,000 awarded *Spangen* First Class. This number is also too high. Nimmergut estimates a total of both *Spangen* First and Second Class at 100,000 (ditto, page 2156) which seems to be correct based on the contemporary documents.

13 Veit Scherzer, *Ritterkreuzträger 1939 - 1945,* Scherzers Militaire-Verlag Ranis/Jena 2005. (Scherzer did unfortunately not number the entries)

14 Dietrich Maerz, *The German Cross*, B&D Publishing LLC, Richmond, 2009, page 66 ff.

15 Bernd Hartmann, *Die Kriegsauszeichnungen des Deutschen Heeres*, Erfstadt, Eigenverlag 2011, page 1.17

16 *International Medal Collector*, B&D Publishing LLC, 2010, Vol.1/No. 4, page 45 ff

17 *International Medal Collector*, B&D Publishing LLC, Vol.3/No. 1, page 7 ff

18 Detlev Niemann, *Bewertungskatalog Orden und Ehrenzeichen*, Niemann Verlag 2004, Hamburg, page 471.

19 Gordon Williamson, *The Iron Cross of 1939*, Bender Publishing, San Jose 2002, page 409-411

20 For more information refer to Dietrich Maerz, *The Knights Cross of the Iron Cross*, B&D Publishing, 2007, page 184 ff

21 Maerz/Stimson, *The Iron Cross First Class*, page 418 ff

BIBLIOGRAPHY

Bowen, V.E, , *The Prussian and German Iron Cross*, Research Publications

Doehle, Dr. Heinrich, *Die Auszeichnungen des Grossdeutschen Reichs*, Berlin 1945

Dombrowski, Hanns, *Orden, Ehrenzeichen und Titel*, Franz Wahlen, 1940

Geeb, *Deutsche Orden und Ehrenzeichen*, Heymanns Verlag, 1985

Geissler, Harald, *Das Eiserne Kreuz*, Patzwall-Verlag, 1995

Klietmann, Kurt, *Auszeichnungen des Deutschen Reiches 1936-1945*, Motorbuch

Klietmann, Kurt, *Deutsche Auszeichnungen*, Die Ordens-Sammlung, Berlin, 1971

Maerz, Dietrich, *The Knights Cross of the Iron Cross*, B&D Publishing, 2007

Maerz, Dietrich/Stimson, George, *The Iron Cross 1. Class*, B&D Publishing, 2010

Merkblatt 15/5, *Orden und Ehrenzeichen*, Biblio-Verlag, 1992

Niemann, Detlev, *Bewertungskatalog 1871-1945*, Niemann-Verlag, 2004/2009

Nimmergut, Jörg, *Das Eiserne Kreuz 1813-1939*, Edition Deutsches Ordensmuseum

Nimmergut, Jörg, *Deutsche Orden und Ehrenzeichen*, Vol. IV, München, 2004

Previtera, Stephen, *The Iron Time*, Winidore Press, 2008

Reichel, Arthur, *127 Jahre Eisernes Kreuz,* 2nd Edition, Dresden 1942

Scherzer, Veit, *Ritterkreuzträger*, Scherzers Militaire-Verlag, Jena, 2005

Williamson, Gordon, *The Iron Cross of 1939*, Bender Publishing, 2002

Der Uniformen-Markt, Volumes 1939-1945

Schwert und Spaten, Volumes 1939-1942

Chapter 2

The Honor Roll of the Heer

EHRENBLATT

DES DEUTSCHEN HEERES

Auf dem Schlachtfeld haben sich durch besondere Tapferkeit hervorgetan:

Oberst [illegible],
Kommandeur eines Infanterie-Regiments

Oberst An[illegible],
Komm[illegible]

Oberst Hoßbach,
Kommandeur eines Infanterie-Regiments

Oberst Seyffardt,
Kommandeur eines Infanterie-Regiments

Oberst Casper,
Kommandeur eines Infanterie-Regiments

Oberstleutnant von Stolzmann,
Bataillons-Kommandeur in einem Infanterie-Regiment

Major Gutman,
Kommandeur eines Schützen-Bataillons

Major Oehmi[illegible]
Kommand[illegible]

Hauptmann [illegible]
Komp[illegible]

Hauptmann [illegible]
Kom[illegible]

Oberleutnant [illegible]
in eine[illegible]

Oberleutnant [illegible]
in einem [illegible]

Oberleutnant [illegible],
in einem [illegible]-Regiment

Oberleutnant Nebe,
Führer einer Voraus-Abteilung

Knights Cross winner *Hauptmann* Günter Braake in his *Waffenrock* with the Honor Roll Clasp on the ribbon of the Iron Cross 2. Class of 1939. He was named in the Honor Roll for his bravery as commander of *I.Btl/GrenRgt 422 (126. InfDiv)* during action near Preekulln in the Kurland pocket on 22. February 1945.

Table of Contents

THE HONOR ROLL CLASP

HISTORY

Already some time before the foundation of the Order of the German Cross 1941, which was an award to fill the gap between the Iron Cross First Class and the Knights Cross of the Iron Cross, it was recognized that some wartime bravery deeds needed to be recognized in a specific way.

The first step of this type of recognition was the naming of the soldier in the *Wehrmachtsbericht (*Armed Forces Report*)*. This procedure was instituted by the Supreme Commander of the Army, *Generalfeldmarschall* von Brauchitsch, on April 27, 1940.[1] It is also noted in the first regulations that the naming is a special recognition which is reserved for the *Führer* to give in exceptional cases.

From the end of July 1941 soldiers which had performed exceptional bravery deeds, which were not deemed sufficient for the award of the Knights Cross of the Iron Cross, were announced within the newly created *Ehrenblatt des Deutschen Heeres* (Honor Roll of the German Army). The regulation was issued on 15. July 1941 (OKH/Gen St d H/H Wes Abt Nr. 2310/41). The first Honor Roll with 27 names was dated 22. July 1941 and was issued as a supplement to the *Heeresverordnungsblatt* (Army Ordinance Gazette).[2]

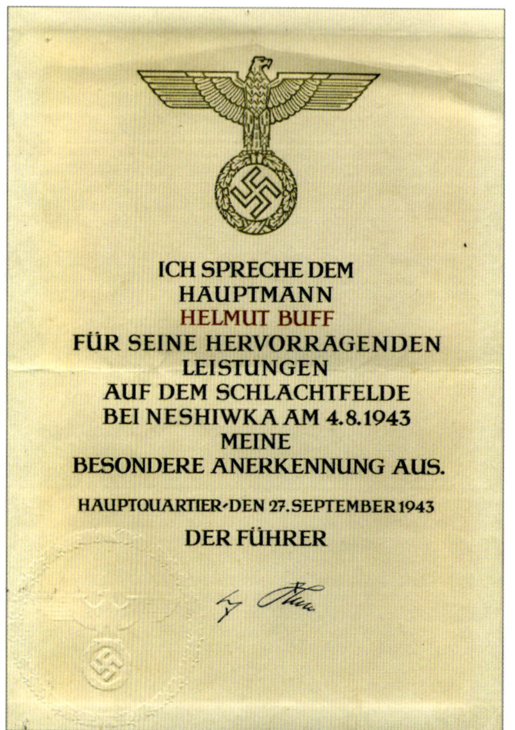

ICH SPRECHE DEM
HAUPTMANN
HELMUT BUFF
FÜR SEINE HERVORRAGENDEN
LEISTUNGEN
AUF DEM SCHLACHTFELDE
BEI NESHIWKA AM 4.8.1943
MEINE
BESONDERE ANERKENNUNG AUS.

HAUPTQUARTIER, DEN 27. SEPTEMBER 1943

DER FÜHRER

The regulations made it very clear that a "sharp measuring stick" had to be applied for naming in the Honor Roll. It was also stipulated that it was possible to name complete small units up to company strength.

In addition to naming in the Honor Roll, the named soldier also received a Certificate of Recognition (*Anerkennungsurkunde*), signed by the *Führer* personally (left).

This procedure continued until the beginning of 1944 when the actual Honor Roll Clasp was introduced as a visual sign of achievement to be worn on the uniform.

EHRENBLATT
DES DEUTSCHEN HEERES

Auf dem Schlachtfeld haben sich durch besondere Tapferkeit hervorgetan:

Oberst **Pflaum**,
Kommandeur eines Infanterie-Regiments

Oberst **Angern**,
Kommandeur einer Schützen-Brigade

Oberst **Hoßbach**,
Kommandeur eines Infanterie-Regiments

Oberst **Seyffardt**,
Kommandeur eines Infanterie-Regiments

Oberst **Casper**,
Kommandeur eines Infanterie-Regiments

Oberstleutnant **von Stolzmann**,
Bataillons-Kommandeur in einem Infanterie-Regiment

Major **Gutman**,
Kommandeur eines Schützen-Bataillons

Major **Oehmichen**,
Kommandeur einer Panzer-Jäger-Abteilung

Hauptmann **Borchardt**,
Kompanie-Chef in einer Aufklärungs-Abteilung

Hauptmann **Unger**,
Kompanie-Chef in einem Schützen-Regiment

Oberleutnant **Eichert**,
in einem Schützen-Regiment

Oberleutnant **Erdl**,
in einem Kradschützen-Bataillon

Oberleutnant **Gröpler**,
in einem Artillerie-Regiment

Oberleutnant **Nebe**,
Führer einer Voraus-Abteilung

Leutnant **Bertra**
in einem Artille

Leutnant **Fromm**
in einem Panzer

Leutnant **Hauck**,
Kompanie-Führ

Leutnant **Kirchn**
in einem Schütz

Leutnant **Kurz**,
in einem Panzer

Leutnant **Süßen**
in einem Schütz

Oberfeldwebel **Ja**
in einer schw. I

Oberfeldwebel **Ty**
in einem Schütz

Feldwebel **Pliska**
in einem Panzer

Unteroffizier **Rot**
in einer Panzer-

Gefreiter **Rothe**
in einem Krads

Gefreiter **Schmi**
in einem Infant

Schütze **Haiß**,
in einem Infant

Hauptquartier O.K.H., den 22. Juli 1941

Der Oberbefehlshaber des Heeres

von Brauchitsch

Generalfeldmarschall

The very first issue of the Honor Roll of the German Army, dated 22. July 1941 and signed by *Generalfeldmarschall* von Brauchitsch.

REGULATIONS

There are no real regulations for the Honor Roll Clasp itself. The clasp was instituted on 30. January 1944 with a simple decree by Adolf Hitler:

> *"The soldiers, who are named in the Honor Roll of the German Army, will receive as a visible identification the Honor Roll Clasp. The gilded clasp consists of a swastika inside an oak leaf wreath. It is worn with the ribbon of the Iron Cross of 1939."*

The original regulations stayed unchanged. It is noteworthy that the regulation specifically stated that merits for commanding the troops or achievements of the troops are not sufficient reasons for the naming in the Honor Roll. The Honor Roll and the Honor Roll Clasp was a dedicated bravery decoration.

Award proposals had to be formulated and commented upon in the same fashion it was required for the Knights Cross of the Iron Cross or German Cross. The OKH/HPA (personnel office of the army) conducted a preliminary examination and gave their recommendations to the final decision maker, which was:

from 1. July 1941 - 19. December 1941	Supreme Commander of the Army *Generalfeldmarschall* Walther von Brauchitsch
20. December 1941 - 22. April 1945	The *Führer* and Supreme Commander of the *Wehrmacht* Adolf Hitler
23. April 1945 - 8. May 1945	Supreme Commanders of Army Groups and independent armies.

Actual award numbers are very sketchy and differ. One source mentions a total of 4,272 awards to the soldiers of the army and *Waffen-SS* (114)[3], other sources name 4,556[4] or 4,547 (including 165 for the Waffen-SS).[5] The vast majority of Honor Roll Clasps were awarded in 1944 and approximately 700 were awarded in the last months of the war in 1945. It is noteworthy that the Honor Roll Clasp was awarded far more sparsely than the Knights Cross of the Iron Cross and it is clear that actual awarded pieces are extremely rare.

The naming of groups or units was extremely rare and only 35 are documented. Only 14 awards to foreigners are recorded, 13 of them to members of the Waffen-SS.[6]

The Honor Roll Clasps for the *Luftwaffe* (*Ehrenblattspange der Luftwaffe)* and for the Navy (*Ehrentafelspange der Kriegsmarine*)[7] were instituted at a later date: on 5. July 1944 for the *Luftwaffe* and on 15. July 1944 for the *Kriegsmarine*.

DESIGN

Contrary to most of the other orders and awards of the Third Reich which show a so-called "running" or "dynamic" swastika as a representation of the government, the Honor Roll Clasp of the *Heer* exhibits a so-called "static" swastika. This is the type that can be found on the political flags, like the standards of the SA organizations.

The swastika is encircled by an oak leaves wreath with a prominent ribbon bow at the bottom. A circumferential trim line is stamped into the surface of the swastika. The clasp is gilded and is presented together with a piece of ribbon of the Iron Cross Second Class of 1939.

Above: Depiction of the Honor Roll Clasp in the publication *Lohn der Tat*. It is titled "Tscherkassy, march to freedom"

THE HONOR ROLL CLASP

The Honor Roll Clasp of the *Heer* is always made of two main parts: the wreath and the swastika. Both parts are stamped from *Tombak* sheet metal. The solid swastika is soldered to the wreath with four attachment points at the end of each swastika arm.

Four round prongs with a diameter of 0.7 mm and blunt tips are soldered to the reverse of the clasp. The complete assembly was gilded after completion.

The size is 24 mm wide and 25 mm high. The swastika has a dimension of 11.5 mm across. The weight is 3.5 g (w/o ribbon).

The reverse of the clasp shows the solder points of the swastika and the arrangement of the four prongs, which are about 10 mm long. The clasps do not have any maker markings.

The company of Otto Klein/Hanau was the only manufacturer of the Honor Roll Clasp of the *Heer*.[8]

AWARD DOCUMENT

There was no specific award document for the Honor Roll Clasp since the clasp was the visible sign for the naming in the Honor Roll itself. The document which went along with the recording into the Honor Roll was the Certificate of Recognition as shown below.

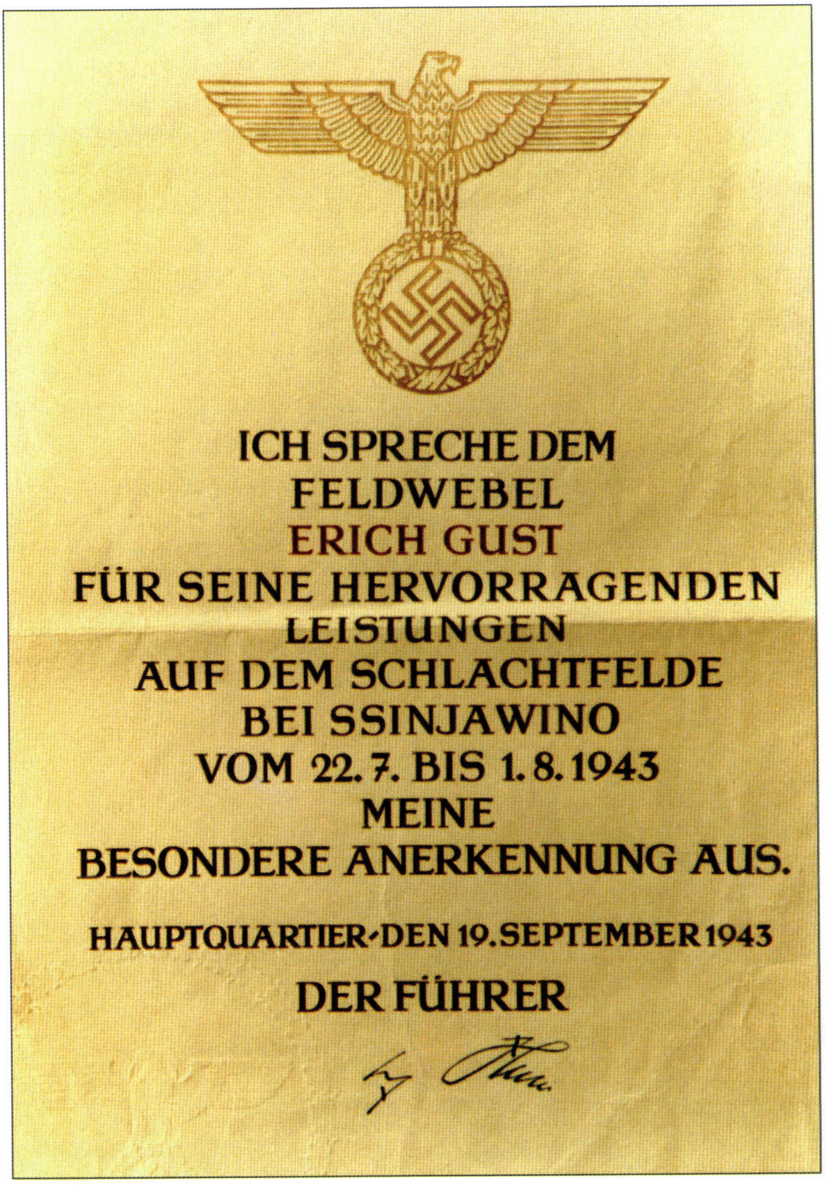

ICH SPRECHE DEM
FELDWEBEL
ERICH GUST
FÜR SEINE HERVORRAGENDEN
LEISTUNGEN
AUF DEM SCHLACHTFELDE
BEI SSINJAWINO
VOM 22.7. BIS 1.8.1943
MEINE
BESONDERE ANERKENNUNG AUS.

HAUPTQUARTIER, DEN 19. SEPTEMBER 1943

DER FÜHRER

Above: Certificate of Recognition for *Feldwebel* Erich Gust, dated 19. September 1943 (cropped size).

THE CASE

The Honor Roll Clasp of the *Heer* was presented in a black case with the dimensions 100 mm long, 68 mm wide, and 23 mm high.

The clasp was crimped to the red, white, and black ribbon of the Iron Cross of 1939 and this ribbon was attached to a carton insert. This insert is covered with an off-white velour and could be lifted out of the case with a piece of ribbon attached to the top right corner of the insert.

The company logos of Otto Klein, the "K" in a circle and three chevrons in a circle, are embossed in the lower left corner of the insert.

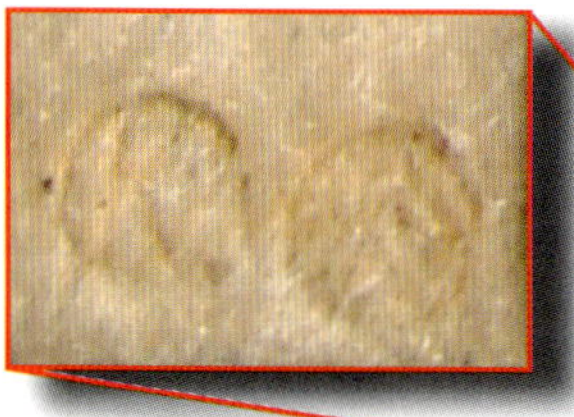

THE CLASP IN WEAR

Due to the relative late institution date of the clasp itself, not too many photographs of the clasp in wear are still in existence. The clasp was worn in the second button hole of the tunic, attached to the ribbon of the Iron Cross Second Class of 1939. Wearing of the *Wiederholungsspange* of the Iron Cross Second Class of 1914 on the black -white ribbon together with the Honor Roll Clasp was not permitted.

There was no provision for the Honor Roll Clasp to be worn on the parade medal bar or on the small ribbon bar. There is no miniature version of the Honor Roll Clasp.

Left: *Leutnant* Erich Gust was awarded with the Honor Roll Clasp on 19. September 1943 (below) holding the rank of *Feldwebel* in *6.Kp/GrenRgt 23*.

He also wears a Close Combat Bar in Silver and the ribbon for the East Front medal.

The Honor Roll Clasp shown below is his actual awarded piece.

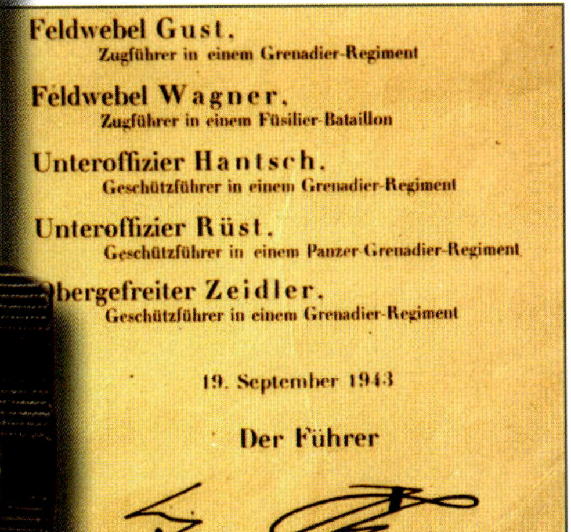

Feldwebel Gust.
Zugführer in einem Grenadier-Regiment

Feldwebel Wagner.
Zugführer in einem Füsilier-Bataillon

Unteroffizier Hantsch.
Geschützführer in einem Grenadier-Regiment

Unteroffizier Rüst.
Geschützführer in einem Panzer-Grenadier-Regiment

Obergefreiter Zeidler.
Geschützführer in einem Grenadier-Regiment

19. September 1943

Der Führer

Right: *Hauptmann* Dr. Karl-Wilhelm Knauth (Knights Cross on 14. November 1943, *Lt. d. R., Fhr. 3.Kp/sPzAbt 505)* wears his Honor Roll Clasp (awarded 7. September 1943) on his *Panzer* wrapper. He was awarded the German Cross in Gold on 20. January 1945. Knauth was killed in the Halbe cauldron on 25. April 1945.

Left: *Hauptmann d.R.* Wilhelm Kubel (Knights Cross 30. September 1944 as *Führer II.Btl/GrenRgt 162*) was awarded with the Honor Roll Clasp on 7. May 1943. He survived the war and later served in the *Bundeswehr* which he left in 1964 with the rank of *Oberstleutnant*.

Above: *Major* Georg Wenzelburger (Knights Cross 26. December 1944 as *Hauptmann* and *Führer II. Btl/GrenRgt 1098*) was awarded with the Honor Roll Clasp on 5. May 1944. The German Cross in Gold was awarded earlier on 18. March 1943. *Mayor* Wenzelburger was also awarded with the Close Combat Bar in Gold (18. February 1945). He had accumulated a total of 78 close combat days, which is the second highest number. He survived the war and died in 2000 at the age of 89.

FAKES AND REPRODUCTIONS

It goes without saying that the Honor Roll Clasp is also reproduced, respectively faked. One needs to remember that at this point in time (2011) the research says that only one manufacturer supplied the *Präsidialkanzlei des Führers* with the Honor Roll Clasp. This maker was Otto Klein/Hanau.

The clasps shown in this chapter are all from this very company and they are all absolutely genuine examples. By comparing the fingerprints of the shown clasps with possible examples it should be fairly easy to determine originality. One should also take into consideration that the Honor Roll Clasp is a very rare decoration.

THE 1957 VERSION OF THE ORDER

The Honor Roll Clasp was authorized in the new "Law about Titles, Orders and Medals", dated 26. July 1957, of course in a de-nazified version. The central swastika was replaced with two crossed swords.

Left: Honor Roll Clasp of the Army in the denazified version as shown in the attachment to the actual law of 1957.

Right: The 1957 version of the Honor Roll Clasp in its simple carton box. Note the 57-style ribbon with the typical grey-white stripes.

Left: The method of wear for the daily services for members of the former *Wehrmacht*, who now served in the newly founded *Bundeswehr*, was in form of a 25 x 12 mm ribbon bar worn above the left breast pocket.

FOOTNOTES

1 Merkblatt 5/15, page 73 ff

2 J. Nimmergut states the first publication date of the Honor Roll as 22. January 1941 (*Deutsche Orden und Ehrenzeichen*, Vol. IV, page 2214) which is incorrect. Hormann in his book *Die Ehrenblattspangen der Wehrmachtteile* mentions a date of 5. August 1941, which is also incorrect.

3 J.M. Hormann, *Die Ehrenblattspangen der Wehrmacht*, Münchner Ordenskundliche Studien, Vol.2, page 16, Hannover

4 R. Absolon, *Wehrgesetz und Wehrdienst*, 1960, *Schriften des Bundesarchivs*, page 263. H. Geissler mentions the same number in his book *Das Eiserne Kreuz von 1813 bis heute*, page 262

5 J. Nimmergut, *Orden und Ehrenzeichen*, Vol IV, page 2215

6 J. Nimmergut, *Orden und Ehrenzeichen*, Vol. IV, page 2215

7 Weber/Skora, *The Kriegsmarine Awards*, Vol. 2, page 997 ff, B&D Publishing, 2011

8 J. Nimmergut mentions C.E. Juncker/Berlin as a second manufacturer. This is doubtful. (*Orden und Ehrenzeichen*, Vol. IV, page 2215)

BIBLIOGRAPHY

Doehle, Dr. Heinrich, *Die Auszeichnungen des Grossdeutschen Reichs*, Berlin 1945

Dombrowski, Hanns, *Orden, Ehrenzeichen und Titel*, Franz Wahlen, 1940

Geeb, *Deutsche Orden und Ehrenzeichen*, Heymanns Verlag, 1985

Geissler, Harald, *Das Eiserne Kreuz*, Patzwall-Verlag, 1995

Klietmann, Kurt, *Auszeichnungen des Deutschen Reiches 1936-1945*, Motorbuch

Merkblatt 15/5, *Orden und Ehrenzeichen*, Biblio-Verlag, 1992

Niemann, Detlev, *Bewertungskatalog 1871-1945*, Niemann-Verlag, 2004/2009

Nimmergut, Jörg, *Deutsche Orden und Ehrenzeichen*, Vol. IV, München, 2004

Scheibert, Horst, *Die Träger der Ehrenblatt-Spange des Heeres*, Podzun-Pallas, 1986

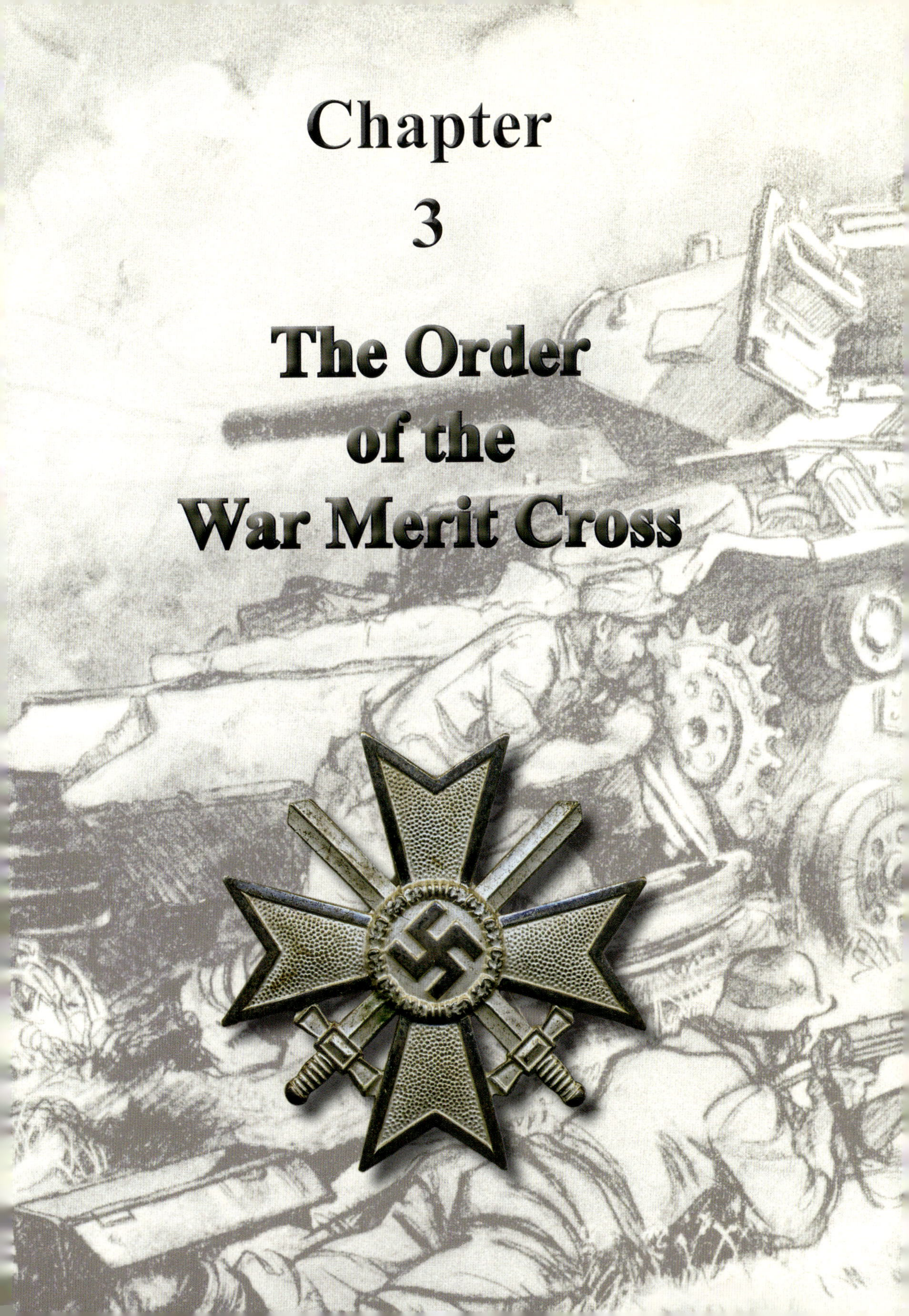

Chapter 3

The Order of the War Merit Cross

Professor Dr. Ferdinand Sauerbruch, one of the most influential surgeons of the 20th century, was awarded the Knights Cross of the War Merit Cross with Swords on 10. December 1943 for his services within the *Wehrmacht*. The photograph shows him in Brüssel/ Belgium in his uniform as *Generalarzt d.R.*

Table of Contents

THE ORDER OF THE WAR MERIT CROSS

HISTORY

The award of a medal or an order in war for other deeds than pure bravery in the face of the enemy has a long tradition. The latest version of such an award before the introduction of the 1939 Order of War Merit Cross was the *Preußisches Verdienstkreuz für Kriegshilfe* (Prussian Cross of Merit for War Auxiliaries), founded 5. December 1916 by Kaiser Wilhelm II. This cross had the form of an eight-pointed star (*Spitzkreuz*), and was issued in one class only in very high numbers. The cross was made of zinc and the ribbon had a

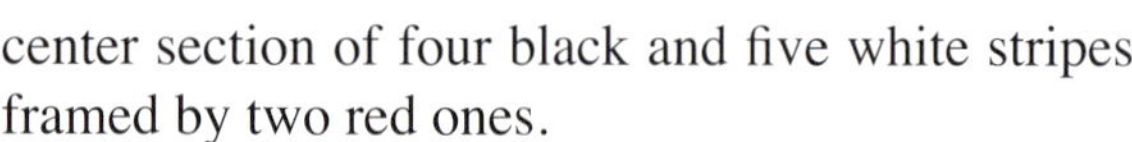

center section of four black and five white stripes framed by two red ones.

This cross (left) could be (and was) awarded to all kinds of military or civilian personnel who distinguished themselves in the war effort. The reason for the foundation of this cross was to be able to recognize the efforts of non-combatant citizens in this first time modern total war, which required not only the sacrifices of the common soldier but also those of the people at the home front.

Since it was obvious from the very beginning of the Second World War that efforts outside the pure military realm had to be recognized and awarded, Adolf Hitler as *Führer* and Commander of the Armed Forces founded the Order of the War Merit Cross on 24. October, 1939.

Links: II. Kl. ohne Schwerter in Bronze, daneben mit Schwertern. Rechts: I. Kl. in Silber, und zwar ohne Schwerter (oben) und mit Schwertern (unten). Aufn. Scherl (K)

The foundation of the new order was announced in the *Uniformen-Markt*, issue 1. November 1939. Initially it was founded only in two classes, with and without swords. Note the design similarity to the Prussian Cross of Merit for War Auxiliaries.

REGULATIONS

The foundation stated that the new order was meant *"as a sign of recognition for those merits in the war which was forced upon us, for which there cannot be any appreciation with the Order of the Iron Cross."*

The order was initially founded in two classes, with and without swords, and served also as a consolidation of the Order of the Iron Cross as a pure bravery and military merit decoration. With a second decree dated 28. August 1940 the order was expanded to include the Knights Cross of the War Merit Cross with and without Swords (at the top end of the award series) and the War Merit Medal (at the lower end).

The Supreme Command of the Army issued special guidelines for the War Merit Cross[1] (emphasis in the original text) for the award procedures within the *Heer*:

> The Knights Cross of the War Merit Cross with Swords was to be awarded for outstanding merits with d e c i s i v e implications for the conduct of the war.
>
> The First Class with Swords was to be awarded for special and s i g n i f i c a n t merits under enemy fire or for s p e c i a l merits in the conduct of the war.
>
> The Second Class with Swords was to be awarded for merits during deployment under enemy fire or for merits in the conduct of the war (such as merits within the forces and for the forces as far as they are not special bravery deeds or battle-decisive leadership decisions).
>
> The Knights Cross w/o Swords was to be awarded for outstanding merits with d e c i s i v e implications for the conduct of war functions.
>
> The First Class w/o Swords for special merits with s u b s t a n t i a l implications on the implementation of war functions (and also for special merits in the administration and economy).
>
> The Second Class w/o Swords for merits in the conduct of general war-related tasks.
>
> The War Merit Medal was to be awarded for commendable deeds during the conduct of war functions within the army (commendable activities mainly in the arms industry).

It must be understood that the award criteria outside of the *Heer* were formulated differently, especially those for persons on the home front (which is not subject of this book[2]).

The last official change to the regulations of the Order of the War Merit Cross was done on 8. July 1944 when the additional grade of the Golden Knights Cross of the War Merit Cross with and without Swords was added.

Initially it was not allowed to continue to wear the War Merit Cross if the Iron Cross was awarded later on. This was changed in 1941 and from that point on both orders could be worn at the same time.

The First and Second Class award procedures were handled the same way as this was done with the Iron Cross. As was the case with the Knights Cross of the Iron Cross, the regular Knights Cross and the Golden Knights Cross in both grades was considered by Hitler as a very special award and could only be awarded by him.

The lower classes of the order, especially the Medal and the Second Class, were awarded in extremely high numbers in the last two years of the war, which led to a certain disdain amongst the front soldiers. Nicknames like "canteen order," "remote fighter medal," and "breakfast order" were amongst the degrading designations.

It will most likely never be possible to determine the actual award numbers for the medal and the Second and First Class of both grades.[3] However, it must be noted that the Knights Cross of the War Merit Cross constitutes a stark contrast to the lower grades.

The Knights Cross with Swords was awarded only 265[4] times, which makes this award a lot rarer than the Oakleaves to the Knights Cross of the Iron Cross. Among the awardees were such prominent names as Professor Werner von Braun, Dr. Jur Ernst Kaltenbrunner, Heinrich Müller ("Gestapo Müller"), and Franz von Papen.

The Knights Cross of the War Merit Cross w/o Swords was even rarer and was only awarded 57 times, much less frequently than the Oakleaves with Swords to the Knights Cross of the Iron Cross. Famous awardees were Willy Messerschmitt and Prof. Dr. Ing. Ferdinand Porsche.

The Golden Knights Cross of the War Merit Cross was only awarded twice and in both cases in the grade without Swords. The two recipients were Franz Hahne (Director of the arms factory Altmärkische Kettenfabrik Alkett) and Dipl. Ing. Karl-Otto Saur (State Secretary Armament Ministry).

DESIGN

The Order of the War Merit Cross is in the form of a Maltese cross (*Malteser Kreuz* or *Spitzkreuz*) with a round oak leaf wreath on the center of the obverse and the reverse (but not for the reverse of the First Class which held the pin system). The field inside the obverse wreath shows a "running" swastika; the reverse field has the date of the institution "1939". In the case of the War Merit Medal the reverse shows the inscription "*Für Kriegsverdienst 1939*" (For War Merit 1939) in *Fraktur* font.

Right and above: Two of the popular post card series about the orders and medals of the Third Reich, showing the War Merit Cross Second and First Class with Swords.

THE ORDER

The complete set of the Order of the War Merit Cross consists of a total of nine awards, starting with the War Merit Medal and ending with the extremely rare and never-awarded Golden Knights Cross of the War Merit Cross without Swords. This variety and the great number of medals and maker variations available up to and including the First Class make this order very collectable. It is a bit astonishing that the order of the War Merit Cross never seems to have caught up with the popularity of the Order of the Iron Cross or the German Cross.

The War Merit Medal

The War Merit Medal was no precondition for the award of the Second Class and was as such a stand-alone medal. It was also stated in the regular statutes[5] that the War Merit Medal would not be awarded to any member of the *Wehrmacht*. Therefore it should not be part of this book, but since one can find award documents made out to (as an example) a switchboard operator with military stamp and signature[6], it is appropriate to include the medal in this chapter.

Left: Obverse of the War Merit Medal. Note that the ribbon has a central red stripe.

Right: Reverse of the War Merit Medal

THE WAR MERIT CROSS SECOND CLASS

Obverse and reverse of a War Merit Cross Second Class w/o Swords. The order is made of *Tombak* and unmarked, which is an indication of relatively early manufacture. Later examples of both classes were made of zinc and finished with a bronze wash.

Obverse and reverse of a War Merit Cross Second Class with Swords. It is also made of *Tombak*.

THE KNOWN MAKERS OF THE WAR MERIT CROSS SECOND CLASS WITH SWORDS[7]

MANUFACTURER	LDO #	PKZ #	Material
Deschler & Sohn, München	-*	1	*Tombak* & zinc
C.E. Juncker	L/12	2	*Tombak*
Wilhelm Deumer, Lüdenscheid	L/11	3	*Tombak* & zinc
Steinhauer & Lück, Lüdenscheid	L/16	4	*Tombak*
Hermann Wernstein, Jena-Löbstedt	-	5	*Tombak*
Fritz Zimmermann, Stuttgart	-	6	*Tombak*
Paul Meybauer, Berlin	-	7	*Tombak* & zinc
Otto Schickle, Pforzheim	L/15	-	*Tombak*
Ferdinand Hoffstätter, Bonn	-	8	zinc
Liefergemeinschaft Pforzheimer Handwerker	-	9	*Tombak*
Foerster & Barth, Pforzheim	-	10	*Tombak* & zinc
Grossmann & Co., Wien	-	11	*Tombak*
Frank & Reif, Stuttgart*	-	-	*Tombak*
Gustav Brehmer, Markneukirchen	-	13	*Tombak* & zinc
L. Chr. Lauer, Nürnberg	-	14	*Tombak*
Friedrich Orth, Wien	-	15	zinc
Alois Rettenmaier, Schwäbisch Gmünd	-	16	*Tombak*
Karl Wurster KG, Markneukirchen	-	18	*Tombak* & zinc
E. Ferd. Wiedmann, Frankfurt/Main	-	19	*Tombak* & zinc
Gebrüder Godet & Co., Berlin*	-	-	*Tombak*
B.H. Mayer, Pforzheim	-	26	*Tombak*
Eugen Schmidthäussler, Pforzheim**	-	28	??
Hans Gnad, Wien	-	31	*Tombak*
W. Hobacher, Wien	-	32	*Tombak* & zinc
Friedrich Linden, Lüdenscheid	-	33	*Tombak*
Willy Annetsberger, München	-	34	*Tombak*
Josef Bergs & Co., Gablonz	-	38	*Tombak*
Rudolf Bergs, Gablonz	-	39	*Tombak*
Berg & Nolte AG, Lüdenscheid	-	40	*Tombak*
Gebrüder Bender, Oberstein	-	41	*Tombak*

MANUFACTURER	LDO #	PKZ #	Material
Biedermann & Co., Oberkassel bei Bonn	-	42	zinc
Jakob Bengel, Oberstein*	-	44	??
Franz Jungwirth, Wien	-	45	*Tombak* & zinc
Richard Feix, Gablonz	-	48	*Tombak*
Eduard Görlach & Söhne, Gablonz	-	51	*Tombak*
Glaser & Sohn, Dresden	-	53	*Tombak*
J.E. Hammer & Söhne, Geringswalde	-	55	*Tombak* & zinc
Robert Hauschild, Pforzheim	-	56	*Tombak*
Karl Hensler, Pforzheim	-	57	zinc
Rudolf A. Karneth & Sohn, Gablonz	-	61	*Tombak*
Franz J. Klamt & Söhne, Gablonz	-	63	*Tombak*
Gottlieb Friedrich Keck & Sohn, Pforzheim	-	64	*Tombak* & zinc
Klein & Quenzer AG, Oberstein	-	65	*Tombak* & zinc
Robert H. Kreisel, Gablonz	-	67	*Tombak* & zinc
Alfred Knobloch, Gablonz	-	68	*Tombak*
Alois Klammer, Innsbruck**	-	69	?
Rudolf Leukert, Gablonz	-	71	*Tombak*
Franz Lipp, Pforzheim	-	72	*Tombak*
Franz Mänert, Gablonz	-	73	*Tombak*
Carl Maurer & Sohn, Oberstein	-	74	*Tombak* & zinc
G.H. Osang, Dresden	-	80	*Tombak*
Overhoff & Cie., Lüdenscheid*	-	81	*Tombak* & zinc
Augustin Prager, Gablonz	-	82	*Tombak*
Emil Peukert, Gablonz	-	83	*Tombak*
Carl Poellath, Schrobenhausen**	-	-	zinc
Julius Pietsch, Gablonz	-	85	*Tombak*
Roman Palme, Gablonz	-	87	*Tombak*
Rudolf Richter, Schlag bei Gablonz	-	89	*Tombak*
August F. Richter KG, Hamburg	-	90	*Tombak*
Josef Rössler & Co., Gablonz	-	91	*Tombak*
Josef Rücker & Sohn, Gablonz	-	92	*Tombak*
Richard Simm & Söhne, Gablonz	-	93	*Tombak* & zinc

MANUFACTURER	LDO #	PKZ #	Material
Adolf Scholze, Grünwald	-	95	*Tombak*
unknown	-	97	*Tombak*
Rudolf Souval, Wien*	-	98	??
R. Wächtler & Lange, Mittweida	-	100	*Tombak* & zinc
Rudolf Tham, Gablonz	-	101	*Tombak*
Phillip Türk's Witwe, Wien*	-	102	??
Carl Wild, Hamburg	-	107	*Tombak* & zinc
Arno Wallpach, Salzburg	-	108	*Tombak* & zinc
Otto Zappe, Gablonz	-	110	*Tombak* & zinc
Hermann Aurich, Dresden	-	113	zinc
Franz Petzl, Wien	-	120	zinc
Moriz Hausch AG, Pforzheim	-	127	*Tombak* & zinc
unknown	-	133	*Tombak*
Julius Moser sen., Oberstein	-	135	zinc
Albin Hopf, Gablonz***	-	-	?
Hermann Bauer, Schwäbisch-Gmünd***	-	-	?
Gustav Hörter, Pforzheim**	-	-	?
Gebr. Gengenbach & Co., Pforzheim***	-	-	?
Emil Herrmann & Co., Gablonz***	-	-	?
Rudolf Stärz, Gablonz***	-	-	?
Petz & Lorenz, Unterreichenbach***	-	-	?

* The table shows the known markings. A "-" indicates that this type of marking has not been encountered in the research.
** Identified as a maker by the existence of a named award bag.
*** Companies identified as makers which do not have either an LDO code nor a *Präsidialkanzlei* number.

A similar list of the known makers of the War Merit Cross without Swords has not yet been compiled. It is fairly reasonable to assume that the majority of such makers are identical to the ones who produced the class with swords. Preliminary investigations, however, indicate that the number of makers of the Second Class without Swords is considerably lower.

THE WAR MERIT CROSS FIRST CLASS

Right and below: War Merit Cross w/o Swords First Class, made by Deumer and marked on the center reverse with "L/11".

Above and left: War Merit Cross w/o Swords First Class, screwback, made by Deumer. Note the anti rotation pin, the indicator line for placing the hinge of the pinback version and the "L/11" marking on the reverse of the lower arm.

Left and below: War Merit Cross with Swords First Class, made by Julius Bauer & Söhne.

Above and right: War Merit Cross with Swords First Class, screwback, made by C.F. Zimmermann. The cross is marked "L/52" on the reverse of the lower arm.

THE KNOWN MAKERS OF THE WAR MERIT CROSS FIRST CLASS WITHOUT SWORDS[8]

MANUFACTURER	LDO #	PKZ #	Material
Deschler & Sohn, München	-*	1	*Tombak*
Wilhelm Deumer, Lüdenscheid	L/11	3	*Tombak* & zinc
Steinhauer & Lück, Lüdenscheid	-	4	*Tombak*
Otto Schickle, Pforzheim	L/15	-	*Tombak*
Hermann Wernstein, Jena-Lobstedt	L/17	-	zinc
Foerster & Barth, Pforzheim	L/21	-	*Tombak* & zinc
Friedrich Orth, Wien	-	15	*Tombak*
C.F. Zimmermann, Pforzheim	L/52	-	silver
Karl Gschiermeister, Wien	-	50	*Tombak*
Petz & Lorenz, Unterreichenbach**	-	-	??

* The table shows the known markings. A "-" indicates that this type of marking has not been encountered in the research.
** Company identified as a maker due to their catalog.

THE KNOWN MAKERS OF THE WAR MERIT CROSS FIRST CLASS WITH SWORDS[8,9]

MANUFACTURER	LDO #	PKZ #	Material
Deschler & Sohn, München	L/10	1	*Tombak*
C.E. Juncker, Berlin	L/12	2	*Tombak*
Wilhelm Deumer, Lüdenscheid	L/11	3	*Tombak* & zinc
Steinhauer & Lück, Lüdenscheid	L/16	4	*Tombak* & zinc
Paul Meybauer, Berlin	L/13	-*	*Tombak* & zinc
Friedrich Orth, Wien	-	15	*Tombak*
Otto Schickle, Pforzheim	L/15	-	*Tombak*
Hermann Wernstein, Jena-Lobstedt	L/17	-	*Tombak*
B.H. Mayer, Pforzheim	L/18	-	*Tombak* & zinc
Foerster & Barth, Pforzheim	L/21	-	*Tombak* & zinc
C.F. Zimmermann, Pforzheim	L/52	-	silver
Hymmen & Co., Lüdenscheid	L/53	-	zinc
Wächtler & Lange, Mittweida	L/55	100	*Tombak* & zinc

MANUFACTURER	LDO #	PKZ #	Material
Funcke & Brüninghaus, Lüdenscheid	L/56		*Tombak*
Boerger & Co., Berlin	L/57	-	zinc
Julius Bauer & Söhne, Zella-Mehlis	-	43	*Tombak*
Klein & Quenzer, Oberstein	-	65	*Tombak* & zinc
Rudolf Souval, Wien	L/58	-	*Tombak* & zinc
Carl Poellath, Schrobenhausen	-	84	*Tombak*
Carl Wild, Hamburg	-	107	zinc
Petz & Lorenz, Unterreichenbach[**]	-	-	*Tombak*

* The table shows the known markings. A "-" indicates that this type of marking has not been encountered in the research.

* Company identified as a maker due to their catalog.

THE SPANISH VERSION OF THE WAR MERIT CROSS FIRST AND SECOND CLASS

Per regulations the War Merit Cross could not be awarded to foreigners. However, foreign volunteers who took an oath to the *Führer* Adolf Hitler were treated the same as regular German soldiers and were therefore eligible for the order.

This applied to the volunteers of the Blue Legion (*Legión Española de Voluntarios),* a total force of about 47,000 Spanish soldiers fighting at the Eastern Front as 250. Infanterie-Division (span.) under *General* Agustín Muñoz Grandes. It is recorded that 36 soldiers of the Blue Division got the War Merit Cross with Swords First Class and 2,329 the Second Class with Swords.

Left: Divisional sign of the Blue Legion.

Right: General Agustín Muñoz Grandes (Knights Cross 12. March 1943, Oakleaves 13. December 1942).

Right: Spanish-made War Merit Cross with Swords Second Class. Note the typical ribbon clasp.

Above and right: Spanish-made War Merit Cross First Class with Swords. The bronze color is against regulations. However, there do exist versions which are silver colored.

THE KNIGHTS CROSS OF THE WAR MERIT CROSS

Left: Obverse of the Knights Cross of the War Merit Cross without Swords. It is made of solid silver and marked "900" and "1" on the outside of the lower arm for Deschler, München (below).

Right: Reverse of the Knights Cross of the War Merit Cross without Swords.

Right: Obverse of the Knights Cross of the War Merit Cross with Swords, made of solid silver and marked "900" and "1" for Deschler, München at the usual spot.

Left: Reverse of the Knights Cross of the War Merit Cross with Swords.

THE GOLDEN KNIGHTS CROSS OF THE WAR MERIT CROSS

Left and below: Obverse and reverse of the extremely rare Golden Knights Cross of the War Merit Cross without Swords. It is made of gilded solid silver and marked "900" and "1" for Deschler, München at the lower arm as usual.

Several cased crosses with and without swords of this and the previous class were recovered from the *Schloss* Klessheim by soldiers of the 3rd Infantry Division. Castle Klessheim was Hilter's guesthouse and also the last storage place of the remaining stock of the *Präsidialkanzlei*.[11]

Above: Obverse of the Golden Knights Cross of the War Merit Cross with Swords, made by company Deschler. Both obverse and reverse are identical to the version in Silver. This grade was never issued.

THE KNOWN MAKERS OF THE KNIGHTS CROSS OF THE WAR MERIT CROSS (WITH AND WITHOUT SWORDS)[10]

MANUFACTURER	PKZ #	Material
Deschler & Sohn, München	1	silver 900
Steinhauer & Lück, Lüdenscheid	4	silver 935
C.F. Zimmermann, Pforzheim	20	silver 900

THE KNOWN MAKERS OF THE KNIGHTS CROSS OF THE WAR MERIT CROSS IN GOLD (WITH AND WITHOUT SWORDS)

MANUFACTURER	PKZ #	Material
Deschler & Sohn, München	1	silver 900, gilded
C.F. Zimmermann, Pforzheim	20	silver 900, gilded

Left: German propaganda poster "Just as we fight - You work for victory!" addressing the home front, which was the main pool of recipients of the War Merit Cross without Swords.

AWARD DOCUMENTS

The amount of variations of the award documents for the War Merit Cross is very high. The reason for this is in one part the extremely high award numbers, especially of the lower grades, and on the other side the great range of awardees, ranging from military personnel to civil servants to civilians.

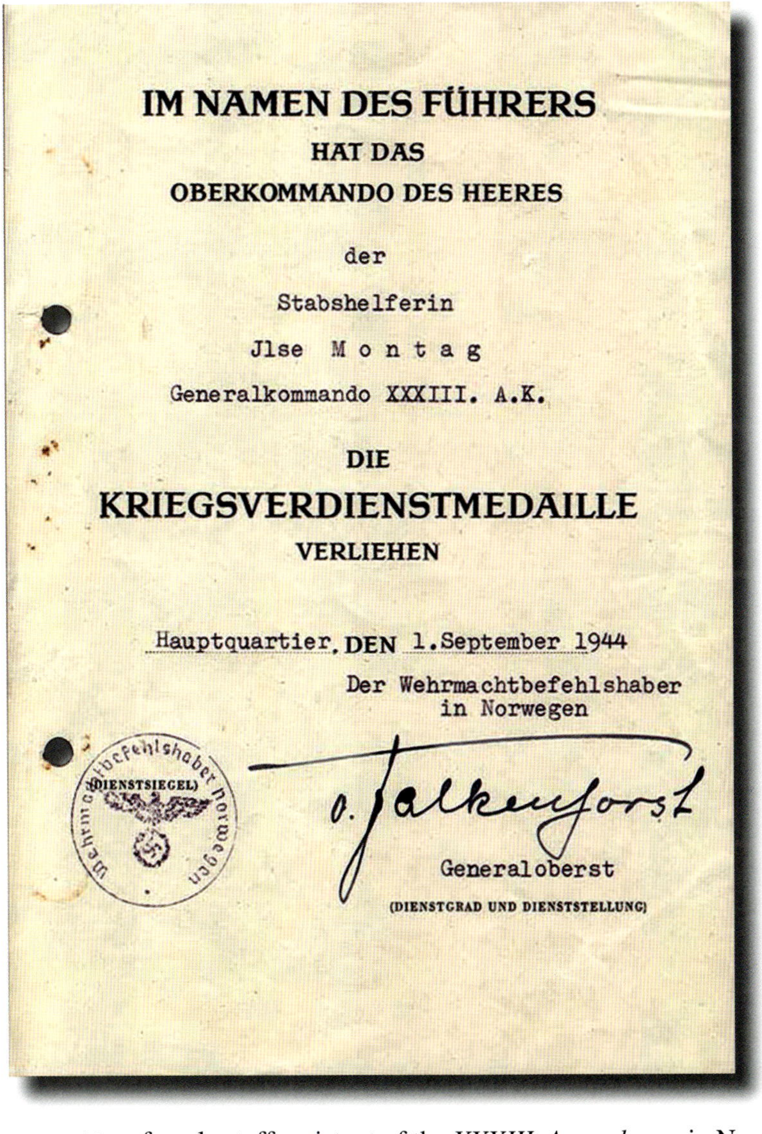

IM NAMEN DES FÜHRERS
HAT DAS
OBERKOMMANDO DES HEERES

der

Stabshelferin

Jlse Montag

Generalkommando XXXIII. A.K.

DIE

KRIEGSVERDIENSTMEDAILLE

VERLIEHEN

Hauptquartier, DEN 1.September 1944

Der Wehrmachtbefehlshaber
in Norwegen

Wehrmachtbefehlshaber Norwegen
(DIENSTSIEGEL)

v. Falkenhorst

Generaloberst
(DIENSTGRAD UND DIENSTSTELLUNG)

Very rare document to a female staff assistant of the *XXXIII. Armeekorps* in Norway. The document is signed by *Generaloberst* von Falkenhorst.

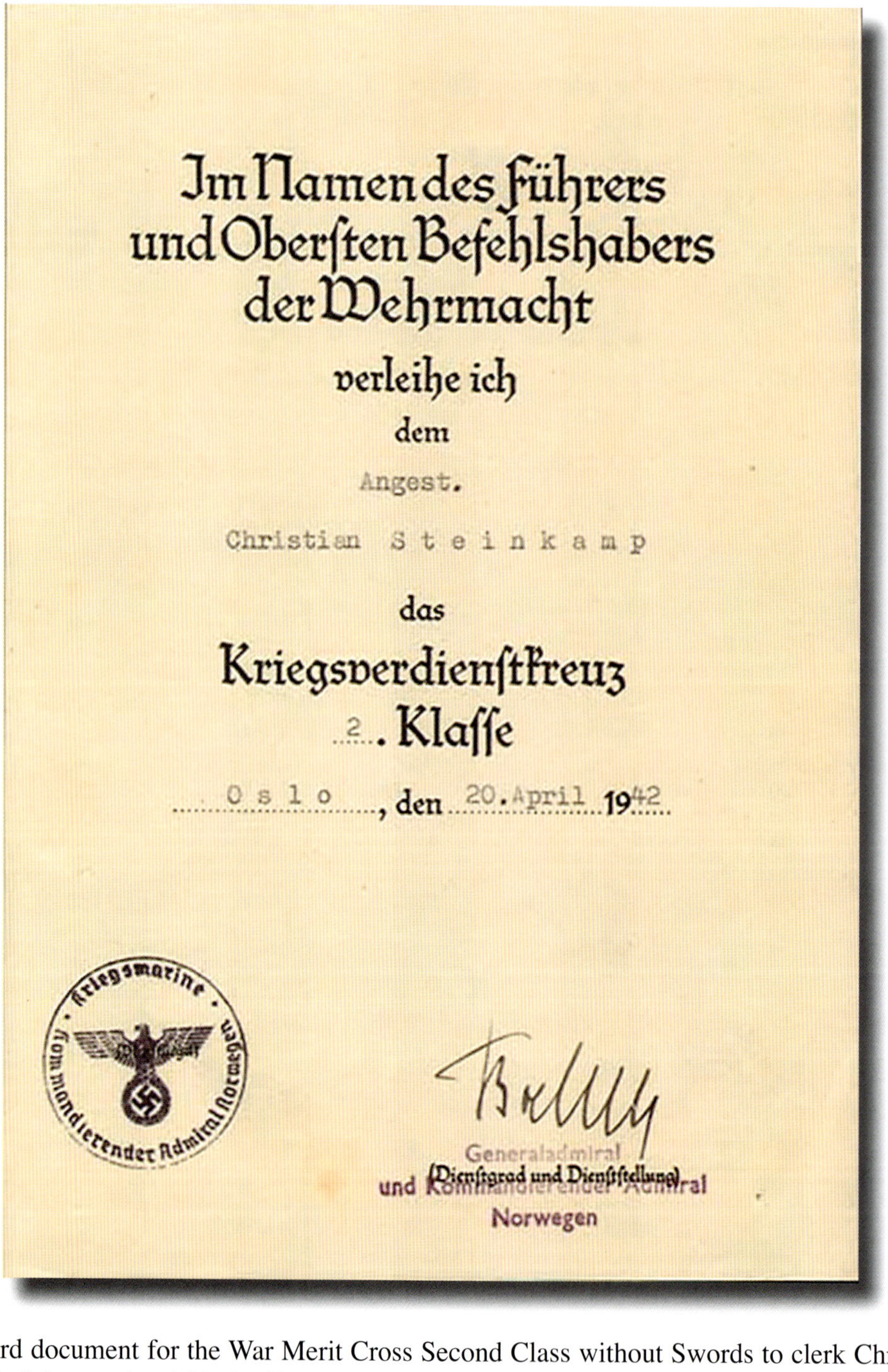

Im Namen des Führers
und Oberſten Befehlshabers
der Wehrmacht

verleihe ich

dem

Angest.

Christian S t e i n k a m p

das

Kriegsverdienſtkreuz

2. Klaſſe

O s l o, den 20. April 1942

Kriegsmarine · Kommandierender Admiral Norwegen

Generaladmiral
(Dienſtgrad und Dienſtſtellung)
und Kommandierender Admiral
Norwegen

Award document for the War Merit Cross Second Class without Swords to clerk Christian Steinkamp, dated 20. April 1942 and made out while serving in Norway.

Im Namen des Führers

und

Obersten Befehlshabers der Wehrmacht

verleihe ich

dem

Oberst

Rudolf K e i l

das Kriegsverdienstkreuz 2. Klasse

mit Schwertern.

Führerhauptquartier, den 30. Januar 1941.

Generalfeldmarschall
und Chef des Oberkommandos
der Wehrmacht

Oberst Rudolf Keil received the War Merit Cross Second Class with Swords on 30. January 1941.

— 234 —

Anlage 1
zu S. 220

IM NAMEN DES FÜHRERS
HAT DAS
OBERKOMMANDO DES HEERES
DEM

DAS
KRIEGSVERDIENSTKREUZ
________ KLASSE
MIT SCHWERTERN
VERLIEHEN

____________, DEN ____________

(DIENSTSIEGEL)

(DIENSTGRAD UND DIENSTSTELLUNG)

One of two official pre-printed forms as directed in the *Merkblatt 15/5*, page 234.

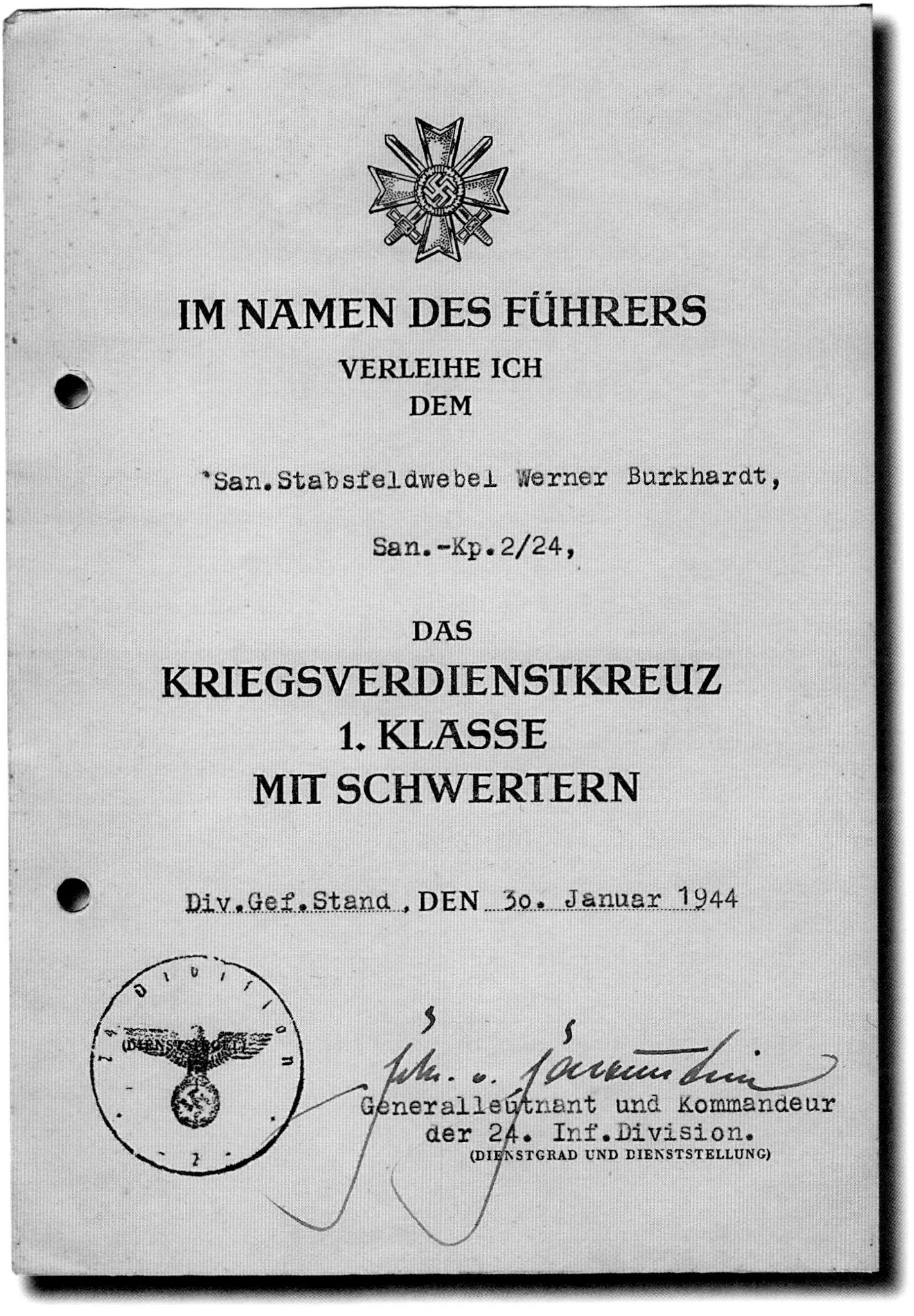

IM NAMEN DES FÜHRERS

VERLEIHE ICH

DEM

San.Stabsfeldwebel Werner Burkhardt,

San.-Kp.2/24,

DAS

KRIEGSVERDIENSTKREUZ

1. KLASSE

MIT SCHWERTERN

Div.Gef.Stand, DEN 30. Januar 1944

Generalleutnant und Kommandeur
der 24. Inf.Division.
(DIENSTGRAD UND DIENSTSTELLUNG)

This award document (in the other prescribed form) to *Sanitäts-Stabsfeldwebel* for the War Merit Cross First Class with Swords is dated 30. January 1944 and signed by *Generalleutnant Freiherr* von Falkenstein.

VORLÄUFIGES BESITZZEUGNIS

IM NAMEN
DES DEUTSCHEN VOLKES
HABE ICH
DEM

Direktor
Dr. Ulrich Hoffmann

DAS RITTERKREUZ
DES KRIEGSVERDIENSTKREUZES
MIT SCHWERTERN
VERLIEHEN.
DIE BESITZURKUNDE FOLGT NACH.

Führer-Hauptquartier, den 22.Mai 1944

DER FÜHRER

Preliminary award document for the Knights Cross of the War Merit Cross with Swords to Dr. Ulrich Hoffmann, dated 22. May 1944. Dr. Hoffmann was director of the propaganda department in the Armaments Ministry.

IM NAMEN
DES DEUTSCHEN VOLKES
VERLEIHE ICH
DEM BAUER
KURT HECHT
DAS RITTERKREUZ
DES KRIEGSVERDIENSTKREUZES
FÜHRERHAUPTQUARTIER
DEN 1. OKTOBER 1944
DER FÜHRER
UND OBERSTE BEFEHLSHABER
DER WEHRMACHT

Award document to farmer Kurt Hecht, dated 1. October 1944 with the formal *Mappe* in blue leather with a golden national eagle. This is one of the very few formal documents signed by Hitler.

PACKETS AND CASES

Just as was the case with the Order of the Iron Cross, each grade of the Order of the War Merit Cross also came within a package or a case. The lower grades like the *Kriegsverdienstmedaille* and the War Merit Crosses of the Second Class were packed in bags with the imprint of the content. The crosses of the First Class were awarded in cases very similar to the ones of the Iron Cross First Class.

The Knights Crosses of the War Merit Cross were presented in relatively large cases which are unique to this order.

Left: Bag for the War Merit Medal with the maker name Rudolf Bergs on the reverse. The medal inside is unmarked.

Right: Package for the War Merit Cross Second Class with Swords, maker Carl Poellath.

Right: War Merit First Class with Swords in its case. The inside of the lid is imprinted with “Deschler & Sohn - München”.

Cases with the imprint of the order to the outside of the lid (with or without swords) do exist (below).

Above: Imprint of the War Merit Cross First Class without Swords.

Left: Late war case for the War Merit Cross without Swords. This case has no pushbutton opening mechanism. The cover paper and the inside lining serve as a hinge.

Left: Knights Cross of the War Merit Cross in its original presentation case. The case is covered with dark blue leather imitation. The size is 180 x 140 x 30 mm.

Below: The cases for the four grades and styles of the Knights Cross of the War Merit Cross are the same. There are no imprints on the outside lids.

THE ORDER IN WEAR

The War Merit Medal and the War Merit Cross Second Class were not worn on the uniform; only the ribbon was attached to the button hole just as the ribbon for the Iron Cross Second Class and the ribbon for the East Medal. The First Class was worn like the Iron Cross First Class and the Knights Cross was a neck order like the Knights Cross of the Iron Cross.

Gefreiter Albert Sebald was awarded on 20. April 1943 with the War Merit Medal in his capacity as storage foreman in Oslo, Norway. He was declared MIA in the Kurland pocket in 1945.

This unknown *Gefreiter* had himself painted in oil on a wood panel on the occasion of the award of the War Merit Cross Second Class. The painting is signed Schuklin, Kursk and dated 1941.

The unknown *Oberleutnant* had his picture taken with the War Merit Cross Second Class.

Oberstleutnant August Fohr of the *ArtillerieRgt 77* had his picture taken in June 1943. He wears the War Merit Cross First Class with Swords above the Wound Badge in Black of the Great War.

Generalmajor Curt Souchay, commander of the *72. Infanterie-Division*, wears the interesting combination of the War Merit Cross First Class with Swords next to the Iron Cross First Class of the Great War and the *Wiederholungsspange* First Class, early pattern.

General der Artillerie Herbert Osterkamp was awarded with the Knights Cross of the War Merit Cross with Swords on 7. November 1944. He was awarded both classes of the Iron Cross of the Great War while serving as Oberleutnant and again both classes in the early months of the Second World War. The German Cross in Silver was awarded on 18. September 1943.

MINIATURES AND STICKPINS

All classes but one of the Order of the War Merit Cross were available in miniature size 16 mm and some also in 9 mm. The only grade not produced was the Knights Cross of the War Merit Cross in Gold, both classes.

Right: 9 mm stickpin and 16 mm miniature of the *Kriegs-verdienstmedaille*

Left: 16 mm stickpin of the War Merit Cross Second Class with Swords.

Left: 28 mm so-called "half miniatures" of both versions of the War Merit Cross First Class.

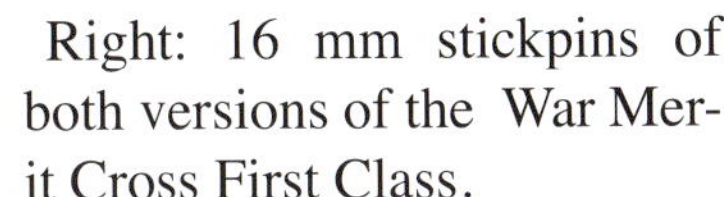

Right: 16 mm stickpins of both versions of the War Merit Cross First Class.

Left: Rare 16 mm stickpin of the Knights Cross of the War Merit Cross without Swords. The miniature is made of silver and marked "900" on the reverse but bears no maker mark.

Right: Cased deluxe LDO-version of the War Merit Cross with Swords as a buttonhole device. The reverse of the button shows the LDO logo and the maker "Steinhauer & Lück - Lüdenscheid."

FAKES AND REPRODUCTIONS

The so-called "Austrian" fake with its coke bottle-shaped pin and (sometimes) marking "L 15" or "L 11" (without "/") are the most prominent fakes of the War Merit Cross First Class with and without Swords.

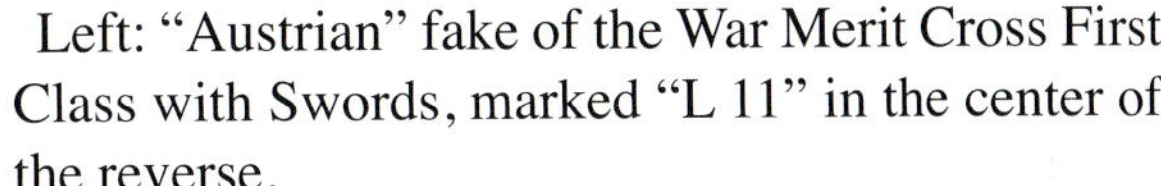

Left: "Austrian" fake of the War Merit Cross First Class with Swords, marked "L 11" in the center of the reverse.

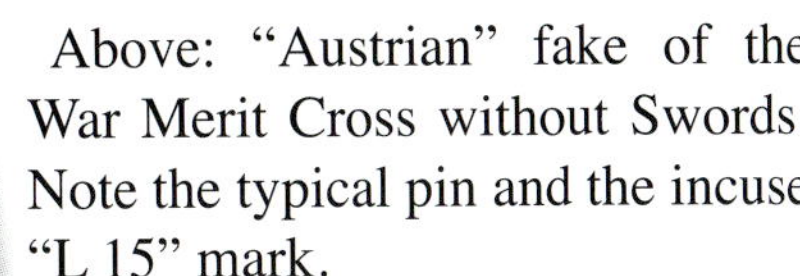

Above: "Austrian" fake of the War Merit Cross without Swords. Note the typical pin and the incuse "L 15" mark.

Left: Reproduction of the Knights Cross of the War Merit Cross. Note the loop and the missing white thread on the edge of the ribbon.

THE 1957 VERSION OF THE ORDER

The post-war versions as authorized under the law of 1957was very easily done: the reverse was made the obverse. Instead of the prominent swastika the date "1939" was now the obverse and the center field of the reverse was left empty.

Kriegsverdienstkreuz 2. Kl. mit Schwertern

Kriegsverdienstkreuz 2. Klasse ohne Schwerter (Vorderseite)

Left: Early 1957 version of the War Merit Cross First Class.

Below: Ribbon for the War Merit Cross First Class for daily wear on the Bundeswehr uniform.

FOOTNOTES

1 *Merkblatt 15/5*, OKW, 13.3.43 29c20 - 6668/43, page 224

2 For a broader study refer to Maerz/Stimson, *The War Merit Cross 1. Class and Higher* (projected 2013) and also to Williamson/Charita, *The War Merit Cross*.

3 Nimmergut gives the following numbers: Medal over 4 Million, 2. Class with Swords over 6 Million, w/o Swords over 2 Million, 1. Class with Swords between 450,000 - 500,000, 1. Class w/o Swords about 92,000.

4 Numbers and names listed in Williamson/Charita, *The War Merit Cross*, Bender Publishing, 2008 and Patzwall, *Die Ritterkreuzträger des Kriegsverdienstkreuzes 1942-1945,* 1984

5 Merkblatt 15/5, page 224

6 Williamson/Charita, *The War Merit Cross*, page 45

7 Table generated based on *Das Kriegsverdienstkreuz 2. Klasse mit Schwertern*, Michael Falk

8 Table generated based on *The War Merit Cross 1. Class and Higher,* Maerz/Stimson, B&D Publishing LLC (projected 2013)

9 Williamson/Charita list the following additional makers: Hoffstätter (8), Jakob Bengel (44), Gottlieb & Wagner (52), Glaser & Sohn (53), Gebrüder Godet (L/50) and Schauerte & Höhfeld (L/54). This could not be verified by the authors; no examples have been encountered.

10 Williamson reports that Klein & Quenzer was also a maker of the Knights Cross of the War Merit Cross with a marking of "65" on the lower arm. This could not be verified and such pieces are most likely (if in existence at all) post war productions.

11 The travel of the PKZ stock is reported in documented detail in "*Die Ritterkreuzträger*", Veit Scherzer , Scherzers Militaire-Verlag 2005 (German language) or "*The Knights Cross of the Iron Cross*", Dietrich Maerz, B&D Publishing LLC, 2007.

BIBLIOGRAPHY

Doehle, Dr. Heinrich, *Die Auszeichnungen des Grossdeutschen Reichs*, Berlin 1945

Dombrowski, Hanns, *Orden, Ehrenzeichen und Titel*, Franz Wahlen, 1940

Falk, Michael, *Das Kriegsverdienstkreuz 2. Klasse mit Schwertern*, Verlag Weber, Schönau, 2012

Geeb, *Deutsche Orden und Ehrenzeichen*, Heymanns Verlag, 1985

Klietmann, Kurt, *Auszeichnungen des Deutschen Reiches 1936-1945*, Motorbuch

Klietmann, Kurt, *Deutsche Auszeichnungen*, Die Ordens-Sammlung, Berlin, 1971

Maerz/Stimson, *The War Merit Cross 1. Class*, B&D Publishing, projected 2013

Merkblatt 15/5, *Orden und Ehrenzeichen*, Biblio-Verlag, 1992

Niemann, Detlev, *Bewertungskatalog 1871-1945*, Niemann-Verlag, 2004/2009

Nimmergut, Jörg, *Deutsche Orden und Ehrenzeichen*, Vol. IV, München, 2004

Patzwall, Klaus, *Die Ritterkreuzträger des Kriegsverdienstkreuzes 1942-1945*, Verlag Militaria-Archiv Klaus D. Patzwall, Hamburg, 1984

Scharfenberg/Thiede, *Lexikon der Ordenskunde*, Battenberg, 2010

Williamson/Charita, *The War Merit Cross*, Bender Publishing, 2008

Der Uniformen-Markt, Volumes 1939-1945

Schwert und Spaten, Volumes 1939-1942

Chapter 3

The Order of the German Cross

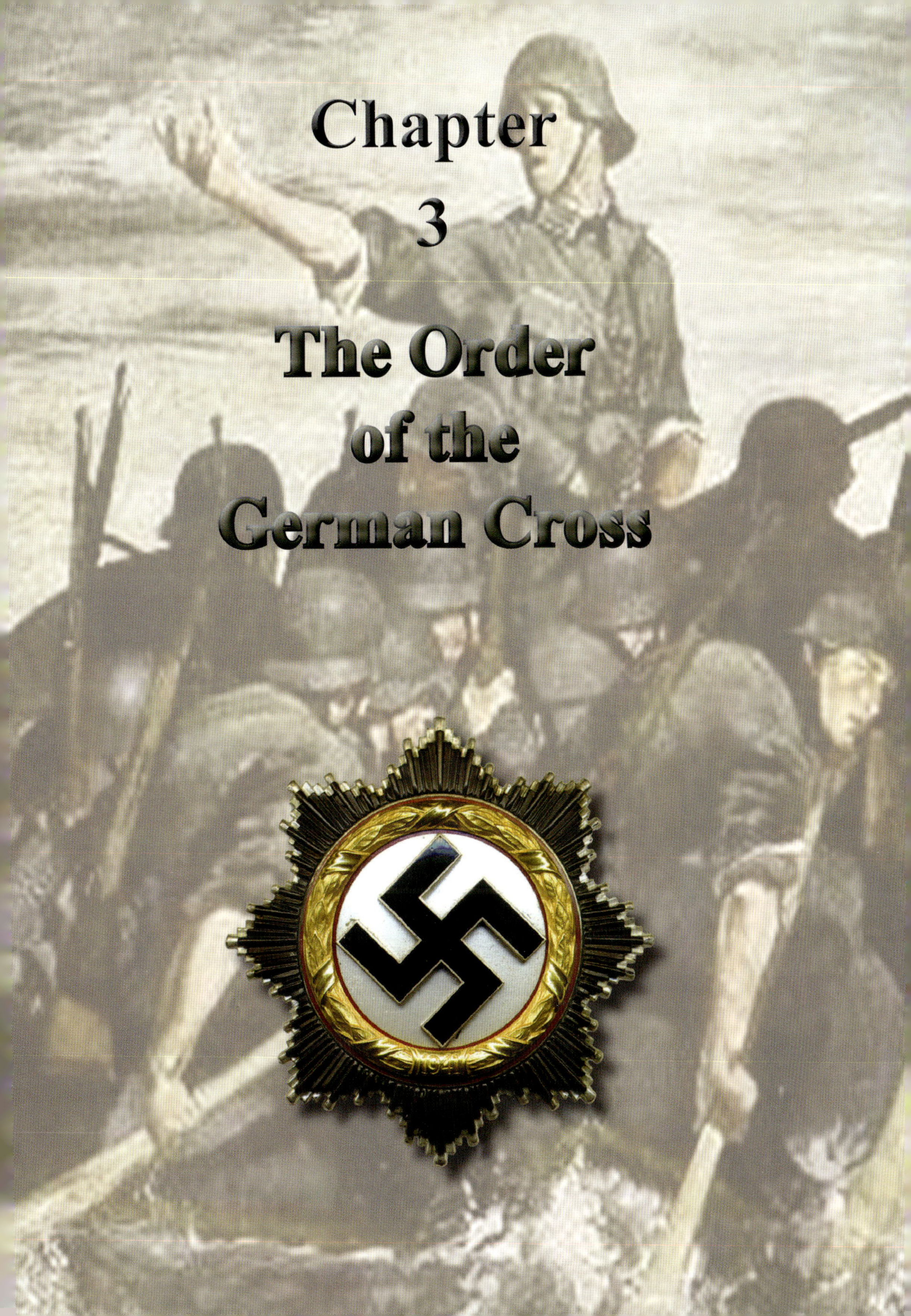

Oberfeldwebel Emil Schareina of the *4/IR 24* was awarded the German Cross in Gold on February 2, 1942 and later the Knights Cross of the Iron Cross on May 15, 1943. The ribbon bar shows the Iron Cross Second Class, the East Medal and the Army Long Service Medal in Silver (18 years of service).

Table of Contents

THE ORDER OF THE GERMAN CROSS

HISTORY

It was recognized in the war year 1941 that the two orders, the Iron Cross First Class and the War Merit Cross First Class, were no longer sufficient to honor the repeatedly occurring acts of bravery and merit. It was not possible, for example, to honor any act of bravery which would have warranted the award of the Iron Cross First Class if the soldier was already awarded this class previously. The same applied for deeds in the area of war merit and the War Merit Cross First Class with Swords.

To fill the gap between the requirements for the Iron Cross First Class (and War Merit Cross with Swords) and the Knights Cross grades, the Order of the German Cross was instituted on September 28, 1941, as the second highest military order of the Third Reich. There is no previous history or any connection to Imperial awards to report - this order was a completely new creation.

Kriegsorden des Deutschen Kreuzes

VERORDNUNG ÜBER DIE STIFTUNG DES DEUTSCHEN KREUZES

Zur Anerkennung vielfacher außergewöhnlicher Tapferkeits- oder Führungstaten stifte ich den Kriegsorden des Deutschen Kreuzes

ARTIKEL 1. Der Orden des Deutschen Kreuzes ist ein Wehrmachtorden. Er wird in folgender Ausführung verliehen: Das Deutsche Kreuz in Silber, das Deutsche Kreuz in Gold.

ARTIKEL 2 Der Orden besteht aus einem achtzackigen, dunkelgrauen, silbergeränderten Stern von 62 mm Durchmesser, der in einem silbernen bzw. goldenen Lorbeerkranz auf mattsilbernem Feld ein schwarzes, silbergerändertes Hakenkreuz trägt. Der Lorbeerkranz zeigt unten die Jahreszahl 1941. Das Deutsche Kreuz wird ohne Band auf der rechten Seite getragen.

ARTIKEL 3. Das Deutsche Kreuz in Silber wird verliehen für vielfache außergewöhnliche Verdienste in der militärischen Kriegführung. Das Deutsche Kreuz in Gold wird verliehen für vielfach bewiesene außergewöhnliche Tapferkeit oder für vielfache hervorragende Verdienste in der Truppenführung. Voraussetzung für die Verleihung des Deutschen Kreuzes in Silber und Gold ist der Besitz des Eisernen Kreuzes 1. Klasse von 1939 oder Spange zum Eisernen Kreuz 1. Klasse des Weltkrieges oder des Kriegsverdienstkreuzes 1. Klasse mit Schwertern.

Führerhauptquartier, den 28. September 1941

Der Führer Adolf Hitler

Above: The original text of the three articles of institution for the War Order of the German Cross.

REGULATIONS

This order was not a gap-filler between the Iron Cross First Class and the Knights Cross of the Iron Cross as is sometimes assumed. It was not necessary to be a recipient of the Order of the German Cross in order to be awarded the Knights Cross, nor was the opposite true. There is, however, a close connection between the two orders in that the previous award of the Iron Cross First Class respectively the War Merit Cross First Class with Swords was a prerequisite for the award of the German Cross in Gold respectively the Silver grade.

The Order was founded in two grades which were both absolutely equal, that is the Silver version is not a lower grade than the Gold one. The regulations clearly state that the Order of the German Cross will be awarded "as a recognition of multiple exceptional bravery or command deeds." The order was awarded in the name of the *Führer* and every award was issued by the chiefs of the personnel offices of the army, air force, and navy.

This makes clear that the two grades, Gold and Silver, are absolutely equal but are awarded for different deeds: the gold grade for bravery, the silver grade for merits in the conduct of the war. Concurring with the general award principle during the Third Reich that "only the deed and the achievement, not rank, status nor length of service" was the basis for an award, the Order of the German Cross was awarded in relatively low numbers. The Gold grade was awarded 25,964 times, the Silver grade only 2,471 times.[1]

It was possible to receive both grades, in which case the Silver one was no longer allowed to be worn - a regulation which was not obeyed by most. A total of eleven recipients received both grades.[2]

A total of 46 German Crosses were awarded to members of allied troops, most of them from Lithuania, Italy, and Finland.[3]

The awarded orders were sent out from the *Präsidialkanzlei*. The private sale of any versions, metal or cloth, was not allowed.

Right: *Kapitän zur See* R. Paul-Hermann Meixner wears both grades of the Order of the German Cross on his uniform.

DESIGN

The Order of the German Cross is - despite the name "cross" - an eight-pointed star with a circular laurel wreath and the prominent swastika in the center. It was to be worn on the lower right breast of the tunic.

The construction is fairly elaborate: the eight-pointed base plate, which was usually made of either *Tombak,* or later on, of *Cupal*[4], is covered by an also eight-pointed grey-black ray plate on which the wreath and the swastika are located. The complete badge is held together by rivets. Depending on the maker and style, the rivet count goes from at least four up to ten on genuine examples.

The grade of the order is distinguished only by the color of the wreath, which is either gilded or silvered.

Above: Contemporary depiction of the Gold and Silver grades.

Due to the material, size, and construction, the decoration is very heavy. Also, the enamel was subject to damage in close quarters. Consequently, in June 1942 a cloth version for the grade in Gold was authorized. The only remaining metal part was the wreath; the balance of the order was embroidered on cloth with the color of the uniform of the bearer.

The embroidered version of the Silver grade was never officially authorized, but genuine examples with different background cloth certainly do exist, made in the same style and by the same companies as the Gold grade.

The German Cross in Gold with Diamonds was never officially instituted and the existing 20 examples which were found at Castle Klessheim were never issued.

THE ORDER

The Gold Grade

Collectors all over the world consider the German Cross as highly collectible. One reason is the relatively lower price when compared to the next higher order, i.e. the Knights Cross of the Iron Cross. Another reason might be the visual appeal with its bold display of the swastika. But certainly part of the order's appeal is the variation in style and makers, which ranges from the extremely rare 10-rivet examples[5] and Type 1 Juncker to the readily available so-called "light" models from C.F. Zimmermann and Otto Klein.

There are five proven manufacturers with a total of 18 known variations for the Gold grade identified at this point in time.

THE KNOWN MAKERS OF THE GERMAN CROSS IN GOLD

Company	Type	Weight [gr]
Deschler & Sohn	Ten rivets, heavy*	65.3
	Six rivets, heavy, short pin	65.5
	Four rivets, heavy, unmarked	68.5
	Four rivets, heavy, "1"	70.5
	Four rivets, light, "1"	54.9
Gebrüder Godet	Six rivets, heavy, unmarked	70.3
	Six rivets, heavy, "21"	71.4
	Six rivets, light, "21"	49.7
C.E. Juncker	Type 1, seven rivets, heavy*	63.3
	Type 1, five rivets, heavy*	66.5
	Type 2, five rivets, heavy	58.7
	Type 2, five rivets, light	52.0
	Type 2, five rivets, light, "2"	45.0
C.F. Zimmermann	Four rivets, heavy, "L/52"*	67.2
	Four Rivets, heavy, "20"	66.5
	Four rivets, light, "20"	44.5
	Four rivets, light, "dotted date", "20"	44.5
Otto Klein	Four rivets, light, "134"	45.4

* : very rare.

Left and below: Heavy version, made by Deschler & Sohn, marked "1".

Right and above: Light version, made by Gebrüder Godet, marked "21" on the underside of the pin.

Right and below: Heavy version, made by C.E. Juncker. The fifth rivet is in the center under the pin.

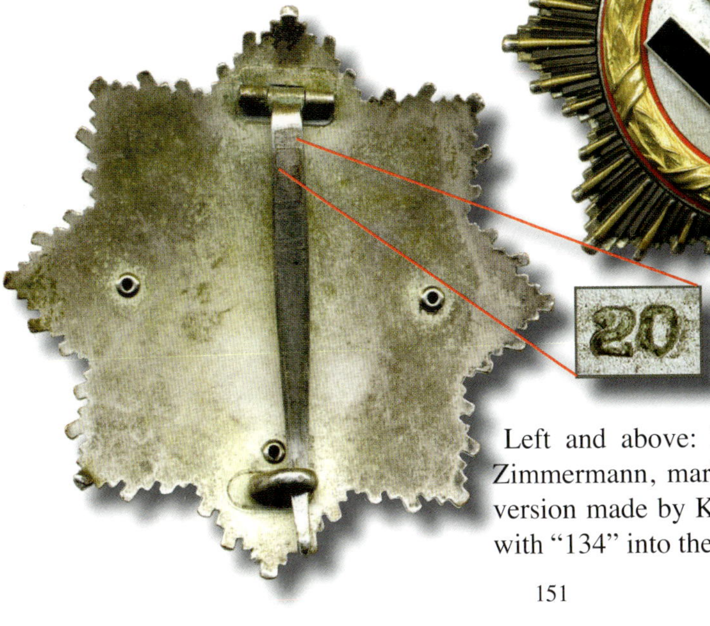

Left and above: Light version made by C.F. Zimmermann, marked "20" under the pin. The version made by Klein is identical, but stamped with "134" into the back plate.

The Silver Grade

The Silver grade is far rarer than the Gold grade, roughly by a factor of ten. In addition there are not as many variations to be found as with the Gold grade. The make and material of the Silver grade is absolutely identical to the Gold grade; the silver wreath is the only difference.

It is theoretically possible that all styles and types of the Gold version could also be found in the Silver version. However, data so far seems to indicate that this is not true and the table below shows the versions known as of today.

THE KNOWN MAKERS OF THE GERMAN CROSS IN SILVER

Company	Type	Weight [gr]
Deschler & Sohn	Six rivets, heavy, long pin	65.5
	Four rivets, heavy, unmarked	68.5
	Four rivets, heavy, "1"	70.5
Gebrüder Godet	Six rivets, heavy, unmarked	70.3
C.E. Juncker	Type 2, five rivets, heavy, "2"	58.7
C.F. Zimmermann	Four rivets, light, "20"	44.5

Left and below: Heavy version, made by Deschler & Sohn. Note that the center rivet of each vertical row is slightly offset to the center.

Right and below: Heavy version, made by Gebrüder Godet. Note that the three rivets are in line.

Left and above: Light version made by C.F. Zimmermann, marked "20" under the pin. This is the most common version of the silver grade.

The Cloth Versions

For tank, self-propelled gun, and aircraft crews, the original award in metal was not only so heavy and bulky that it tended to get caught in close quarters, but the enamel of the swastika was also very easily damaged. Thus, nearly a year after the institution of the award, cloth versions were allowed to be worn on the uniform. The star rays and the swastika were embroidered on a piece of cloth which normally had the same color as the uniform of the branch of service. The table below shows the official colors.

Field Gray		Army (*Wehrmacht-Heer*)
Dark Blue		Navy (*Kriegsmarine*)
Blue Gray		Airforce (*Luftwaffe*)
Black		*Panzer* Troops
Stone Gray		*Waffen-SS*/Assault Gun Units
Olive-colored		*Afrikakorps, Heer*
Light Khaki		*Afrikakorps, Luftwaffe*
White		Tropical (Summer) Uniform

Most of the cloth versions in Gold and in Silver use the same type of wreath, the Type 2 of C.E. Juncker. This type can easily be identified by a flaw in the upper area of the "9" in the date "1941" (picture to the left).

Despite the official decree that the cloth version in Silver was not authorized, various genuine examples do exist and are constructed in the same style and with the same wreath type as the Gold versions, but with the wreath silvered.[6]

There are three known types of the cloth versions, but most likely more do exist. The difference between Type 1 and 2 is the embroidering of the rays. Type 3 has a smaller swastika. All three types use the same wreath.

The versions in stone-gray, olive, light khaki, and white are considered rare.

Left: Cloth version of the German Cross in Gold on field gray backing. This is a Type 1, recognizable by the shorter ray tips. They are often stamped with "SH" (Hermann Schmuck & Cie) on the reverse.

Right: Cloth version in Gold on black backing for *Panzer* units. This is the Type 2 with the longer ray tips.

Left: Gold version on a very dark field gray. This is a Type 3 with the smaller swastika.

Right: Worn cloth version in silver on field gray backing. This is also a Type 2.

The German Cross in Gold with Diamonds

It seems that there were some plans to introduce a higher version of the German Cross in Gold, one with Diamonds set into the gold wreath. Twenty examples were made and were found by soldiers of the 3rd US-Infantry Division in Castle Klessheim near Salzburg (today in Austria). The grade was never instituted and there is no official mention of this grade of the order in any period documentation.

Above: *Schloss* Klessheim shortly after its occupation by American forces. The right side is still covered with camouflage netting.

Three examples of the German Cross in Gold with Diamonds made it to the museum of the West Point Academy in the state of New York. The remaining examples are either in collections or were destroyed.

All twenty examples were made by the Munich jeweler Peter Rath. Each example is unique inasmuch as the number of diamonds in the wreaths varies between 92 and 98. The outside of the pin is engraved with "Rath München".

Left: one of the twenty examples of the German Cross in Gold with Diamonds. The wreath is made of gold.

Above: Six hollow rivets hold the star together. The backplate is silvered.

Left: The order rests in a red presentation case with a golden national eagle on the outside lid. The case is marked "Rath - München."

AWARD DOCUMENTS

Due to the award procedures, which were different for each branch of the *Wehrmacht*, there are three distinct types of award documents in existence: army, air force and navy. Since this book is about the awards of the *Heer*, we will only examine documents from this branch of the armed forces.[7]

Vorläufiges Besitzzeugnis

Im Namen des Führers
und Obersten Befehlshabers
der Wehrmacht

verleihe ich
dem

Hauptmann B u s c h h a u s e n ,
Kp.Chef 6./Schtz.Rgt.lo

das

Deutsche Kreuz in Gold

HQu OKH, den 24.Dezember 19 41

Oberkommando des Heeres
~~Der Oberbefehlshaber des Heeres~~

Generalfeldmarschall

Der Oberbefehlshaber des Heeres

Above: Preliminary award document for the German Cross in Gold to *Hauptmann* Buschhausen, *KpChef 6/Schützenregiment 10 (9. Panzerdivision)*, dated December 24, 1941 and signed by *Generalfeldmarschall* Wilhelm Keitel. Size is DIN A5.

IM NAMEN DES FÜHRERS
UND OBERSTEN BEFEHLSHABERS
DER WEHRMACHT
VERLEIHE ICH
DEM

HAUPTMANN
FRIEDRICH BUSCHHAUSEN
KOMPANIECHEF 6./S. R.10

DAS DEUTSCHE KREUZ
IN GOLD

HAUPTQUARTIER, DEN 28. DEZEMBER 1941

OBERKOMMANDO DES HEERES

GENERALFELDMARSCHALL

Above: The formal award document to *Hauptmann* Friedrich Buschhausen is dated four days later. The size is 356 x 256 mm. The rank, name, and unit of the awardee is handwritten.

The award documents for the Silver grade are basically identical to those of the Gold grade, but the name of the order is changed to "*Das Deutsche Kreuz in Silber*."

VORLÄUFIGES BESITZZEUGNIS

IM NAMEN DES FÜHRERS
UND OBERSTEN BEFEHLSHABERS
DER WEHRMACHT
HAT DAS
OBERKOMMANDO DES HEERES
DEM

Major

Fritz Rödlich

DAS
DEUTSCHE KREUZ
IN SILBER
VERLIEHEN

H.Qu./OKH, DEN 30. November 1944

I.A.

(DIENSTSIEGEL)

Generalleutnant
(DIENSTGRAD UND DIENSTSTELLUNG)

Above: Preliminary award document for the German Cross in Silver to *Major* Fritz Rödlich. The size is DIN A5.

IM NAMEN DES FÜHRERS
UND OBERSTEN BEFEHLSHABERS
DER WEHRMACHT
VERLEIHE ICH
DEM
OBERFELDARZT
DR. GUSTAV GRETHER
STAB 299. INF. DIV.
DAS DEUTSCHE KREUZ
IN SILBER

HAUPTQUARTIER, DEN 24. NOVEMBER 1944

OBERKOMMANDO DES HEERES

Keitel

GENERALFELDMARSCHALL

Above: The formal award document to *Oberfeldarzt* Dr. Gustav Grether for the German Cross in Silver. The size is 356 x 256 mm, the rank and name are printed, and the document is signed by *Generalfeldmarschall* Wilhelm Keitel.

CASES

The German Cross in Gold and Silver was always presented in a case. There are basically two case styles with some variations within the later version.

The early awards were presented in a small case. Later cases (which are by far the more numerous than early examples) are larger (below).

Depending on the grade in the case, the upper lid had either a gold- or silver-colored strip imprinted around its edge. The picture to the right shows a small case for a Gold grade with the corresponding gold around the sides of the lid.

Right: Unissued examples, such as the ones found in *Schloss* Klessheim, have the award still wrapped in cellophane. The condition of such pieces is absolutely stunning and gives an impression of the craftsmanship which went into the manufacture of this order.

Left: Some of the later examples were awarded in a simplified case which no longer had any opening or closing mechanism. The usual metal hinge was replaced by one made of paper. This type is rare.

THE ORDER IN WEAR

Contrary to most of the other awards and decorations of the Germany Army, which were worn on the left side of the breast, the German Cross was to be worn on the right side. This method of wear on the otherwise empty breast side shows the order very prominently.

Above: *Generalleutnant* Walther Lucht wears his German Cross (awarded 12. March 1942) on the right side of his tunic. Lucht was awarded with the Knights Cross on 30. January 1943 and with the Oakleaves (# 691) on 9. January 1945 in connection with the Operation *Wacht am Rhein* (Battle of the Bulge).

Above: *Waffen-SS Sturmbannführer* Franz Hack, *Kommandeur III.Btl./SS-PzGrenRgt 9 "Germania"*, was awarded with the German Cross in Gold on January 8, 1943 and wears a cloth version on his tunic. He also displays the Knights Cross of the Iron Cross (May 14, 1944), the Close Combat Bar in Silver, the Iron Cross First Class, and the Wound Badge in Silver. Note the loops for the missing General Assault Badge.

MINIATURES AND STICKPINS

The Order of the German Cross in the miniature version was only allowed to be worn singly, either in 16 mm with a ring to be worn on a chain or as a 16 mm size pin.

Both grades are known to exist in miniature. The miniatures were sold through private retail shops and examples with markings “L/12”, L/50”, and “L/57” are known.

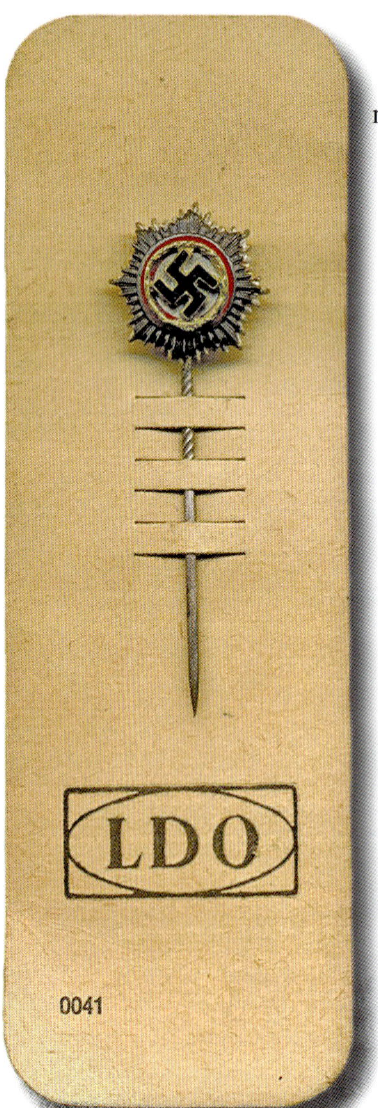

Left: 16 mm miniature of a German Cross in Gold, marked “L/50” on an LDO cardboard strip.

Above: 16 mm miniature with a ring for the award chain.

Right: 16 mm miniature of the Silver grade on a pin with the typical knurling.

FAKES AND REPRODUCTIONS

The German Cross in Gold and Silver is also faked, but these reproductions are not very convincing when compared to original pieces. It is fairly easy to memorize the fingerprints of the five proven makers. All known fakes are unique designs, meaning that they are not trying to copy existing and documented examples of the known makers. The rumors of nearly perfect copies of German Crosses in Gold by Otto Klein and Juncker are just that - rumors. Nor are there any nearly perfect copies of crosses by any other maker.

(A word regarding the often-used term "perfect copy": If a copy is perfect, then it cannot be distinguished from an original piece. If there is no distinction between a "copy" and a documented original - meaning that there is no deviation that cannot be explained by wear, repair, damage, etc. - then the piece in question is original by definition. In other words, there *are* no "perfect copies." Fakes or reproductions always have different and recordable differences from the original.)

Besides the easily detectable fakes there is another consideration, namely those German Crosses produced by the maker Steinhauer & Lück (S&L). As is the case with certain types of the Knights Cross of the Iron Cross by this maker, there are also German Crosses by S&L which have not been proven to be of wartime manufacture. As of this writing there is no solid evidence that any of the crosses made by this company were received for distribution by the *Präsidialkanzlei,* nor have any been determined to have been given to awardees. Two versions exist, one with the typical "4" mark of S&L and the other without the mark. Based on our knowledge of the PKZ numbering system, any version without a "4" cannot have been made before May 1945 because all other manufacturers who delivered to the *Präsidialkanzlei* had their products marked with the appropriate code. This fact proves that Steinhauer & Lück produced the German Cross after the war, and at this point in time there is no evidence at all that Steinhauer & Lück was a legitimate supplier of the award.[8,9,10,11]

There are enough genuine examples of the proven makers on the market so that there is no need to venture into undocumented versions or types from undocumented makers. It might very well be that future research will shed more light on the subject, however.

The cloth version of the German Cross has also been faked, but these copies are easily detectable by the metal wreath, which is in most cases extremely crude. There are also versions which are completely embroidered. Despite the fact that such versions existed before the war's end, there is no clear documentation of style and make and therefore a comparison is not possible. However, most of these fully embroidered versions are so ridiculously made - most of them without the date "1941" - that a comparison is not necessary anyway.

THE 1957 VERSION OF THE ORDER

The post-war versions of the German Cross as authorized under the law of 1957 fall back on the award regulations which state the prerequisite of the Iron Cross First Class or the War Merit Cross First Class with Swords for the awarding of the corresponding grades (Gold or Silver) of the order.

Consequently, the prominent swastika was replaced with the Iron Cross First Class (of course also in the de-nazified version) for the Gold grade and with the War Merit Cross First Class with Swords (also de-nazified) for the Silver grade.

Above: German Cross in Gold in the 1957 version with a typical Deschler wreath, most likely made by that company.

Above: German Cross in Silver made by Steinhauer & Lück.

The early 1957 examples are very well made and are already highly sought after by collectors. For the soldiers and officers of the *Bundeswehr* both versions could be worn on the ribbon bar, the so-called *Bandschnalle* (below the versions in gold and silver).

FOOTNOTES

1 Klaus Patzwall/Veit Scherzer, *Das Deutsche Kreuz 1941-1945*, Volume I, page 39, Verlag Klaus Patzwall, Norderstedt.

2 ibid., page 41

3 Dietrich Maerz, *The German Cross*, page 54 and further expanded in *Das Deutsche Kreuz*, page 56 ff.

4 *Tombak* is a high copper content (at least 80%) brass alloy with the balance material being zinc. *Cupal* is an artificial composite material consisting of aluminum and copper pressed together in a sandwich style, whereas the outer and thinner layer is the aluminum and the inner layer is the copper. See also *The German Cross*, page 25 ff.

5 Detlev Niemann (*Bewertungskatalog, Orden und Ehrenzeichen*) lists an example with 14 rivets in the gold as well as silver version. They are proven to be fakes.

6 D. Niemann states (*Bewertungskatalog, Orden und Ehrenzeichen*) that the cloth versions in silver would be privately made examples. The Silver examples are made in the same industrial style as the Gold versions.

7 A detailed examination of all types of the documents can be found in *The German Cross*, B&D Publishing, 2009, pages 346 - 371.

8 Nimmergut lists the "4" marked S&L cross (both grades) in his book (*Deutsche Orden und Ehrenzeichen*) on page 2213 with the remark "production in the last weeks of the war." He forgets to mention that the town of Lüdenscheid was already captured by American Forces on April 16, 1945 (*Wehrmachtsberichte 1939-1945*, dtv, Volume 2, page 539), and there was neither the demand nor the infrastructure to deliver medals to the *Präsidialkanzlei*. Nimmergut does not mention the unmarked examples.

9 Patzwall (*Das Deutsche Kreuz 1941-1957*) lists Steinhauer & Lück as a legitimate maker without any proof. He also lists Meybauer and Souval, also without providing any additional solid information.

10 Gordon Willimason (*The Iron Cross of 1939*, Bender Publishing) names Steinhauer & Lück as a maker with the marking "4" and shows a silver version. Contrary to the "normal" marking of the "4" outside of the pin, this example is marked on the underside of the pin. Williamson does not mention the unmarked examples.

11 Paul Preuss, who was Vice President of Steinhauer & Lück during the war and after, reports in a letter to the editor of the German magazin "Orden & Militaria Journal (No. 26, Sept. 1977), that he personally got an order for German Crosses in Gold from Dr. Doehle on 20. July 1944.

BIBLIOGRAPHY

Doehle, Dr. Heinrich, *Die Auszeichnungen des Grossdeutschen Reichs*, Berlin 1945

Dombrowski, Hanns, *Orden, Ehrenzeichen und Titel*, Franz Wahlen, 1940

Geeb, *Deutsche Orden und Ehrenzeichen*, Heymanns Verlag, 1985

Geissler, Harald, *Das Eiserne Kreuz*, Patzwall-Verlag, 1995

Klietmann, Kurt, *Auszeichnungen des Deutschen Reiches 1936-1945*, Motorbuch

Klietmann, Kurt, *Deutsche Auszeichnungen*, Die Ordens-Sammlung, Berlin, 1971

Maerz, Dietrich, *The German Cross*, B&D Publishing, 2009

Merkblatt 15/5, *Orden und Ehrenzeichen*, Biblio-Verlag, 1992

Niemann, Detlev, *Bewertungskatalog 1871-1945*, Niemann-Verlag, 2004/2009

Nimmergut, Jörg, *Deutsche Orden und Ehrenzeichen*, Vol. IV, München, 2004

Patzwall/Scherzer, *Das Deutsche Kreuz 1941-1945*, Volumes 1 and 2, Verlag Klaus Patzwall, Norderstedt 2007

Scheibert, Horst, *Die Träger des Deutschen Kreuzes in Gold - Das Heer*, Podzun-Pallas Verlag, Friedberg

Scheibert, Horst, *Die Träger des Deutschen Kreuzes in Gold - Kriegsmarine - Luftwaffe - Waffen-SS und des Deutschen Kreuz in Silber*, Podzun-Pallas Verlag, Friedberg

Williamson, Gordon, *The Iron Cross of 1939*, Bender Publishing, 2002

Der Uniformen- Markt, Volumes 1939-1945

Schwert und Spaten, Volumes 1939-1942

The Wound Badge

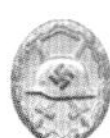

Hauptmann Erwin Kreßmann, *KpChef 1. Kp/sPzJgAbt 519* was awarded with the German Cross in Gold on January 25, 1944 and with the Knights Cross on December 9, 1944. He wears the Wound Badge in Silver, which he received on January 30, 1944, below the Iron Cross First Class as per regulations.

Table of Contents

THE WOUND BADGE

HISTORY

On March 3, 1918, near the closing days of the Great War, Emperor Wilhelm II founded the Wound Badge in three grades: black, matt white (silver) and matt yellow (gold). The actual awarding was initially only authorized for the Prussian soldiers of the *Heer*, but it was later extended to include the soldiers of the other German states and those of the *Luftwaffe* and *Marine*. The badges for the *Heer* and the *Luftwaffe* were hollow stamped and have a German steel helmet, model 1916, on a pebbled background surrounded by a laurel wreath. The Wound Badge for the *Marine* has an anchor with surrounding chain instead of the steel helmet.

The badges were awarded until well after the war during the demobilization phase of the fighting units. From January 1, 1933 until 1936 this design could also be applied for by formally wounded soldiers of the Great War at the local pension office.

Left: The actual design goes back to a design made by Paul Krecklow, a soldier of the Westfront who initially came up with the design and named it *Frontkämpfer Ehrenkreuz 1918* (Honor Cross for Front Soldiers).[1]

Above: The three grades of the Wound Badge of the Great War 1914 - 18.

REGULATIONS

The Wound Badge of the Second World War was instituted on September 1, 1939. The regulations and the design was the same for all three branches of the army. The badge was intended:

> *"as a tribute for those, who were wounded or otherwise damaged by enemy fire during personal brave commitment for the Fatherland."*

The badge was founded in three grades: black, silver, and gold.

The Wound Badge in Black was awarded for one and two wounds. Multiple wounds which were inflicted by the same weapon at the same time, such as multiple shots from a machine gun or fragments from a grenade were to be treated as one wound.

The Wound Badge in Silver was awarded - in consideration of earlier wounds - for three and four wounds. Wounds from the Great War or from the Spanish Civil War were included in the count. Independent of the amount of wounds the Wound Badge in Silver could be awarded for

- the loss of one hand or one arm or one foot or leg or one eye or if the eye became permanently inoperative, or
- complete deafness or hardness of hearing bordering on deafness,
- brain damage, and
- abhorrent deformation of the face.

The Wound Badge in Gold was awarded for more than four wounds. Earlier wounds and such inflicted during the Great War and the Spanish Civil War did count. Independent of the amount of wounds the gold grade was to be awarded for:

- the loss or permanent incapacitation of both hands, or both arms, or both feet respectively legs, or
- the loss or permanent incapacitation of one hand or arm and one foot or leg, or
- loss or complete blindness in both eyes.

After one wound for which the Black Wound Badge was already awarded, any additional "heavy" wound such as the loss of an arm or a leg or an eye was sufficient grounds to award the Wound Badge in Gold.[2]

When a higher grade of the Wound Badge was awarded, the lower grade was no longer worn. Accidents during war duty without enemy fire did not count towards any Wound badge. The only exception was suffered blindness which was grounds to award the Wound Badge in Gold.[3]

DESIGN

The design of the Wound Badge of 1939-1945 was basically the same as the one introduced at the end of the Great War. The badge is oval-shaped with a width of 37 mm and a height of 43 mm and is framed by a laurel wreath. The badge background is pebbled and on that background two crossed swords with an overlaid steel helmet with a prominent swastika form the central motif. Each grade is fully colored in the respective color of the grade, i.e. black, matt white (silver), or matt yellow (gold).

Das neue Verwundeten-Abzeichen.
Bei Verleihung sind andere abzulegen.
Aufnahme: Presse-Hoffmann (M)

There are two basic designs in existence. The first one is officially called "Wound Badge for the German Volunteers in the Spanish Freedom Fight 1936/1939."[4] This type, which was instituted on 22. May 1939, used the same design as the Great War version with an additional swastika in the center. Officially only 182 Wound Badges in Black and one Wound Badge in Silver of this type were awarded. However, this design was also awarded until autumn 1940[5] and was still available for private purchase in 1943 in some retail shops.[6] The name "First Type" is therefore more appropriate for this design. The picture (left) shows the depiction in the *Uniformenmarkt*, issue September 15, 1939.

The second design was introduced after March 1940 and is the one which can be found made by numerous manufacturers. The major change is the steel helmet which is now a Model 1935 instead of the Great War Model 1916. The overall size stayed the same. The picture (right) shows the second design as depicted in Dr. Doehle's book.

Verwundetenabzeichen (1939)

Verwundetenabzeichen des 20. Juli 1944

The design of the special edition for the 20. July 1944 Wound Badge uses the same theme as the second design but moves the steel helmet up and opens the crossing angle of the swords to make room for the date and Hitler's signature.

THE BADGE

The Grades

The Wound Badge in Black is always hollow stamped from either brass or steel. The badge can be found either without any maker mark, with an LDO stamp, or with a *Präsidialkanzlei* number. It is estimated that approximately 2.5 million in Black, 1.0 million in Silver and 0.5 million of the Gold grade were awarded.[7]

Right: Obverse of a first type Wound Badge in Black. The badge is made from brass sheet metal which can be seen where the black paint has worn off.

Left: The reverse of the badge shows the hollow stamped feature. The badge is unmarked which is normal for the first type.

The second type Wound Badge in Black has a steel helmet Model 1935 with a swastika on top as the central motif.

Left: Obverse of an LDO-marked badge made of steel sheet metal.

Right: The LDO number "L/21" is stamped below the steel helmet and indicates the maker Förster & Barth, Pforzheim.

Right: Another Wound Badge in Black made of steel sheet metal.

Left: This example is marked with the *Präsidialkanzlei* number "26" on the pin, which stands for the maker B.H. Mayer, Pforzheim.

Left: Obverse of the first type Wound Badge in Silver with the M16 steel helmet.

Right: The majority of the Wound Badges in Silver (both types) are solid. This one is *hohl verbödet,* which means that it is stamped hollow and then filled with metallic material.

Right: Wound Badge in Silver, second type.

Left: This example is made by the company Wächtler & Lange and stamped "100" on the catch plate (below, rotated 180 degrees for clarity).

Left: Obverse of another second type.

Right: This type is a hollow-back example made by the firm of Assmann. It displays Assmann's distinctive logo (below).

Right: Wound Badge in Gold, first type.

Left: This example was awarded during the Polish campaign 1939.

Left: Obverse of a second type Wound Badge in Gold.

Right: This example is stamped "30", which is the *Präsidialkanzlei* number of the *Hauptmünzamt Wien*.

Right: Wound Badge in Gold, first type. This badge comes from the estate of Oakleaves winner *Major* Bruno Kahl.

Left: This is a fairly rare semi-hollow example, stamped "L 24" for Fritz Zimmermann, Stuttgart.

The Wound Badges of 20th July 1944

On July 20, 1944 an unsuccessful attempt on the life of Adolf Hitler was carried out by *Oberst* Claus Schenk Graf von Stauffenberg. A timed bomb was set off in the barracks where the daily briefing took place. Four persons were killed and another twenty members of the briefing were wounded, some seriously.

The special Wound Badge of the 20th of July was founded by Hitler shortly afterwards on August 28, 1944. The following persons received the badge[8]:

Name	Rank	Grade
Heinz Assmann	*Kapitän z. See*	Black
Nikolaus von Below	*Oberst*	Black
Heinrich Berger	Stenographer	Gold (posthumous)
Karl Bodenschatz	*General der Flieger*	Gold
Heinrich Borgmann	*Oberstleutnant*	Silver
Heinz Brandt	*Oberst i.G.*	Gold (posthumous)
Heinz Bucholz	Stenographer	?
Herbert Büchs	*Major i.G.*	?
Walther Buhle	*General der Infanterie*	Gold
Hermann Fegelein	*SS-Gruppenführer*	Silver
Otto Günsche	*SS-Hauptsturmführer*	?
Adolf Heusinger	*Generalleutnant*	Silver
Alfred Jodl	*Generaloberst*	Black
Ernst John von Freyend	*Major*	?
Wilhelm Keitel	*Generalfeldmarschall*	Black
Günther Korten	*General der Flieger*	Gold (posthumous)
Karl-Jesco von Puttkammer	*Konteradmiral*	Black
Walter Scherff	*Generalmajor*	Gold
Rudolf Schmundt	*Generalleutnant*	Gold (posthumous)
Franz von Sonnleithner	Emissary	Black
Hans-Erich Voß	*Konteradmiral*	Black[9]
Heinz Waizenegger	*Oberstleutnant*	?
Walter Warlimont	*General der Artillerie*	Black

Hitler also got one example (most likely in the black grade regarding the regulations) but he never wore it. The badges were awarded with a document.

Regarding to Dr. Doehle no specific regulation was stipulated. It also seems, based on the example of *Konteradmiral* Voß, that subsequent grades based on additional received wounds were also of the 20th July type. So it seems that the regulations of the normal Wound Badge applied (which they did also for the special award, meaning that earlier wounds did count towards the grade of the 20th July badge) and that also explains the storage of all grades of the 20th July Wound Badge at the *Präsidialkanzlei*.

All the badges were made of silver by the company C.E. Juncker of Berlin. The reverse is either stamped "2" or "L/12" in addition to the silver grade "800".

Right: The three grades of the 20th July Wound Badge.

THE KNOWN MAKERS OF THE WOUND BADGES[10]

PKZ	LDO	Company	Town	B	S	G
1	L/10	Deschler & Sohn	München	x	x	
2	L/12	C.E. Juncker*	Berlin	x	x	x
3	L/11	Wilhelm Deumer	Lüdenscheid	x	x	x
4	L/16	Steinhauer & Lück	Lüdenscheid	x	x	x
5	L/17	Hermann Wernstein	Jena	(x)	x	x
6	L/24	Fritz Zimmermann	Stuttgart		x	x
7	L/13	Paul Meybauer	Berlin	x	x	
9	-	Liefergemeinschaft Pforzheim	Pforzheim	(x)		
10	L/21	Förster & Barth	Pforzheim	x	x	x
11	-	Grossmann & Co.	Wien	(x)	x	x
12	-	Frank & Reif	Stuttgart	(x)	-	-
13	L/60	Gustav Brehmer	Markneukirchen	x	x	x
15	L/14	Friedrich Orth	Wien	x	x	x
16	-	Alois Rettenmaier	Schwäbisch-Gmünd	x		
18	-	Karl Wurster KG	Markneukirchen			
19	L/51	E. Ferd. Wiedmann	Frankfurt/Main	(x)		
20	L/52	C.F. Zimmermann	Pforzheim	x	x	
21	L/50	Gebrüder Godet & Co.	Berlin		x	x
22	L/57	Boerger & Co.	Berlin	x	x	
26	L/18	B.H. Mayers Hof-Kunstprägeanstalt	Pforzheim	x	x	x
28	-	Eugen Schmidthäussler	Pforzheim	x	x	x
30	-	Hauptmünzamt Wien	Wien	x	x	x
32	-	Wilhelm Hobacher	Wien	x		
33	L/61	Friedrich Linden	Lüdenscheid	(x)		
35	L/64	F.W. Assmann & Söhne	Lüdenscheid	x	x	
39		Rudolf Berge	Gablonz a.d. Neiße			
40		Berg & Nolte AG	Lüdenscheid			
45		Franz Jungwirth	Wien	x		
49		Josef Feix & Söhne	Gablonz a.d. Neiße			
53	L/22	Glaser & Sohn	Dresden	(x)	x	x
57		Karl Hensler	Pforzheim	x		
58		Artur Jäckel & Co.	Gablonz a.d. Neiße	x		
61		Rudolf A. Karneth & Sohn	Gablonz a.d. Neiße	(x)		
63		Franz Klamt & Söhne	Gablonz a.d. Neiße	x		

PKZ	LDO	Company	Town	B	S	G
65	L/26	Klein & Quenzer	Idar-Oberstein	x	x	x
67		Robert H. Kreisel	Gablonz a.d. Neße	x		
73		Franz Mänert	Gablonz a.d. Neiße	(x)		
81		Overhoff & Cie	Lüdenscheid	x		
83		Emil Peukert	Gablonz a.d. Neiße	(x)		
84		Carl Poellath	Schrobenhausen	(x)		
86		Paulmann & Crone	Lüdenscheid			
87		Roman Palme	Gablonz a.d. Neiße	x		
88	L/62	Werner Redo	Saarlautern	x		
91		Josef Rössler & Comp.	Gablonz a.d. Neiße	x		
92		Josef Rücker & Sohn	Gablonz a.d. Neiße		x	x
93		Richard Simm & Söhne	Gablonz a.d. Neiße	x		
95		Adolf Scholze	Grünwald a.d. Neiße	x		
98	L/58	Rudolf Souval	Wien			
100	L/55	Wächtler & Lange	Mittweida	x	x	x
103		August G. Tham	Gablonz a.d. Neiße	x		
107		Carl Wild	Hamburg	x	x	x
108		Arno Wallpach	Salzburg	(x)		
109		Walter & Henlein	Gablonz a.d. Neiße	(x)		
110		Otto Zappe	Gablonz a.d. Neiße	x		
112		Agentorwerke Rust & Hetzel	Wien	(x)		
113		Hermann Aurich	Dresden	x		
114		Ludwig Bertsch	Karlsruhe			
116	L/56	Funcke & Brüninghaus	Lüdenscheid	x	x	x
117		Hugo Lang	Wiesenthal	x		
118		August Menze & Sohn	Wien	x		
124		Rudolf Schanes	Wien	x		
126		Eduard Hahn	Oberstein a.d. Nahe			
127		Moriz Hausch AG	Pforzheim	x	x	x
129		Fritz Kohm	Pforzheim	x		
130		Wilhelm Schröder & Co.	Lüdenscheid	x	(x)	
131		Heinrich Wander	Gablonz a.d. Neiße	(x)		
138	L/23	Julius Maurer	Oberstein a.d. Nahe			
139	L/53	Hymmen & Co.	Lüdenscheid	x	x	x
140	L/54	Schauerte & Hohfeld	Lüdenscheid	x	x	x

PKZ	LDO	Company	Town	B	S	G
	L/15	Otto Schickle	Pforzheim	x	x	x
		Gebr. Gegenbach & Co. GmbH	Pforzheim	(x)		
		Arbeitsgemeinschaft AGMuK	Gablonz a.d. Neiße	(x)		
		Adolf Besson	Schwäbisch-Gmünd	(x)		
		Richard Roßwaag Sohn	Oberstein a.d. Nahe			
		Arbeitsgemeinschaft Gustav Hähl	Pforzheim			
		Arbeitsgemeinschaft Emailleure ..	Berlin	(x)		

The list shows all manufacturers of the Wound Badge which could be identified via markings, naming in period documents, literature, or named packaging. The table does not claim completeness but rather reflects the state of research in 2012.

(x) allocation via named packaging or naming in the documents of the *Präsidialkanzlei*. However, no actual badge with maker marking was available.

x unequivocal allocation with maker marked examples

* sole manufacturer of the 20th July Wound Badge, marked either “2” or “L/12”.

PACKAGES AND CASES

The Wound Badge was awarded in a paper package with the imprint *Verwundetenabzeichen* and the grade (*Schwarz, Silber,* or *Gold*). The name of the manufacturer is printed on the lower reverse of the package.

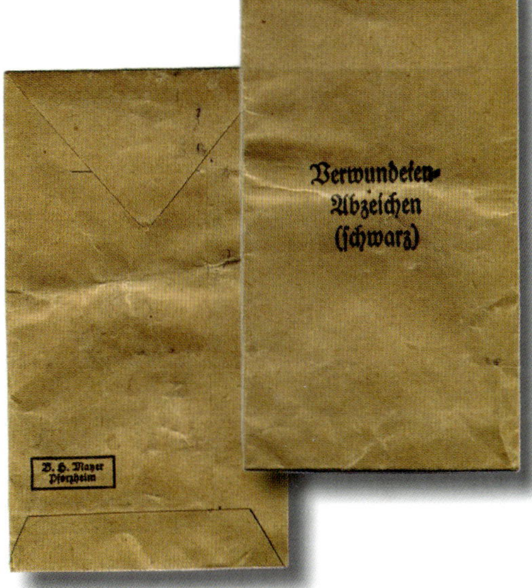

Above: Inside the package the badge was additionally wrapped in thin paper.

For private purchase pieces several types of cases exist. The range goes from the small standardized cardboard box to the high quality satin and velvet-covered boxes.

AWARD DOCUMENTS

The Wound Badge in all grades, but especially the Black Grade, was awarded in very high numbers. Consequently the amount and variations of the award documents are equally diverse.

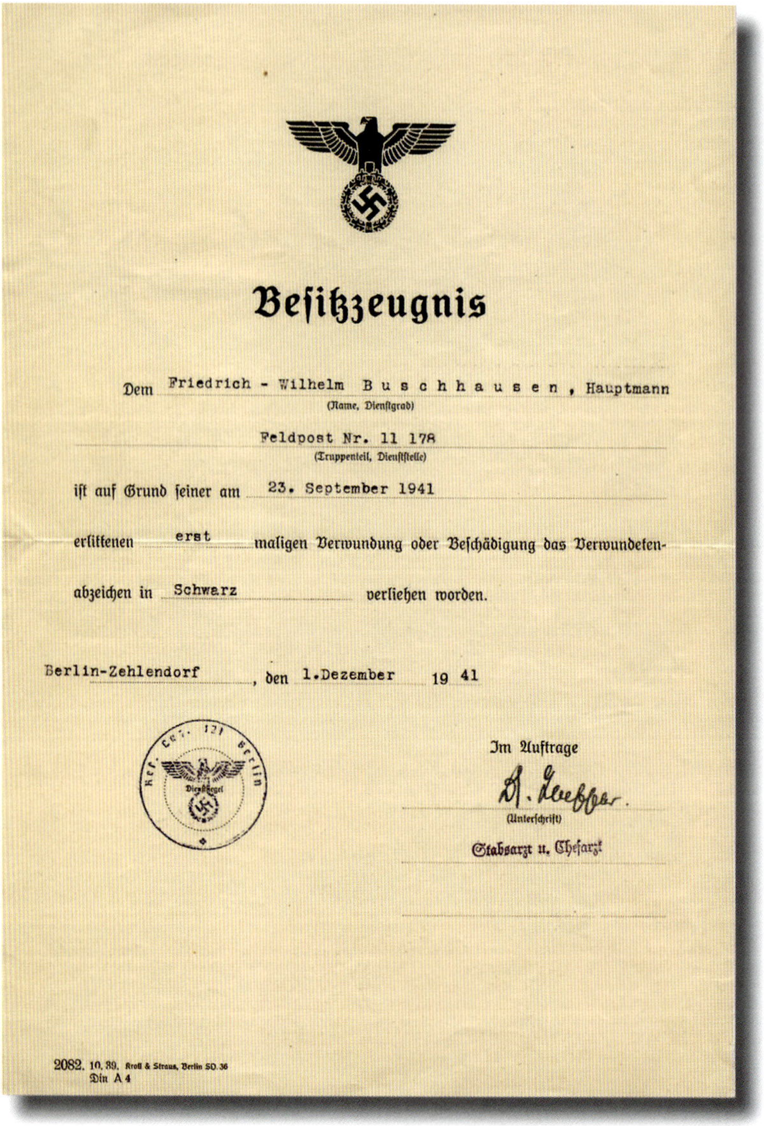

Besitzzeugnis

Dem Friedrich - Wilhelm B u s c h h a u s e n , Hauptmann
(Name, Dienstgrad)

Feldpost Nr. 11 178
(Truppenteil, Dienststelle)

ist auf Grund seiner am 23. September 1941

erlittenen erst maligen Verwundung oder Beschädigung das Verwundetenabzeichen in Schwarz verliehen worden.

Berlin-Zehlendorf, den 1.Dezember 1941

Im Auftrage

(Unterschrift)

Stabsarzt u. Chefarzt

2082. 10.39. Kroll & Straus, Berlin SO 36
Din A 4

Above: Award document for the Wound Badge in Black for *Hauptmann* Friedrich-Wilhelm Buschhausen. Then *Major* Buschhausen was awarded with the Knights Cross later in the war on May 10, 1943 as *Kdr I.Btl/PzGrenR 69*.

H

BESITZZEUGNIS

DEM

Oberleutnant Wolfram K e r t z
(NAME, DIENSTGRAD)

3./Pz.Gren.Rgt.147
(TRUPPENTEIL, DIENSTSTELLE)

IST AUF GRUND

SEINER AM 24.12.1943 ERLITTENEN

1 MALIGEN VERWUNDUNG-BESCHÄDIGUNG

DAS

VERWUNDETENABZEICHEN

IN S c h w a r z

VERLIEHEN WORDEN.

Cosel O/S., DEN 14.Jan. 19 44

(Dr. Preuß)

Stabsarzt und Chefarzt.
(DIENSTGRAD UND DIENSTSTELLE)

1704

Above: Award document for the Wound Badge in Black for *Oberleutnant* Wolfram Kertz, *3. Kp/PzGrenRgt 147* of the *25. Panzer Division*. He was later awarded with the Knights Cross on October 4, 1944 for his bravery at the bridge of Arnheim during the Allied Operation Market Garden (size 13.9 cm x 20.0 cm).

BESITZZEUGNIS

DEM

Kurt F ieb i g Stabsfeldwebel

(NAME, DIENSTGRAD)

Gen. Komp. / Panz. Ers. Abt. 1

(TRUPPENTEIL, DIENSTSTELLE)

IST AUF GRUND

SEINER AM 13.Sept.1941 24.Jan. 1942 14.Sept.1943 ERLITTENEN

dreiMALIGEN VERWUNDUNG-BESCHÄDIGUNG

DAS

VERWUNDETENABZEICHEN

IN Silber

VERLIEHEN WORDEN.

Erfurt DEN 29. Nov. 19 43.

(UNTERSCHRIFT)

Oberst

(DIENSTGRAD UND DIENSTSTELLE)

Above: Award document for the Wound Badge in Silver for *Stabsfeldwebel* Kurt Fiebig of the *Panzerersatzabteilung 1* (size 14.0 cm x 20.0 cm). The three required wounds are noted by date.

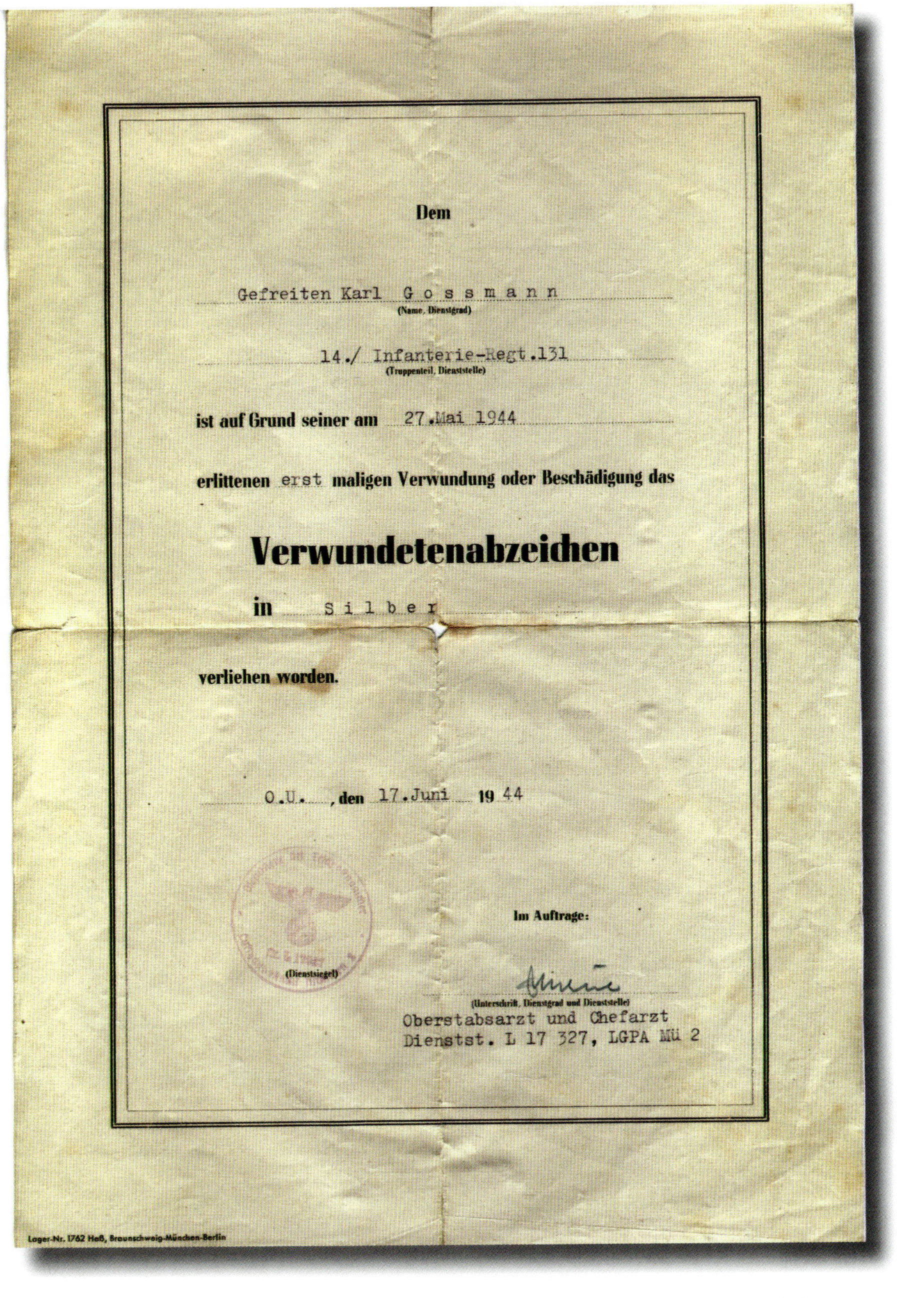

Dem

Gefreiten Karl G o s s m a n n
(Name, Dienstgrad)

14./ Infanterie-Regt.131
(Truppenteil, Dienststelle)

ist auf Grund seiner am 27.Mai 1944

erlittenen erst maligen Verwundung oder Beschädigung das

Verwundetenabzeichen

in S i l b e r

verliehen worden.

O.U., den 17.Juni 19 44

(Dienstsiegel)

Im Auftrage:

(Unterschrift, Dienstgrad und Dienststelle)
Oberstabsarzt und Chefarzt
Dienstst. L 17 327, LGPA Mü 2

Lager-Nr. 1762 Heß, Braunschweig-München-Berlin

Above: Award document for the Wound Badge in Silver for *Gefreiter* Karl Gossmann of the *14. Kp/InfRgt 131*. The document notes that this is a first-time wound, an indication of the severity.

BESITZZEUGNIS

DEM

General der Panzertruppe Walter Nehring
(NAME, DIENSTGRAD)

Komm.General XXIV.Pz.Korps
(TRUPPENTEIL, DIENSTSTELLE)

IST AUF GRUND

SEINER AM 1. 8.1943 ERLITTENEN

5.-MALIGEN VERWUNDUNG-~~BESCHÄDIGUNG~~

DAS

VERWUNDETENABZEICHEN

IN G O L D

VERLIEHEN WORDEN.

A.H.Qu., DEN 5.8. 19 43

Hollidt.

(UNTERSCHRIFT)

General der Infanterie und
Oberbefehlshaber der 6. Armee
(DIENSTGRAD UND DIENSTSTELLE)

Above: Award document for the Wound Badge in Gold for *General der Panzertruppe* Walther* Nehring, award for the fifth wound. The document is signed by Oakleaves winner *General der Infanterie* Karl-Adolf Hollidt (Knights Cross on September 8, 1941, Oakleaves on May 17, 1943) in his position as Commander of the 6. Army.
(*: the document shows "Walter" which is a typo)

Besitzzeugnis

Dem Uffz.
(Dienstgrad)

Jmort, Fritz
(Name)

des 6./ Pz. Gren. Rgt. 4
(Truppenteil und Dienststelle)

ist auf Grund seiner am 17.7.41., 10.9.41., 25.7.43. 17.8.44., 19.8.44 u. 20.8.44 erlittenen

sechs maligen Verwundung oder Beschädigung das

Verwundetenabzeichen

in " Gold "

verliehen worden.

Res. Laz. 182 Schwiebus

Im Auftrage:

Oberstabsarzt und Chefarzt

Schwiebus, den 27. 8. 44.
(Ort und Datum)

A. 1538. DIN A 5. C. Heinrich, Dresden N. III. 43.

Above: Award document for the Wound Badge in Gold for *Unteroffizier* Fritz Jnort, *6. Kp/PzGrenRgt 4* for a total of six wounds received in the time between July 1941 and August 1944. The document is signed by an *Oberstabsarzt* (major physician).

THE BADGE IN WEAR

The Wound Badge was to be worn on the left breast side. If an Iron Cross First Class or a War Merit Cross First Class was awarded, the Wound Badge was to be worn below the order. Only one grade could be worn, and earlier versions, such as a Wound Badge awarded during the Spanish Civil War or during the Great War, were to be discarded in case of the subsequent award of the 1939 version.

Above: Photograph of an unknown *Gefreiter* with a Wound Badge in Black (first type) and the Iron Cross Second Class ribbon in the buttonhole.

Above: Photograph of an unknown *Obergefreiter* with a Wound Badge in Black (second type) and the General Assault Badge. In case of any War Badges present, the Wound Badge was to be worn lower. The button hole holds the ribbons for the Medal for the Winter Campaign in Russia 1941/42 (East Medal) and the Iron Cross Second Class.

Above: *Unteroffizier* Gustav Koller (Knights Cross August 8, 1944 as *Obergefreiter* and *Gruppenführer 1. Kp/PzGrenRgt 21*) wears his Wound Badge in Silver (second type) below the Iron Cross First Class and the Panzer Assault Badge in Bronze. He also was awarded with the Close Combat Bar in Silver.

MINIATURES AND STICKPINS

Miniatures, half miniatures (*Halbminiatur* in the size of approximately 25 mm) and stick pins of all grades of the Wound Badge can be encountered very often. As a singe device and also in combination with other medals, in that case in the 9 mm size. They seem to be the most produced miniature (the grade in black) and also the one with the most variations.

Left: Very large *Halbminiatur* (approx. 35 mm high) of a first type Wound Badge in Black.

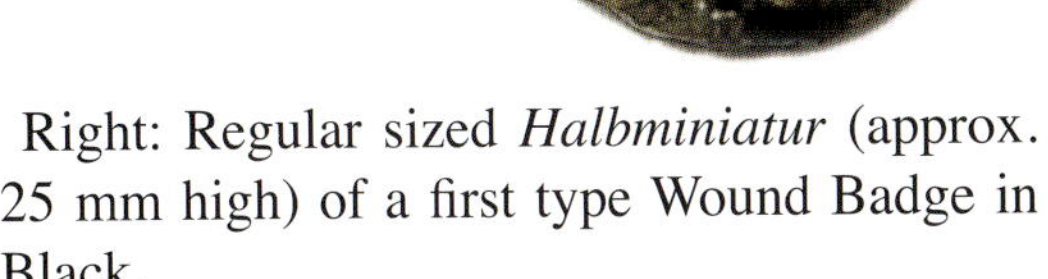

Right: Regular sized *Halbminiatur* (approx. 25 mm high) of a first type Wound Badge in Black.

Left: Two oversized miniature pins. The badges are 20 mm high; the design is of the first type.

Right: 16 mm stick pin of a Wound Badge in Black, second type.

Right: 9 mm stick pin of a Wound Badge in Black, second type.

Left: 9 mm combination with a second type Wound Badge in Silver attached to both classes of the Order of the Iron Cross.

Right: 9 mm stickpin of a Wound Badge in Gold, first type.

FAKES AND REPRODUCTIONS

All grades of the Wound Badge have been faked and are faked. The Silver and Gold grades in particular have been reproduced in all kinds of variations with all possible (and impossible) maker marks. As can be imagined, the most dangerous fakes are those of the 20th July Wound Badge, because the most money can be made by selling one to the unsuspecting and/or gullible buyer.

Most of these fakes are not convincing when compared to the real badges. But most potential buyers do not have the luxury of comparing a potential pickup with a genuine piece. It is therefore advisable to buy such a high-priced award only from a dealer with unconditional return guarantee or only when the unbiased opinion of several knowledgeable experts has been solicited and received.

For the regular versions the best advice that can be given is to buy a specialized book and study the subject before rushing into any purchases. Nothing is more satisfying than to buy a genuine medal or badge with self-acquired solid knowledge.

Above: This fake Wound Badge 20th of July in Silver was sold by Mr. Schiffer from Mühlenramede (one of the early German dealers) to the USA for $ 22.50 - of course as an absolute original - on May 25, 1960. It is not longer in the original collection, but it has still already been in the United States for over 50 years. This fact will allow a possible seller to state that “it comes form a very old collection.” Nevertheless, a fake is a fake no matter how old it is or what the story that comes with it claims.

THE 1957 VERSION OF THE BADGE

The Wound Badge of 1939 was authorized in a de-nazified version in all three grades for wear. The revised badge design was identical to the second type but without the swastika. The production specification from the German Interior Ministry dictates the same style: hollow stamped Wound Badge in Black and solid brass construction for the Gold and Silver grades. The 20th July Wound Badge was not authorized as a 1957 version.

Der Bundesminister des Innern
I A 1 - 11965 A

HERSTELLUNGSVORSCHRIFT für das VERWUNDETEN - ABZEICHEN

Nr. 30
August 1957

Abmessungen: Höhe 44 mm

Material:
Verwundeten-Abzeichen in Schwarz
Hohlprägung: Messing Ms 85 1 mm
Verwundeten-Abzeichen in Silber
Massivprägung: Messing Ms 85 3,5 mm
Verwundeten-Abzeichen in Gold
Massivprägung: Messing Ms 85 3,5 mm

Beschreibung: Das Verwundeten-Abzeichen zeigt auf gekörnten Grund einen Stahlhelm auf zwei gekreuzten Schwertern. Das Ganze wird umrahmt von einem Lorbeerkranz.

Fertigung: Das Abzeichen wird geprägt, geschnitten und entgratet. Auf der Rückseite wird eine Scharniernadel senkrecht hart angelötet. Danach wird das Abzeichen gesandelt und, entsprechend seiner Stufe, wie folgt gefärbt:

in Schwarz: chemisch schwarz färben, mit schwarzem Lack lackieren und im Ofen einbrennen.

in Silber: galvanisch versilbern und mit mattem Zaponlack überziehen.

in Gold: galvanisch vergolden und mit mattem Zaponlack überziehen.

Above: The official design of the 1957 version for all three grades.

Right: Wound Badge in Gold in the 1957 version without the swastika.

FOOTNOTES

1 Andreas Klein, *A Short History of the German Wound Badge*, International Medal Collector Magazine, Vol. 2, No.1, B&D Publishing LLC, 2011

2 Dr. Heinrich Doehle, *Die Auszeichnungen des Grossdeutschen Reichs*, page 26 ff, Berlin 1945

3 *Merkblatt 15/5, Orden und Ehrenzeichen*, Biblio-Verlag, 1992, page 195 ff

4 Dr. Heinrich Doehle, *Die Auszeichnungen des Grossdeutschen Reichs*, page 18, Berlin 1945

5 Hanns Dombrowski, *Orden, Ehrenzeichen und Titel*, Verlag Franz Wahlen, Berlin, 1940

6 Klein/Brücker/Ueberfeld, *Das Verwundetenabzeichen von 1939*, ABuD Publishing GbR (not yet published as of 2012)

7 Rolf Michaelis, *Deutsche Kriegsauszeichnungen 1939-1945 Heer - Waffen-SS - Polizei,* Michaelis-Verlag, 1998

8 H. von der Heyde, *Das Verwundetenabzeichen 20. Juli 1944*, printed in Nimmergut *Deutsche Orden und Ehrenzeichen* (grades added by the authors)

9 *Konteradmiral* Hans-Erich Voß initially received the grade in Black, but was subsequently wounded several more times which awarded him the Silver and Gold grades. He is reportedly the only recipient of all three grades.

10 Klein/Brücker/Ueberfeld, *Das Verwundetenabzeichen von 1939*, ABuD Publishing GbR, projected 2013

BIBLIOGRAPHY

Doehle, Dr. Heinrich, *Die Auszeichnungen des Grossdeutschen Reichs*, Berlin 1945

Dombrowski, Hanns, *Orden, Ehrenzeichen und Titel*, Franz Wahlen, 1940

Geeb, *Deutsche Orden und Ehrenzeichen*, Heymanns Verlag, 1985

Klein/Brücker/Ueberfeld, *Das Verwundetenabzeichen von 1939*, ABuD Publishing

Klietmann, Kurt, *Auszeichnungen des Deutschen Reiches 1936-1945*, Motorbuch

Klietmann, Kurt, *Deutsche Auszeichnungen*, Die Ordens-Sammlung, Berlin, 1971

Merkblatt 15/5, *Orden und Ehrenzeichen*, Biblio-Verlag, 1992

Nimmergut, Jörg, *Deutsche Orden und Ehrenzeichen*, Vol. IV, München, 2004

Der Uniformen-Markt, Volumes 1939-1945

Schwert und Spaten, Volumes 1939-1942

Chapter 6

The Infantry Assault Badge

Leutnant Wolfram Kertz, *5.Kp/InfRgt 193 (69. InDiv)* in a portrait photograph taken in 1940 after the conclusion of the Norway campaign. He wears his Infantry Assault Badge in Silver according to the regulations below his Iron Cross First Class. The small ribbon bar is for the Iron Cross Second Class and the West Wall Medal 1939. On 4. October 1944 then *Oberleutnant* Wolfram Kertz was awarded with the Knights Cross of the Iron Cross for his bravery in Arnheim during the Allied Operation Market Garden.

Table of Contents

THE INFANTRY ASSAULT BADGE

HISTORY

Shortly after the attack on Poland on 1. September 1939 it was contemplated how the brave infantry troops could be awarded with a specific decoration besides the Iron Cross of 1939. As a result of this process the Supreme Commander of the Armed Forces, *Generaloberst* von Brauchitsch, instituted on 20. December 1939 the Infantry Assault Badge (*Infanteriesturmabzeichen*). This became the first in a series of so-called "war badges" (*Kampfabzeichen*), visual signs of achievements in combat and of experienced service.

Das neue Infantrie-Sturmabzeichen
(Siehe „UM" S. 14!)
Aufnahme: Presse-Hoffmann (K)

The picture (left) of the new badge was published in the 15. February issue of the magazine *Uniformen-Markt*. It is credited to "Presse Hofmann" and described as a photo (*Aufnahme*), despite having the looks of a graphic.

The Infantry Assault Badge was first instituted in the Silver grade; the Bronze grade followed on 1. June 1940. Both grades are absolutely equal, the grade difference being based solely on the branch of service of the receiver.

Zum ersten Mal verliehen

Das Infanteriesturmabzeichen. Nach der Teilnahme an drei Sturmangriffen erhält der Infanterist dies am 1. Januar 1940 gestiftete Ehrenzeichen verliehen. Wer es trägt, hat an Entscheidungen teilgehabt, die nur die Infanterie herbeiführen kann im Einsatz von Mann gegen Mann, wobei das Kämpfertum der Persönlichkeit letzte Bewährung erfährt.

Aufn.: J. Mantler.

Das Infanterie-Sturm-Abzeichen

Die ersten Infanteriesturmabzeichen wurden jetzt verliehen. Der junge Leutnant gehört zu den ersten Trägern des Ehrenzeichens.

PK. Pinkornelly-PBZ.

The first awards were given out on 28. May 1940 to a *Gefreiter* and a *Leutnant*. This news was reported in the magazine *Illustrierter Beobachter*, issue 24 of 13. June 1940.

REGULATIONS

The initial grade in Silver was to be awarded to members of the rifle companies of the non-motorized Infantry Divisions and to soldiers of the mountain troops (*Gebirgsjäger*) under the condition that they:

- participated in three assaults
- on three different days
- in the first assault line
- with the weapon in hand, and
- broke into the enemy positions.

Forcible reconnaissance and counter-attacks were also valued as assaults, but only if close combat was involved.

More than three assaults were counted towards the award of the Close Combat Bar (see chapter C 7).

In the early days of awarding the badge was restricted to members of the rifle companies. However, the Infantry regiments also consisted of machine gun, infantry gun, and anti-tank gun companies. On 1. June 1940 this led to the expansion of the awarding to these units, because it was argued that they facilitated the breaking of the enemy line with their specific weapons. However, they needed to be employed in the close combat area, just as the rifle companies.

The same year it was regulated that the Infantry Assault Badge could also be awarded to the accompanying medics, provided they treated the wounded in the same close combat area as the assaulting company members were fighting. (If the medics were part of an independent medical unit, the General Assault Badge was awarded, see chapter C 9.)

Right: Russia, July 1941. These are the foot soldiers the Infantry Assault Badge in Silver was created for.

The grade in Bronze was instituted on 1. June 1940 and is not a lower grade but rather the badge for the motorized units of the infantry divisions. (But not for *Panzergrenadiere*, which were part of the *Panzer* Divisions and the *Panzer* Grenadier Divisions. They were eligible for the Tank Assault Badge in Bronze, see Chapter C6). The requirements for the Bronze grade were exactly the same as for the Infantry Assault Badge in Silver.

Above: An advancing motorized infantry unit as depicted by the famous war painter Walter Gotschke. These are the units which were eligible for the Infantry Assault Badge in Bronze (left).

DESIGN

The Infantry Assault Badge is comprised of an oval-shaped oak leaf wreath with a stylized bow at the bottom holding the wreath together. The wreath is crossed diagonally by a rifle with its barrel pointing upwards from lower right to upper left. The top of the wreath is decorated by a *Heer* eagle looking to its left. The eagle holds the upper arm of a "running" swastika in its claws.[1]

The reverse of the badge is usually flat and holds the vertical pin system. The hinge and the catch are soldered, riveted, or crimped to the badge, depending on the maker. Maker marks, if any at all, are either part of the casting with raised or sunken letters or, as a rarer variation, stamped into the reverse of the badge. Most of the time the mark is in the area of the hinge.[2]

Generally speaking the badge was slightly convex. But there are examples which are more convex and some examples are completely flat.

THE BADGE

While it might be correct to discuss the two grades separately it should also be noted that there is no difference other than the finish between a Silver grade and a Bronze grade of the same maker and the same manufacturing style.

There are three manufacturing styles which can be encountered: massive stamped examples, semi-hollow stamped examples, and those which are hollow-stamped.

Left: A massive stamped Infantry Assault Badge manufactured by the company of Fritz Zimmermann, Stuttgart. It is made of *Tombak*.

Above: A semi hollow Infantry Assault Badge made of zinc by an unknown maker.

Left: A hollow stamped Infantry Assault Badge made by the company B.H. Mayer, Pforzheim. It is made of *Tombak*.

Right: Infantry Assault Badge in Silver

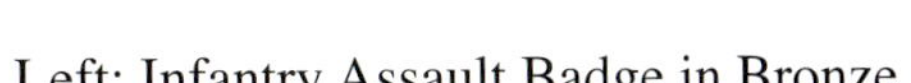

Left: Infantry Assault Badge in Bronze

THE MAKERS OF THE INFANTRY ASSAULT BADGE

Earlier examples from the years 1940 and 1941 are usually hollow-stamped and made of *Tombak*. Starting with the restrictions of valuable raw materials in 1942 the majority of the badges were made of zinc. Very late in the war, pot metal came also into use. Some badges can also be found hollow-stamped from *Cupal* sheets.

The variations in makers markings are plentiful and the table below, which lists all known makers of the Infantry Assault Badge (both grades), shows the more prominent ones in use. One needs to be aware that several variations of a specific maker also might have a different style of marking, including the use of LDO numbers. The vast majority of all the badges, however, are unmarked and a determination of the maker can only be done by comparison.

Maker	Marking*	Variations
Sohni, Heubach & Co., Idar-Oberstein	S.H.u.Co.-O.	(3) variations
Gottlieb & Wagner, Idar-Oberstein	none	(1) variation
Rudolf Souval, Wien	R.S.	(2) variations
Friedrich Orth, Wien	F.O.	(3) variations
Wilhelm Hobacher, Wien	W.H.	(2) variations
Grossmann & Co., Wien	GR.&Co.	(1) variation
Josef Feix & Söhne, Gablonz	J.F.S.	(3) variations
Richard Simm & Söhne, Gablonz	R.S.S	(1) variation
Adolf Scholze, Grünwald**		(1) variation
Metall und Kunststoff, Gablonz	M.K.2.	(8) variations
E. Ferdinand Wiedmann, Frankfurt a.M.		(4) variations
B.H. Mayer Kunstprägeanstalt, Pforzheim	0/1R	(2) variations
Frank & Reif, Stuttgart	FANK&REIF STUTTGART	(3) variations
Gebrüder Schneider AG, Wien		(2) variations
Carl Wild, Hamburg	C W	(1) variation
Deschler & Sohn, München	L/10	(2) variations
Ernst L. Müller, Pforzheim	ERNST L. MÜLLER PFORZHEIM	(3) variations
Friedrich Linden, Lüdenscheid	F L L	(5) variations
Funcke & Brünninghaus, Lüdenscheid	L/56	(5) variations

Maker	Marking*	Variations
F.W. Assmann & Söhne, Lüdenscheid		(6) variations
Fritz Zimmermann, Stuttgart		(4) variations
Gebrüder Wegerhoff, Lüdenscheid		(1) variation
Hermann Aurich, Dresden		(1) variation
Hymmen & Co., Lüdenscheid	L/53	(1) variation
Josef Bergs & Co., Gablonz***	JB&Co	(2) variations
Dr. Franke & Co., Lüdenscheid		(2) variations
Werner Redo, Saarlautern	W.R.42.	(1) variation
Karl Wurster, Markneukirchen		(2) variations
Wilhelm Deumer, Lüdenscheid	none	(6) variations
Schauerte & Höhfeld, Lüdenscheid	none	(2) variations
C.E. Juncker, Berlin	none	(4) variations
Paul Meybauer, Berlin	none	(5) variations
Otto Schickle, Pforzheim	none	(4) variations
Petz & Lorenz, Unterreichenbach	none	(1) variation
Unknown Maker	n/a	at least (18)

* Table does not show all possible variations of maker markings of each individual maker.

** The attribution of the "AS in triangle" maker to Adolf Scholze is circumstantial, based upon ground finds of "AS" products in Gablonz and clues in Scholze's wartime accounting books. The logo has yet to be found in period documentation.

*** Earlier publications show this maker as Julius Bauer. However, the reverse set up with ball hinge and crimped in catch is like other Gablonz maker and the obverse design is very similar as well. Furthermore there are marked packets with this maker, so all signs point to Josef Bergs.

PACKAGES

The Infantry Assault Badge was given to the soldier in an award packet (*Verleihungstüte*), which actually was the standard package developed by the LDO and was generally called a "cellulose bag" (*Zellstoffbeutel*).

The shape of the bags is always the same, but the color and the type setting vary. The common colors are red-brown, light brown, or dark blue. One can also find bags with the imprint of the maker on the reverse.

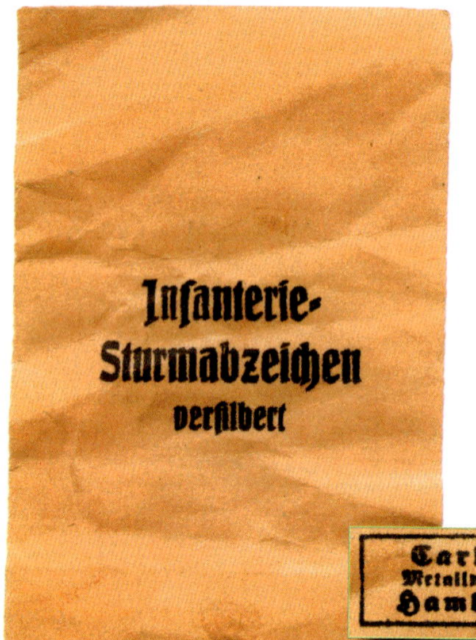

Left: A packet for the Infantry Assault Badge in Silver with the imprint *Infanterie-Sturmabzeichen versilbert* (which means silvered). The name of the manufacturer is printed to the reverse. The size is 71 mm wide x 105 mm high.

Right: A packet for the Infantry Assault Badge in Bronze from the company Josef Feix, Söhne. The size is 60 mm wide x 105 mm high.

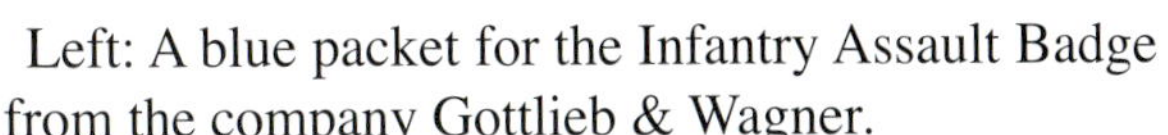

Left: A blue packet for the Infantry Assault Badge from the company Gottlieb & Wagner.

Right: Privately purchased examples were packaged and sold in generic cases like this one with a marbled pattern on the outside of the carton.

AWARD DOCUMENTS

After each assault the commander of the regiment, based on the proposals of his battalion commanders, decided for which unit a recognition for an assault was met. The individual company commanders then recorded the names of the soldiers who fulfilled the requirements of the Infantry Assault Badge regulations. Crucial was the fierce commitment of each soldier at the utmost front line. If three assaults had been recognized, the name of the soldier was given to the regimental headquarters where it was approved and a document and the badge were issued.

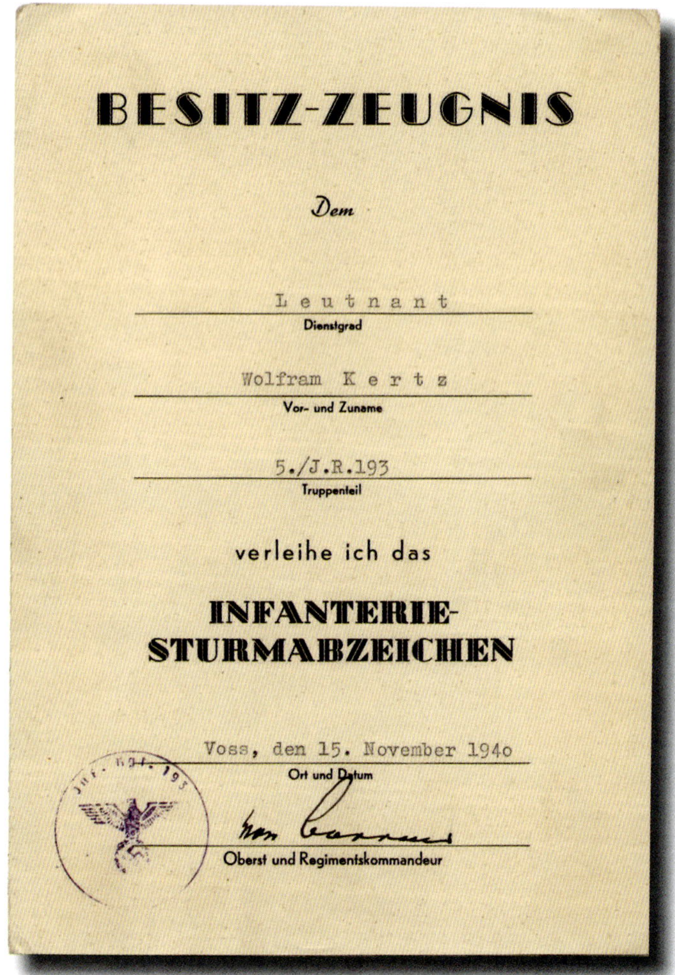

BESITZ-ZEUGNIS

Dem

Leutnant
Dienstgrad

Wolfram Kertz
Vor- und Zuname

5./J.R.193
Truppenteil

verleihe ich das

INFANTERIE-
STURMABZEICHEN

Voss, den 15. November 1940
Ort und Datum

Oberst und Regimentskommandeur

Above: Early award document to *Leutnant* Wolfram Kertz, dated 15. November 1940 and issued in the town of Voss in Southern Norway. Note that the document does not indicate the grade "*in Silber.*" Wolfram Kertz was awarded the Knights Cross on 4. October 1944 , holding the rank of *Oberleutnant* in the *Kampfgruppe Bruhn* near Arnheim.

Besitzzeugnis.

Dem

Gefreiten Karl Maser

Dienstgrad, Name

10./ I.R. 311

Truppenteil

verleihe ich das

Infanterie-Sturmabzeichen.

Im Felde, den 3. Januar 1942.

Oberst und Rgt. Kdr.

Above: A fairly rare ornamental award document for the Infantry Assault Badge in *Silver*. The size is 149 mm x 210 mm (DIN A5). It is made out to *Gefreiter* Karl Maser of the *10. Kp/InfRgt 311* of the 217. Infantry Division. Note that the grade "Silber" is not indicated on the document.

Besitzzeugnis

Dem Feldwebel
(Dienstgrad)

Karl Krauß
(Vor- und Zuname)

11./I.R. 339
(Truppenteil)

verleihe ich das

Infanterie-Sturmabzeichen

— Silber —

Rgts. Gef. Stand, 16. 2. 42
(Ort und Datum)

i.V.

(Unterschrift)

Major

(Dienstgrad und Dienststellung)

Infanterie Regiment 339
Stempel

Above: Filled out by hand, this document for the Infantry Assault Badge was made out to *Feldwebel* Karl Krauss, *11. Kp/InfRgt 339 (167. InfDiv)* on 16. February 1942. Krauss was awarded the German Cross in Gold on 17. October 1943 and on 5. December 1944 the Honor Roll Clasp. He was also an awardee of the Close Combat Bar in Gold (24. December 1944).

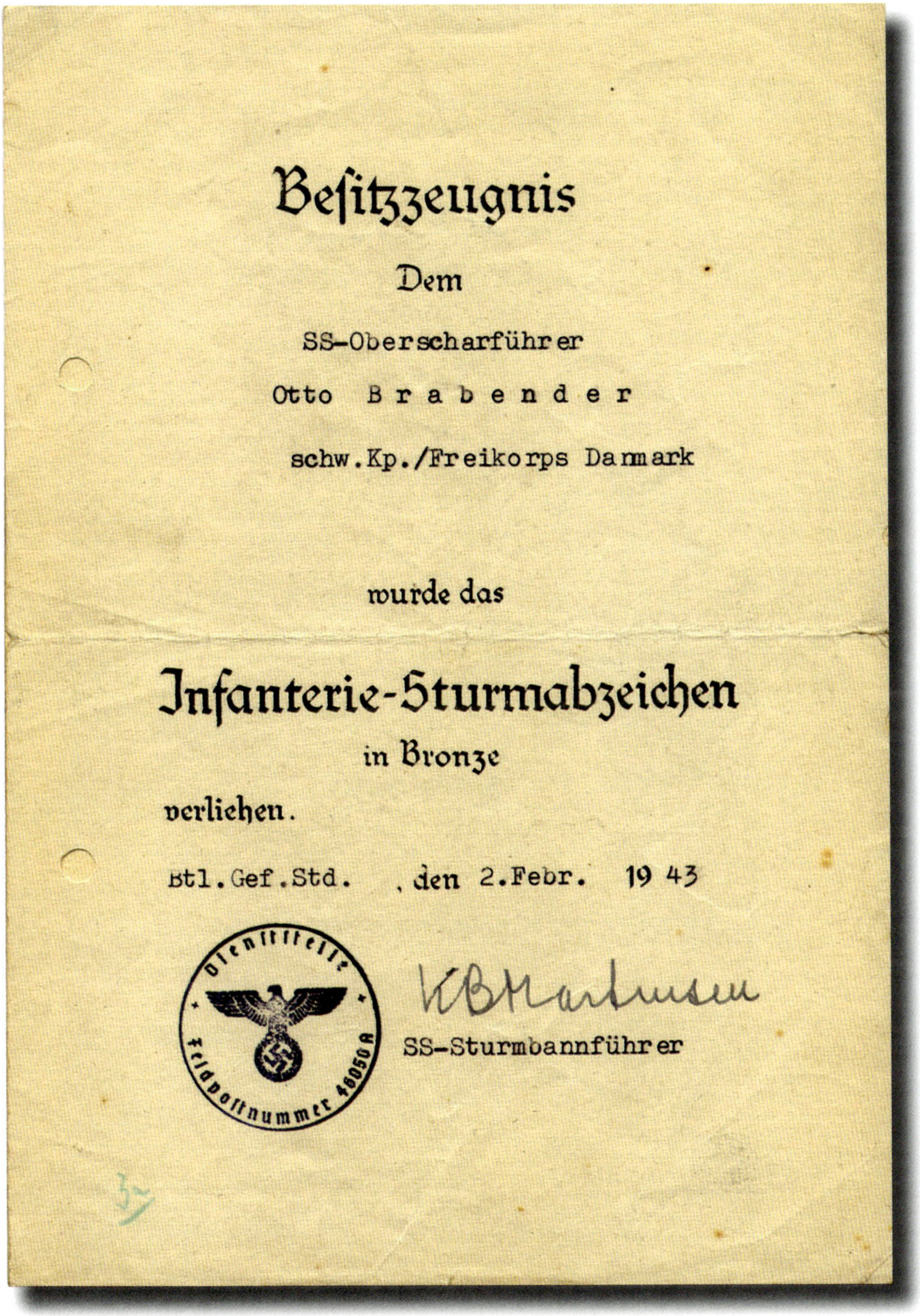

Besitzzeugnis

Dem

SS-Oberscharführer

Otto Brabender

schw.Kp./Freikorps Danmark

wurde das

Infanterie-Sturmabzeichen

in Bronze

verliehen.

Btl.Gef.Std. , den 2.Febr. 1943

Dienststelle Feldpostnummer 46050 A

SS-Sturmbannführer

Above: Award document in size DIN A5 for *SS-Oberscharführer* Otto Brabender of the *schw.Kp./Freikorps Danmark* (*SS-Brigade 1, LIX Armeekorps*) for the Infantry Assault Badge in Bronze, dated 2. February 1943.

THE BADGE IN WEAR

The Infantry Assault Badge in Silver or Bronze was worn on the left breast side. If the recipient was already awarded the Iron Cross First Class, the Infantry Assault Badge was to be worn below the Iron Cross. It the recipient was also awarded the Wound badge, the Infantry Assault Badge was to be worn above that badge.

Above: The NCO in the black *Panzer* wrapper wears an Infantry Assault Badge in Bronze below the Iron Cross First Class next to the Wound Badge in Black. The award of the Bronze grade (and the missing death heads on the collar) makes clear that this *Unteroffizier* was not part of the *Panzertruppe* but rather a member of another unit equipped with motorized armored vehicles.

Above: The *Obergefreiter* wears the Infantry Assault Badge in Silver above the Wound Badge in Silver. The second button hole shows the ribbon for the Iron Cross Second Class of 1939.

Above: *General der Infanterie* and commander of the X. Army Corps Friedrich Köchling (Knights Cross on 31. July 1942) wears his Infantry Assault Badge in Silver below the 1914 Iron Cross and repetition *Spange* and above the Wound Badge in Silver.

STICKPINS

The Infantry Assault Badges in Silver and in Bronze were produced as stickpins in the sizes 16 mm and 9 mm. They can be found in differing levels of quality and were produced by several companies.

Left: 16 mm stickpin of the Infantry Assault Badge in Silver.

Right: 16 mm stickpin of the Infantry Assault Badge in Bronze.

Left: 9 mm stickpin of the Infantry Assault Badge in Bronze.

FAKES AND REPRODUCTIONS

The Infantry Assault Badge is heavily faked. There are too many to list and it is well known that some dealers (and especially one in Germany) are constantly improving the quality of their illegal production and trade.

Some of the fakes are bad castings of real badges, like the crude fakes of Assmann-made badges. Some are post-war productions from companies which made the badge also before May 1945, such as Souval/Wien.

It is impossible to list the multitude of fakes in one book and, besides, that is not the correct approach for a collector to take. It is far easier to learn the limited number of real badges and exclude everything else as either "unknown" or "fake."

THE 1957 VERSION OF THE BADGE

The Infantry Assault Badge was authorized for wear in the 1957 version. The design is identical, only the national eagle and the swastika were removed. Early versions of the badge were made by the same manufacturers who made the badges during the war and are already highly sought by collectors.

Above: Infantry Assault Badge in Silver and in Bronze in the version of the law of 1957.

Right: The Infantry Assault Badge in Silver for the ribbon bar for daily wear on the uniform.

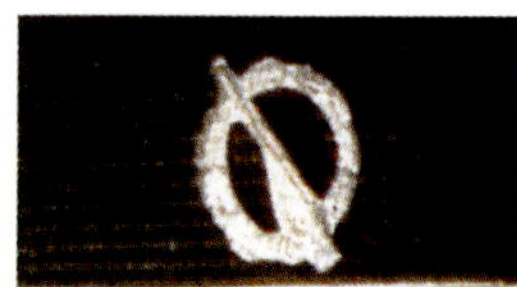

FOOTNOTES

1 Nimmergut mentions in his *Orden und Ehrenzeichen*, Vol. IV, page 2294 a prototype which surfaced in 1978. The eagle has spread wings and holds a round wreath with a swastika inside in its claws. The rifle is crossed by an upwards pointing lightning bolt. The badge is marked for Lauer/ Nürnberg. Nimmergut doubts that it is genuine and so do the authors of this book.

2 Sascha Weber, *The Infantry Assault Badge*, B&D Publishing LLC, page 15

BIBLIOGRAPHY

Doehle, Dr. Heinrich, *Die Auszeichnungen des Grossdeutschen Reichs*, Berlin 1945

Dombrowski, Hanns, *Orden, Ehrenzeichen und Titel*, Franz Wahlen, 1940

Geeb, *Deutsche Orden und Ehrenzeichen*, Heymanns Verlag, 1985

Merkblatt 15/5, *Orden und Ehrenzeichen*, Biblio-Verlag, 1992

Nimmergut, Jörg, *Deutsche Orden und Ehrenzeichen*, Vol. IV, München, 2004

Weber, Sascha, *The Infantry Assault Badge,* B&D Publishing LLC, Richmond, MI 2008

Der Uniformen-Markt, Volumes 1939-1945

Schwert und Spaten, Volumes 1939-1942

Chapter

7

The Close Combat Clasp

Oberleutnant Wolfram Kertz is pictured after the award of the Knights Cross (4. October 1944). He was awarded with the Close Combat Clasp in Bronze only 13 days later, on 17. October 1944, both awards for action during the Allied operation "Market Garden."

Table of Contents

THE CLOSE COMBAT CLASP

HISTORY

The Infantry Assault Badge was intended as a visual sign of a battle-tested front soldier. However, due to the prolonged war the badge was no longer sufficient to honor the months- and years-long deployments of the time-tested infantry soldiers. Another award had to be created to do the soldiers justice.

On 25. November 1942, 17 months into Operation Barbarossa and after 38 months of the Second World War, the Supreme Commander Adolf Hitler founded the Close Combat Clasp in the grades Bronze, Silver, and Gold:

> "*.... as a visible sign of appreciation for the soldier fighting with the bare weapon and close combat means man against man, but also as an incentive for highest acquittal.*"

Close combat days were days during which the soldier saw "the whites in the eye of the enemy" during fights of man against man until a final outcome. This type of close combat could not only occur during an assault, but also during reconnaissance missions or during defensive actions, even in rearward areas of the front line.

Stiftung einer Nahkampfspange

Als sichtbares Zeichen der Anerkennung des mit der blanken Waffe und Nahkampfmitteln Mann gegen Mann kämpfenden Soldaten, zugleich aber auch als Ansporn zu höchster Pflichterfüllung stiftete der Führer am 25. November 1942 die Nahkampfspange. Mit dieser Auszeichnung wird vor allem der deutsche Infanterist für höchsten mannhaften Einsatz belohnt. Sie kann aber jedem Soldaten der deutschen Wehrmacht verliehen werden, der die Bedingungen für ihre Verleihung erfüllt.

Voraussetzung für Verleihung der Nahkampfspange ist, daß der Soldat ungeschützt und zu Fuß sich vielfach im Nahkampf Mann gegen Mann mit der Waffe in der Hand bewährt hat. Die Verleihung erfolgt in drei Stufen. Die erste Stufe in Bronze wird für 15 Nahkampftage, die zweite Stufe in Silber für 30 Nahkampftage und die dritte Stufe in Gold für 50 Nahkampftage verliehen. Die Nahkampftage werden rückwirkend ab 1. Dezember 1939 gerechnet. Die Nahkampfspange wird auf der linken Brust über der Ordensschnalle getragen und zeigt in der Mitte auf schwarzem Grund das Hoheitszeichen mit den gekreuzten Waffen, Seitengewehr und Handgranate, als Symbol des Nahkampfes. Vom Mittelstück der Spange

Aufn.: „DUZ"

gehen Strahlenbündel mit Eichenlaubblättern nach beiden Seiten, die die Bewährung und den Ruhm versinnbildlichen.

The institution of the Close Combat Clasp was announced in the 20. June 1943 issue of the *Uniformen-Markt*. The report mentions wrongly that the counting of the close combat days starts with the 1. December 1939. Correct is the retroactive date of 1. December 1942.

REGULATIONS

The requirements to be awarded with the Close Combat Clasp in Bronze, the first grade, were 15 documented close combat days as defined by being close combat man to man until the ultimate outcome was reached. The requirement to see the "white in the eye of the enemy" was actually mentioned in the regulation.[1] The crediting of the close combat days started retroactive 1. December 1942.

To distinguish the well-tried and experienced front soldier it was regulated that for the uninterrupted service[2] on the Eastern Front[3] starting 22. June 1941 the following allowance could be made:

for 15 months uninterrupted service:	up to 15 close combat days
for 12 months uninterrupted service:	up to 10 close combat days
for 8 months uninterrupted service:	up to 5 close combat days

The decision for the actual allowance of days was in the hands of the company leader.

The commander of a division was authorized to award the Close Combat Clasp to heavily wounded soldiers who could no longer participate in any future close combat actions. The conditions were that the soldier in question had already accumulated 10, 20, or 40 close combat days to be awarded the Bronze, Silver, or Gold grade. This regulation also applied to soldiers killed in action.[4]

The requirements for the Silver grade were a total of 30 close combat days. The awarding of the Gold grade required a staggering accumulation of 50 days of close combat. The first award of the Gold grade was made on 10. August 1943. Every awardee of the Close Combat Clasp in Gold received also 21 days of special leave and could be recommended for the award of the German Cross in Gold without further explanatory statements.

On 8. April 1944 Adolf Hitler decided that he would present (not award) the Close Combat Clasp in Gold personally to the decorated soldiers. The first such ceremony was on 27. August 1944 in which 14 soldiers were presented with this extremely high award.[5,6]

Later on, in autumn of 1944, Heinrich Himmler, as Supreme Commander of the Replacement Army, was assigned to hold the presentation ceremony since the awardees were released from front duty to teach their experience at schools of the Replacement Army.

On 12. December 1944 Himmler presented the Close Combat Clasp in Gold to a total of 81 soldiers of the *Heer* and the *Waffen-SS* in the city hall of Ulm/Baden-Württemberg.

DESIGN

The central motif of the Close Combat Clasp consists of the German stick grenade and a carbine bayonet, the typical close combat weapons, crossed over each other and crowned by a national eagle with the swastika in its claws. This arrangement is surrounded by six oak leaves, forming a square box. This box is underlaid with a black plate.

Extending outwards on both sides of the central rectangle are four oak leaves surrounded by rays, symbolizing the proof in combat and the resulting recognition.[7] The clasp was designed by the Berlin painter and designer Wilhelm Ernst Peekhaus. The clasp was worn above the left breast pocket above the ribbon bar.

Nahkampfspange in Bronze

Nahkampfspange in Silber

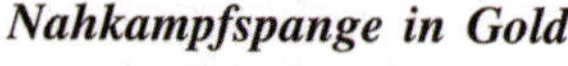

Nahkampfspange in Gold

Above: All three grades of the Close Combat Clasp as depicted in *Die Auszeichnungen des Grossdeutschen Reichs* by Dr. Heinrich Doehle.

THE CLASP

The Close Combat Clasp was produced by several makers and it is reasonable to assume that each maker made all three grades of the award since the difference lies only in the finish. This could be a silver or gold plating or a bronzed *Brennlack* finish or even a colored wash. Most of the Close Combat Clasps are made of zinc; the so-called Presentation Close Combat Clasp was made of *Tombak*.

Above: Close Combat Clasp in Bronze.

Above: Reverse of the same clasp with the marking "FEC W.E. PEEKHAUS BERLIN" on the left side and "AUSF. C.F. (sic!) JUNCKER BERLIN" on the right side. (FEC stands for the latin word "fecit" and means "he did.")

Right: Detail image of the center motif of the Close Combat Clasp. The underlying material zinc shines through the bronze *Brennlack* wash in some exposed areas.

Above: Close Combat Clasp in Silver.

Above: Reverse of the same clasp with the marking "FEC W.E. PEEKHAUS BERLIN" on the left side and "AUSF. A.G.M. u.K. GABLONZ" on the right side.

Left: The detail image of the center motif shows areas where the silver wash finish is disturbed by typical bubbles from the underlying zinc base material.

Above: Close Combat Clasp in Gold.

Above: Reverse of the same clasp with the marking "FEC W.E. PEEKHAUS BERLIN" on the left side and "F","L" and " L" in three circles, the logo of Friedrich Linden, Lüdenscheid.

Right: The gold finish of this clasp is exceptionally well preserved.

When it was announced on 26. March, 1944 that Hitler would from now on present the Close Combat Clasp in Gold to the awardees, it was also clear that this could not be done with the clasps packed in normal carton or cellophane bag as was normally the case.
It was decided that a black case with white inside lining was required, in the same style of the presentation cases for the Oakleaves and higher grades of the Order of the Iron Cross. As a producer the Berlin-based company of Gebrüder Godet was recommended to Dr. Doehle, but the actual version was produced by C.E. Juncker.[8]

The Gold Presentation Close Combat Clasp is made of *Tombak*. The black backplate is fixed to the clasp with a central rivet (on the regular clasps the backplate is crimped) and at the top center reverse a little hook is added to keep the clasp flush to the uniform of the recipient.

There are two types of the Gold Presentation Clasp known, both are made by C.E. Juncker. The difference lies in the attachment of the catch to the clasp body.

Above: Gold Presentation Close Combat Clasp made by C.E. Juncker, Type 2.

Above: Reverse of the Gold Presentation Close Combat Clasp. Note the central rivet, the little hook, and the recessed catch on a small plate (the identification feature of type 2).

THE MAKERS OF THE CLOSE COMBAT CLASP[9]

Arbeitsgemeinschaft Metall und Kunststoff, Gablonz	(16) variations
Deschler & Sohn, München	(4) variations
Funcke & Brüninghaus, Lüdenscheid	(1) variation
Gebrüder Wegerhoff, Lüdenscheid	(3) variations
Wilhelm Hobacher, Wien	(1) variation
Hymmen & Co., Lüdenscheid	(2) variations
Josef Feix Söhne, Gablonz	(2) variations
C.E. Juncker, Berlin (regular clasps)	(2) variations
C.E. Juncker, Berlin (Gold Presentation Clasp)[10]	(2) variations
Friedrich Linden, Lüdenscheid	(3) variations
Rudolf Souval, Wien	(4) variations
Steinhauer & Lück, Lüdenscheid	(6) variations
Unknown Maker	(2) variations

Right: Photograph of the last official presentation of the Close Combat Clasp in Gold. *Generaloberst* Heinz Guderian presented the clasps to 13 recipients in the OKH at Zossen on 10. March 1945.

PACKAGES

The Close Combat Clasps were packaged in grey cardboard boxes with the imprint *Nahkampfspange* or *Nahkampfspangen* (which is the plural despite there being only one clasp in the box). Underneath the grade was spelled out in either *bronze*, *versilbert,* or *vergoldet*.

The Gold Presentation Combat Clasp was presented in a special case, similar to the ones for the Knights Cross and its higher grades. The outside of the rectangular case is covered with black imitation leather paper. The inside lid is white silk. The clasp rests on black velvet. There are two types of cases with the major difference being the shape of the push button.

AWARD DOCUMENTS

As was the case with every order or award of the Third Reich, the recipient of the Close Combat Clasp received also an award document. The most common type is pictured on the following pages. There was no dedicated document for each grade; the individual *Stufe* or grade was typed into the provided space on the document together with the number of combat days achieved.

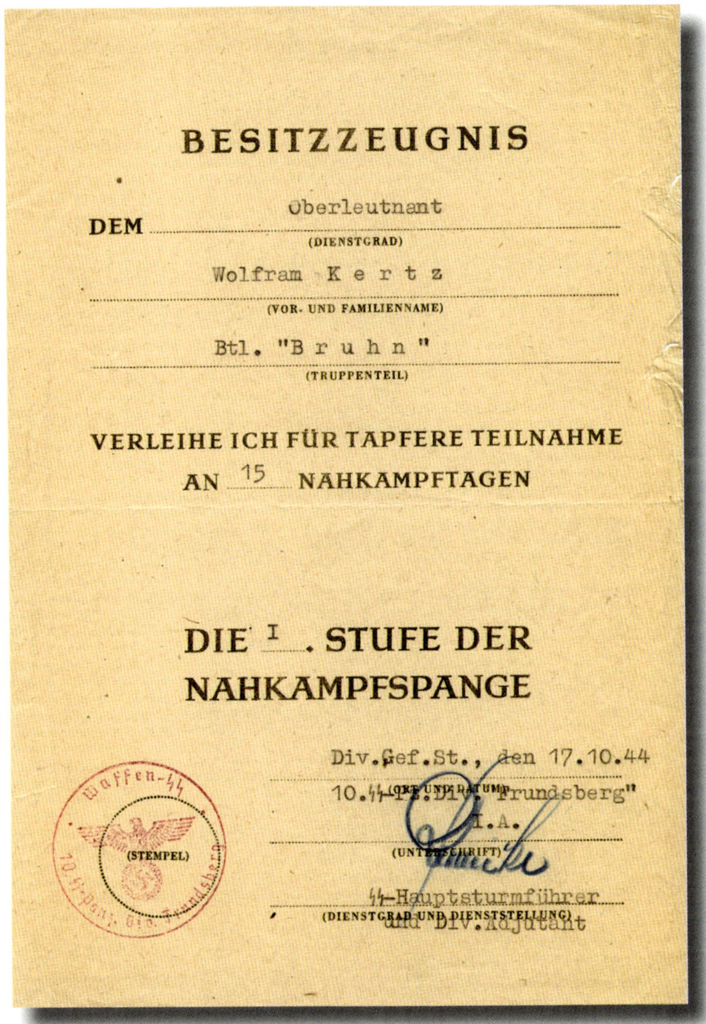

BESITZZEUGNIS

DEM Oberleutnant
(DIENSTGRAD)

Wolfram K e r t z
(VOR- UND FAMILIENNAME)

Btl. "B r u h n"
(TRUPPENTEIL)

VERLEIHE ICH FÜR TAPFERE TEILNAHME
AN 15 NAHKAMPFTAGEN

DIE I. STUFE DER
NAHKAMPFSPANGE

Div.Gef.St., den 17.10.44
(ORT UND DATUM)
10.SS-Pz.Div. "Frundsberg"

(STEMPEL)

I.A.
(UNTERSCHRIFT)

SS-Hauptsturmführer
und Div.Adjutant
(DIENSTGRAD UND DIENSTSTELLUNG)

Above: Award document for *Oberleutnant* Wolfram Kertz. The *Bataillon "Bruhn"* was temporarily subordinated to the *10. SS-PzDiv Frundsberg*, which saw action in the area of Arnheim during Operation Market Garden. The document is for a Close Combat Clasp in Bronze (15 close combat days, *1. Stufe* or 1. grade). The size is DIN A5.

BESITZZEUGNIS

DEM Oberleutnant
(DIENSTGRAD)

Karl K r a u s s
(VOR- UND FAMILIENNAME)

Stab II./ Gren.Rgt. 339
(TRUPPENTEIL)

VERLEIHE ICH FÜR TAPFERE TEILNAHME
AN 30 NAHKAMPFTAGEN

DIE 2. STUFE DER
NAHKAMPFSPANGE

O.U.,den 1.Dez. 1943
(ORT UND DATUM)

(UNTERSCHRIFT)

Oberst u. Rgt.-Kdeur.
(DIENSTGRAD UND DIENSTSTELLUNG)

Above: Award document for the 2. grade (Silver) to *Oberleutnant* Karl Krauss. The document is signed by the Commander of the *Grenadierregiment 339 (167. InfDiv.)*

BESITZZEUGNIS

DEM Oberleutnant d.R.
(DIENSTGRAD)

Karl K r a u s s
(VOR- UND FAMILIENNAME)

Feld-Ers.Btl.85
(TRUPPENTEIL)

VERLEIHE ICH FÜR TAPFERE TEILN
AN 50 NAHKAMPFTAGEN

DIE 3. STUFE DER
NAHKAMPFSPANGE

Div.Gef.St., 24. Dezember 1944
(ORT UND DATUM)

(UNTERSCHRIFT)

Generalmajor und Kommandeur
der 101. Jäger-Division
(DIENSTGRAD UND DIENSTSTELLUNG)

Above: *Oberleutnant* Karl Krauss (previous page) managed to be awarded the Close Combat Clasp in Gold a little over one year after he received the Silver grade. Krauss was also a holder of the German Cross in Gold (17. October 1943) and was named in the Honor Roll of the *Heer* (5. December 1944).

THE CLASP IN WEAR

The Close Combat Bar was worn above the left breast pocket on the highest spot and above the ribbon bar. Only the last grade was to be worn, the earlier grade was to be discarded but remained with the recipient.

Above: The *Unteroffizier* wears the Close Combat Clasp in Bronze per regulations above his ribbon bar for the Iron Cross Second Class, East Front Medal and Remembrance Medal for 13. March 1938. He also wears the Infantry Assault Badge in Silver and the Wound Badge in Black.

Above: *Oberfeldwebel* Johann Baichl, *Zugführer* of the *5.Kp/PzGrenRgt 33 (4. Panzer-division)* was awarded the Close Combat Clasp in Gold on 23. October 1944. The German Cross in Gold was awarded on 23. May 1944. The ribbon below the one for the Iron Cross Second Class in the buttonhole is for the East Medal.

Above: A rested *Oberleutnant* Wolfram Kertz in the field grey *Panzer* wrapper for the *Panzergrenadiere*. He wears the Close Combat Clasp in Bronze above the Iron Cross First Class. He was also awarded with the Infantry Assault Badge (15. November 1940) and the Wound Badge in Black (14. January 1944). The Knights Cross was awarded for actions at the famous bridge over the river Rhein in Arnheim. (Compare to photos on pages 208 and 232.)

STICKPINS

Stickpins for the Close Combat Bar are extremely rare and have so far only been encountered in the 9 mm size. This is due to the regulation which was announced in the 15. July issue of the *Uniformen-Markt* by the *Präsidialkanzlei* that all miniatures of combat badges be produced in 9 mm size only. Since this new regulation was announced barely 8 months after the introduction of the Close Combat Clasp it is doubtful whether any companies had the intention to produce a 16 mm miniature.

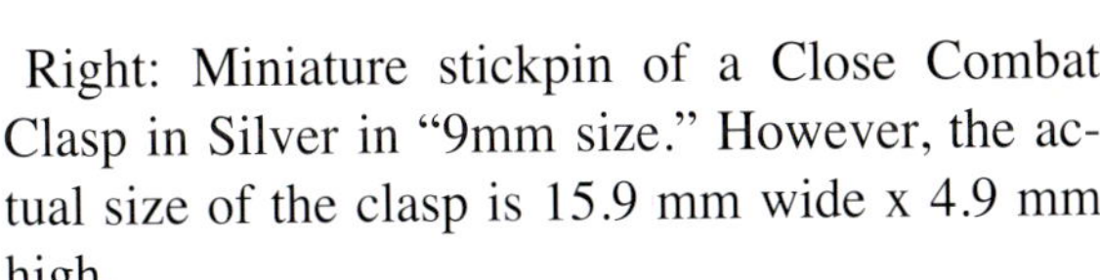

Right: Miniature stickpin of a Close Combat Clasp in Silver in "9mm size." However, the actual size of the clasp is 15.9 mm wide x 4.9 mm high.

Amtliche Mitteilungen der Präsidialkanzlei

„Durch Erlaß vom 5. Juli 1943 hat das Oberkommando der Wehrmacht im Einvernehmen mit den Oberkommandos der drei Wehrmachtteile der Präsidialkanzlei die Ueberwachung der Herstellung sowie des Vertriebs von Waffenabzeichen der Wehrmacht im freien Handel übertragen. Der Staatsminister und Chef der Präsidialkanzlei hat darauf die nachstehende Anordnung erlassen:

Auf Grund der Verordnung über die verbindliche Einführung von Normen-, Geschäfts- und Lieferbedingungen sowie von Güte- und Bezeichnungsvorschriften vom 8. 9. 1939 (RGBl. I S. 1745) in Verbindung mit dem Erlaß des Reichswirtschaftsministers vom 5. 7. 1940 — III BL 16. 40 — ordne ich an was folgt:

Die Bestimmungen meiner Anordnungen vom 25. 7. 1940 (RMBliV S. 1869), vom 1. 11. 1940 (RMBliV S. 2045) und vom 8. 1. 1941 (RMBliV S. 126) werden mit sofortiger Wirkung auf die Waffenabzeichen der Wehrmacht erstreckt.

Berlin, den 7. Juli 1943

Der Staatsminister und Chef der Präsidialkanzlei.

In Vertretung
gez. Dr. Doehle.

Sämtliche Herstellerfirmen werden nachdrücklichst auf die Einhaltung der vorstehenden Anordnung hingewiesen, insbesondere auf die Verpflichtung, vor weiterer mengenmäßiger Herstellung von Waffenabzeichen der Wehrmacht oder deren Verkleinerungen der Präsidialkanzlei Muster zur Genehmigung vorzulegen. Verkleinerungen für den Rockaufschlag des Zivilrocks dürfen zukünftig nur in der auch für die Verkleinerungen von Orden und Ehrenzeichen vorgeschriebenen Größe von 9 mm hergestellt werden.

Alle Firmen, die bisher Waffenabzeichen der Wehrmacht oder deren Verkleinerungen hergestellt haben, werden ersucht, unverzüglich ihre Anschrift unter Angabe der von ihnen hergestellten Abzeichen oder Verkleinerungen der Präsidialkanzlei zwecks Prüfung der Frage der Erteilung der Genehmigung zur weiteren Anfertigung mitzuteilen."

*

Das Ritterkreuz des Kriegsverdienstkreuzes mit Schwertern und ohne Schwerter darf durch den Ordenseinzelhandel vorläufig nicht verkauft werden. Träger dieser Auszeichnung sind wegen Beschaffung von Ersatzstücken oder Zweitstücken an die Präsidialkanzlei, Berlin W 8, Voßstr. 4, zu verweisen.

*

Es ist festgestellt worden, daß die Firma Richard Roßwaag Sohn in Idar-Oberstein Verwundetenabzeichen in Schwarz hergestellt und durch Vermittlung der Firma Sterner in Fürstenfeldbruck/Oberbayern in den Handel gebracht hat. Weder der Firma Roßwaag noch der Firma Sterner ist die hierzu erforderliche Genehmigung durch die Präsidialkanzlei des Führers erteilt worden. Von den beiden genannten Firmen dürfen Verwundetenabzeichen und auch andere Nachbildungen staatlicher Orden und Ehrenzeichen oder deren Verkleinerungen nicht bezogen werden. Bei Zuwiderhandlungen erfolgt Entziehung der Genehmigung zum Vertrieb von Orden und Ehrenzeichen.

Left: The announcement in the *Uniformen-Markt* that only 9 mm miniatures of combat badges are allowed to be produced.

FAKES AND REPRODUCTIONS

The Close Combat Clasp is as much faked as every other badge and order of the Third Reich and it would be futile to list all known fakes in this book.[11] As a rule of thumb all non-zinc clasps should be viewed with great suspicion. Fake clasps with the maker marks of A.G.M.u.K, F&BL, FLLGWL, JFS, and L/58 have been observed. Of course the Gold Presentation Clasp has also been faked, just as have the cellophane and paper packages.

The only defense against these fakes is a well founded study of the genuine pieces since they are the only constant in this ever expanding hobby.

THE 1957 VERSION OF THE BADGE

All three grades of the Close Combat Clasp were authorized for wear in the de-nazified version. The 1957 clasps have the same design, only the national eagle and the swastika were removed.

Above: De-nazified Close Combat Clasp in Silver.

Left: 1957 Close Combat Clasp in Bronze on the ribbon bar for daily wear on the uniform.

FOOTNOTES

1 *Merkblatt 15/5*, page 114, OKH., 3.12.42 - 14521/42 - PA/PZ V/V (f).

2 Command post, hospitalization, or leave up to a quarter of the scheduled time frames are not considered interruptions of the service. Merkblatt 15/5, page 115, footnote 2.

3 On 26. March 1943 this allowance of days for time was extended to the service in Africa, starting also with 22. June 1941 (OKH., 26.3.43 - 12354/43 - PA/P5 (f), *Merkblatt 15/5*, page 115.

4 Merkblatt 15/5, page 115, footnote 3.

5 A full list of all award ceremonies can be found in the book *The German Close Combat Clasp of World War II,* Thomas M. Durante, 2007, page 255.

6 Nimmergut mentions in *Orden und Ehrenzeichen, Vol. IV*, page 2291 two presentations made by Hitler to one or two persons, one being *SS-Sturmbannführer* Léon Degrelle together with the Oak-leaves on 15. September 1944 and the other presentation was to *SS-Hauptscharführer* Hermann Maringgele and *SS-Obersturmführer* Joachim Boosfeld. Both broke out of the Budapest pocket and reported to Hitler on 21. February 1945, who spontaneously awarded both with the Knights Cross of the Iron Cross and the Close Combat Clasp in Gold.

7 The description of the design is taken from *Uniformen-Markt*, June 1943 issue.

8 For a complete accounting of the creation of the Presentation Clasp refer to T. Durante, *The German Close Combat Clasp of World War II,* page 250 ff

9 Table is compiled based on the book by Thomas Durante.

10 Nimmergut states a complete number of 172 for the awarded Presentation Close Combat Badge in Gold (*Orden und Ehrenzeichen, Vol. IV,* page 2291) with a total of 585 awards of the gold grade, including three to soldiers of the *Luftwaffe*.

11 T. Durante gives a very good overviev of the known fakes in his book. pages 278 - 295.

BIBLIOGRAPHY

Doehle, Dr. Heinrich, *Die Auszeichnungen des Grossdeutschen Reichs*, Berlin 1945

Dörr, Manfred, *Die Träger der Nahkampfspange in Gold*, Biblio Verlag, Osnabrück, 1996

Dombrowski, Hanns, *Orden, Ehrenzeichen und Titel*, Franz Wahlen, 1940

Durante, Thomas M., *The German Close Combat Clasp of World War II,* PaPJay Publishing, Belgium, 2007

Geeb, *Deutsche Orden und Ehrenzeichen*, Heymanns Verlag, 1985

Merkblatt 15/5, *Orden und Ehrenzeichen*, Biblio-Verlag, 1992

Nimmergut, Jörg, *Deutsche Orden und Ehrenzeichen*, Vol. IV, München, 2004

Der Uniformen- Markt, Volumes 1939-1945

Schwert und Spaten, Volumes 1939-1942

Chapter 8

The Panzer Assault Badge

Waffen-SS Obersturmführer Michael Wittmann, arguably the most famous *Panzer* commander of World War II, in a photograph together with his wife Hildegard, taken on their wedding day 1. March 1944. Wittmann wears the Knights Cross of the Iron Cross with Oakleaves (14. January 1944 and 30. January 1944), his Iron Cross First Class, the Panzer Assault Badge in Silver, and his Wound Badge in Black. He was awarded the Swords on 22. June 1944 (no. 71). Wittmann and his *Tiger* crew were killed in Normandy six weeks later on 8. August 1944.

Table of Contents

THE PANZER ASSAULT BADGE

HISTORY

The *Kampfwagen* Badge of the Great War 1921

In 1921, when the Great War was already over, the Defense Minister of the Weimar Republic, Dr. jur. Otto Karl Geßler introduced the *Kampfwagen-Abzeichen* (literally Combat Car Badge) with the words:

> *To bear in remembrance in the minds of the German people the deeds of the combat car units, which had to be dissolved after the peace treaty, a remembrance badge for the former crews of the combat cars will be instituted with the name the Combat Car Badge.*

The badge shows a German tank of the Great War (a model A7V) surrounded by a wreath and crowned by a death head with crossed bones underneath. This martial symbol had its origin in the death head emblem employed by the Imperial Hussars and was a visual indication that the new tank force saw itself as a continuation of the old cavalry tradition. (The death head was later to be found on the collar tabs of the German *Panzertruppe* between 1934 - 1945 and should not be confused with the death head on the caps of the *Waffen-SS*.)

The badge was manufactured by C.E. Juncker of Berlin and only 99 former members of the new Panzer force were awarded with it.

Above: *Feldmarschall* August von Mackensen with his *Husarenfellmütze* with the death head symbol.

Left: The badge of 1921 with the A7V tank and the same death head symbol.

The *Legion Condor* Tank Badge 1936 -1939

Between November 1936 - March 1939 German volunteers fought in Spain on the side of the troops of General Franco. German tank troops were mainly employed in training Spanish tank troops, but were also actively taking part in the fight. The commander of the German *Panzer* troops in Spain was *Oberst* Wilhelm Ritter von Thoma, who founded on his own initiative the so-called *Panzertruppenabzeichen* (Tank Troop Badge) at the end of 1936. The badge was awarded a total of 415 times in Spain and was later authorized for wear by *Generaloberst* von Brauchitsch. The award conditions were at least three months long deployment and irreproachable behavior.

The design employed the same basic scheme as the *Kampfwagen* Badge of 1921: a large death head with crossed bones and a small tank below, all surrounded by a laurel wreath (right).

Left: A German *Panzermann* of the Legion Condor with the death head of the tank troops on his cap. He wears the Spanish Cross with Swords, the Spanish Campaign Medal, and the Legion Condor Tank Badge.

REGULATIONS

Already during the very early days of the Second World War it became clear to the German Supreme Command that the decisive role in winning battles and campaigns went over from the infantry to the *Panzertruppe*. Together with the *Luftwaffe* spectacular results could be achieved. However, so far no extensive combat operations with a comparable armored adversary had taken place.

Consequently the Supreme Commander of the *Wehrmacht*, *Generaloberst* von Brauchitsch, introduced on December 20, 1939 (together with the Infantry Assault Badge) the *Panzerkampfabzeichen*[1] (Tank Assault Badge, also called Panzer Assault Badge).

Left: The *Scherl-Bilderdienst* published the first picture of the *Panzerkampfabzeichen* on 29. December, only nine days after the institution.[2] This is a clear indication that the badge was already in the making long before the institution. The maker of the first series and also of the badge in this picture was C.E. Juncker/Berlin.

Panzerkampfwagenabzeichen
Aufnahme: Presse-Hoffmann (K)

Right: The *Uniformen-Markt* published this picture on January 15, 1940. The pictured badge is also made by C.E. Juncker.
In both cases no mention of the initial grade "*in Silber*" is made.

Right: *Generaloberst* Heinz Guderian is titled as the "creator of our victorious tank force" in this picture from an August 1940 calender sheet. The artist is the famous Wolfgang Willrich.

The initial **Grade in Silver** (which was not named like that initially but only after the introduction of the grade in bronze) was to be awarded to officers, NCOs, and service men of the *Panzertruppe*, who distinguished themselves actively as:

- tank commander, or
- command tank commander, or
- tank cannoneer, or
- tank driver, or
- tank wireless operator

in at least three deployments on three different days. Medical personnel could also be awarded with the badge if they were part of the tank crew and also took part on three different engagements in rescue and recovery operations of wounded personnel. Similar regulations applied to the *Kradmelder* (dispatch rider) and maintenance troops, always under the condition of operating under fire and enemy contact.

Starting December 1944, the members of the tank destroyer units, equipped with *Jagdpanzer 38, Jagdpanzer IV, Jagdpanther, Jagdtiger, Sturmgeschütz III* and *IV*, were to be awarded with the Panzer Assault Badge in Silver. The other remaining tank destroyer units were awarded, still as before, with the General Assault Badge.

Above: Heraldic display of the units of the *Panzertruppe*, named "Spearhead of the Army." Part of an illustration called *Waffengattungen des Heeres* (branches of the army) from February 1945.

The **Grade in Bronze** was introduced on 1. June 1940, simultaneous with the bronze grade of the Infantry Assault Badge and the newly founded General Assault Badge. The Tank Assault Badge in Bronze is an equal grade to the silver badge. It was to be awarded to members of the

- *Panzer-Grenadieregimenter*[3], or
- motorcycle rifle battalions, and
- armored reconnaissance units

For the members of the *Panzer-Grenadierregimenter* and motorcycle rifle battalions the same award conditions as for the Infantry Assault Badge in Bronze applied (refer to Chapter 6), for the armored reconnaissance units the same conditions as those for the Infantry Assault Badge in silver applied.

Above: *Panzergrenadiere*, a postcard with a motif from the artist Walter Gotschke, 1942.

The Tank Assault Badge was not only issued in the equal versions "*Silber*" and "*Bronze*" but also in several grades depending on the days of countable deployment days, also in the versions silver and bronze.

These additional grades were authorized on 22. June 1944 and were divided into the following steps (*Stufen*):

II. *Stufe* with the deployment number "25"
III. *Stufe* with the deployment number "50"
IV. *Stufe* with the deployment number "75"
Stufe IV. could be awarded again with the deployment number "100"

The requirements for the days were always the same, the additional grades simply showed the accumulation of those days. Counting for the higher grades started with 1. July 1943. For an already earlier awarded Tank Assault Badge three days were added without specific documentation, counting towards a possible higher grade.

To award proven front soldiers it was furthermore decreed that for uninterrupted service at the Russian Front or in Africa past 22. June 1941 the following days could be added:

25 days for 15 months of uninterrupted service
15 days for 12 months of uninterrupted service
10 days for 8 months of uninterrupted service

Hospital stays due to injuries or vacation days did not count as an interruption. Also, the division commander had the authority to award the next higher grade with a reduced number of required days if the soldier would not be able to accumulate additional days due to an injury, as follows:

Stufe II after 18 days of deployment
Stufe III after 35 days of deployment
Stufe IV with "75" after 60 days of deployment

DESIGN

The Panzer Assault Badge design follows the other design schemes of the German combat badges: the central motif is surrounded by an oak leaves wreath and the top of the wreath is crowned by the national eagle. The central motif in this case is of course a stylized *Panzer* with some features of the Mark III and some of the Mark IV.

The badges were designed, as were many of the German war badges also, by Berlin-based artist and designer Wilhelm Ernst Peekhaus. The picture below shows a Panzer Assault Badge in Silver by the maker Rudolf Richter/Schlag bei Gablonz with the maker mark "R.R.S."

The design of the grades or versions in Silver and Bronze were absolutely identical save for the finish.

The design for the *Stufe* II. and III. is different to the *Stufe* I, the difference between *Stufe* II and *Stufe* III is the number in the small box at the bottom of the wreath (either "25" or "50"). The silver or bronze grade is indicated by the color of the wreath and the national eagle, either silver or bronze.

The design for the *Stufe* IV ("75" and "100") is again different to the previous ones. The grade is indicated by either a silver or bronze tank, the wider wreath is always gilded. The difference in days is indicated by the numbers "75" or "100" in the small box at the bottom of the wreath.

Die Stufen zum Panzerabzeichen und allgemeinen Sturmabzeichen

Der Führer hat als Anerkennung der immer erneut bewiesenen Einsatzfreudigkeit der im Panzer angreifenden Angehörigen der schweren Waffen die Einführung höherer Stufen zum Panzerkampfabzeichen genehmigt.
Die höheren Stufen zum Panzerkampfabzeichen und Sturmabzeichen werden nach besonderem Muster mit der Zahl 25 in der II. Stufe, der Zahl 50 in der III. Stufe, der Zahl 75 und der Zahl 100 in der IV. Stufe gefertigt. Es kann verliehen werden:
nach 25 anrechnungsfähigen Einsätzen die . . . . II. Stufe
nach 50 anrechnungsfähigen Einsätzen die . . . . III. Stufe
nach 75 anrechnungsfähigen Einsätzen die . . . . IV. Stufe
und zwar das Panzerkampfabzeichen in Silber an Panzerbesatzungen der Panzereinheiten, das Panzerkampfabzeichen in Bronze an Panzerbesatzungen der Panzerspäheinheiten, das Sturmabzeichen an Angehörige der Sturmgeschützeinheiten, der Sturmpanzereinheiten und Panzerjägereinheiten der Panzerjägerabteilungen. Die IV. Stufe kann nach 100 Einsätzen mit der Zahl 100 erneut verliehen werden.

20

Above: Excerpt of the informational brochure of the Supreme Command of the Army "*Der Lohn der Tat. Die Auszeichnungen des Heeres*."

THE BADGE

Left: Panzer Assault Badge in Silver, *Stufe I*.

Right: Panzer Assault Badge in Bronze, *Stufe I*

Right: Panzer Assault Badge in Silver, *Stufe II*. (Josef Feix Söhne, Gablonz).

Left: Panzer Assault Badge in Bronze, *Stufe II*. (Josef Feix Söhne, Gablonz).

Left: Panzer Assault Badge in Silver, *Stufe III* (Josef Feix Söhne, Gablonz).

Right: Panzer Assault Badge in Bronze, *Stufe III* (Josef Feix Söhne, Gablonz).

Right: Panzer Assault Badge in Silver, *Stufe IV* - 75 deployment days. (Josef Feix Söhne, Gablonz).

The zinc-made badges of later manufacture tend to lose their gilding nearly completely over time. The bronze example below shows just some traces of remaining gilding at the upper part of the talons.

Left: Panzer Assault Badge in Bronze, *Stufe IV* - 75 deployment days. (Josef Feix Söhne, Gablonz).

Left: Panzer Assault Badge in Gold, *Stufe IV* - 100 deployment days. (C.E. Juncker, Berlin).

The earlier examples made by Juncker hold the gilding far better and give a better representation of the original state of the badges.

Right: Panzer Assault Badge in Bronze, *Stufe IV* - 100 deployment days. (Josef Feix Söhne, Gablonz).

THE MAKERS OF THE PANZER ASSAULT BADGE[4]

Stufe I	C.E. Juncker, Berlin	(6) known variations
	Paul Meybauer, Berlin	(5) known variation
	Karl Wurster, Marktneukirchen	(5) known variations
	Assmann & Söhne, Lüdenscheid	(2) known variations
	Steinhauer & Lück, Lüdenscheid	(9) known variations
	Friedrich Linden, Lüdenscheid	(5) known variations
	Berg & Nolte, Lüdenscheid	(1) known variation
	Gebrüder Wegerhoff, Lüdenscheid	(1) known variation
	Hermann Aurich, Dresden	(1) known variation
	Wilhelm Deumer, Lüdenscheid	(3) known variations
	Hymmen & Co. Lüdenscheid	(4) known variations
	Schauerte & Höhfeld, Lüdenscheid	(2) known variations
	Dr. Franke & Co, Lüdenscheid	(2) known variations
	Adolf Scholze, Gablonz	(4) known variations
	Rudolf Karneth, Gablonz	(1) known variation
	Otto Schickle, Pforzheim	(4) known variation
	B.H. Mayer, Pforzheim	(5) known variations
	Petz & Lorenz, Unterreichenbach	(2) known variation
	Frank & Reif, Stuttgart	(3) known variations
	Rudolf Souval, Wien	(3) known variations
	E. Ferd. Wiedmann, Frankfurt	(3) known variations
	Wilhelm Hobacher, Wien	(3) known variations
	Rudolf Richter, Schlag bei Gablonz	(2) known variations
	Friedrich Orth, Wien	(1) known variation
	Arno Wallpach, Salzburg	(1) known variation
	"EWE"	(1) known variation
	Fritz Zimmermann, Stuttgart	(1) known variation
	(9) Unknown Maker	multiple
Stufe II	C.E. Juncker, Berlin	(2) known variations
(25)	Josef Feix Söhne, Gablonz	(1) known variation
	Gustav Brehmer, Markneukirchen	(2) known variations
Stufe III	C.E. Juncker, Berlin	(2) known variations
(50)	Josef Feix Söhne, Gablonz	(1) known variation
	Gustav Brehmer, Markneukirchen	(2) known variations
Stufe IV	C.E. Juncker, Berlin	(2) known variations
(75 & 100)	Josef Feix Söhne, Gablonz	(1) known variation

Table might not show all variations known as of 2012 due to ongoing research.

PACKAGES

The Panzer Assault Badge was given out at the divisional level and was most likely stored there in greater numbers, at least the initial grade. The individual badge was either stored in a paper bag with the description of the content and the grade. It is also known that carton cases holding 50 pieces were used to supply the badges to the divisions. Even the higher grades were stored in the usual *Zellstoff* bag. Privately purchased badges were either supplied with the standard LDO paper bag with inscription of the content or inside the standardized LDO-cases.

Left: Regular paper bag for a Panzer Assault Badge in Bronze, *Stufe* III.

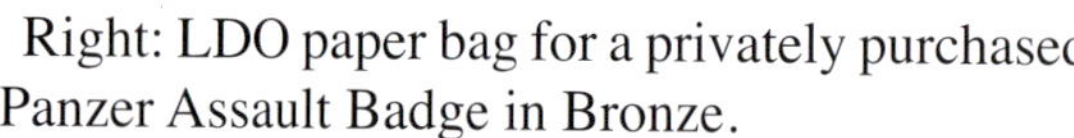

Right: LDO paper bag for a privately purchased Panzer Assault Badge in Bronze.

AWARD DOCUMENTS

Since the Panzer Assault Badge was awarded on the divisional level a lot of variations of award documents exist, and it is nearly impossible (and also not necessary) to categorize them all. The variations range from pre-printed documents for a specific badge grade and *Stufe* to one completely written with a typewriter of the divisional clerks office. The documents had to adhere to the style and content as prescribed in the *Merkblatt 15/5* (below). This generic document style was also used for other war badges, mainly the Infantry Assault Badge.

Anlage 2
zu S. 102

BESITZZEUGNIS

DEM ....
(Dienstgrad)

....
(Vor- und Familienname)

....
(Truppenteil)

VERLEIHE ICH DAS

....

....
(Ort und Datum)

....
(Unterschrift)

Stempel

....
(Dienstgrad und Dienststellung)

3. Panzer-Division

B e s i t z z e u g n i s

Dem ......Unteroffizier......................................

...............Helmut Franz...................................

...............5./Panzer-Regiment 5..........................

wurde das

Panzerkampfwagenabzeichen

verliehen.

.Div.St.Qu., den 30. Mai 1940.........
(Ort und Datum)

Stempel

....
(Unterschrift)

Generalmajor u. Div.Kdeur.
....
(Dienstgrad und - stellung

Above: Fully typewritten award document in format DIN A4 to *Unteroffizier* Helmut Franz. This is a very early document, dated 30. May 1940. Note that the badge is still referred to as *Panzerkampfwagenabzeichen*. The document is signed by the division commander *Generalmajor* Horst Stumpff.

Besitzzeugnis

Dem Oberschirrmeister
(Dienstgrad)

Paul - Friedrich K o c h
(Vor- und Zuname)

2. Kompanie Panzer - Regiment 5
(Truppenteil)

wurde das

Panzerkampfabzeichen

— Silber —

verliehen.

In Afrika, den 15.8.1942
(Ort und Datum)

(Unterschrift)

Gen.Major und Div.Kdr.
~~Oberst und Div. Fuehrer~~
(Dienstgrad und Dienststellung)

Above: Award document in the size DIN A5 for the Panzer Assault Badge in Silver for *Oberschirrmeister* Paul-Friedrich Koch (Master Sergeant Motor Pool), signed by *Generalmajor* Heinz von Randow (Commander 21. PzDiv) and dated 15. August 1942.

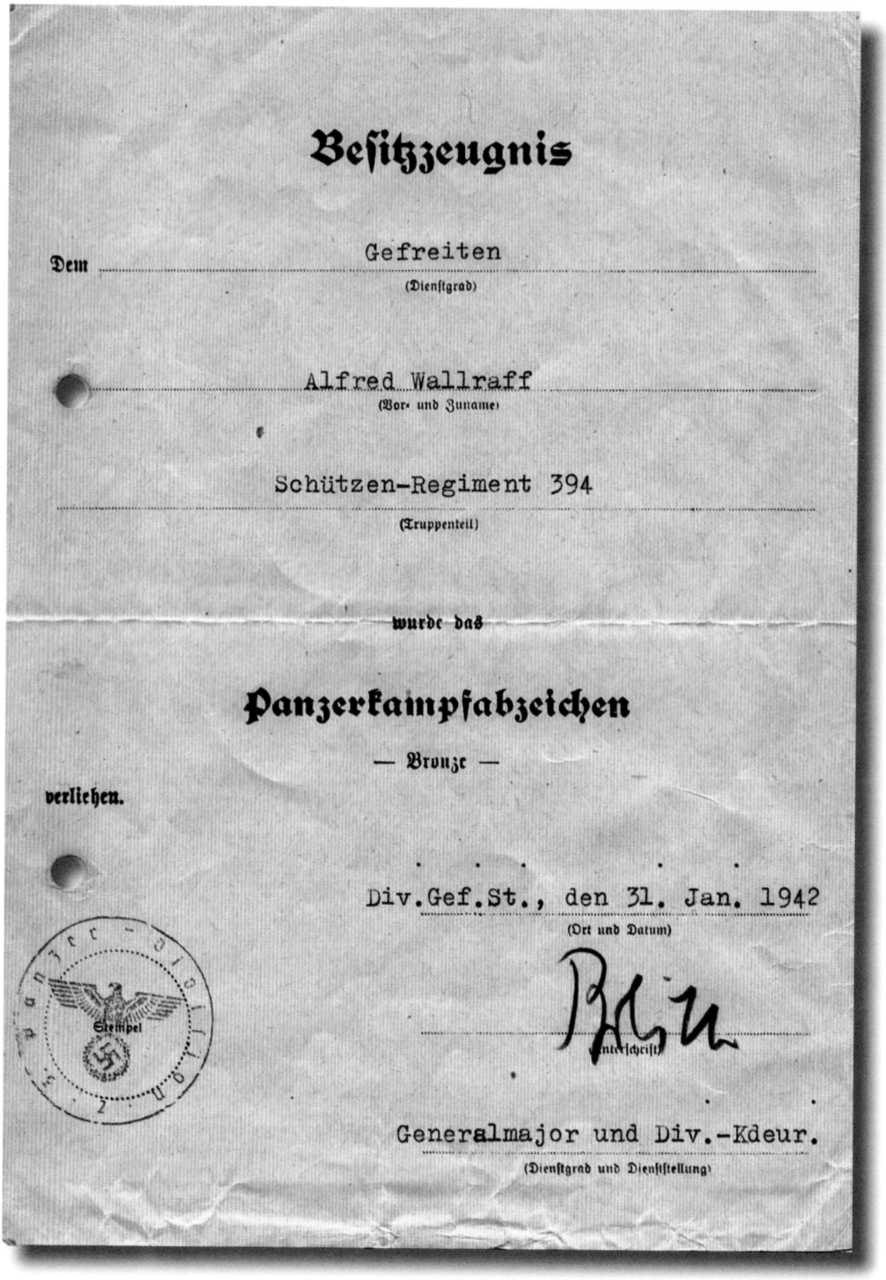

Besitzzeugnis

Dem Gefreiten

(Dienstgrad)

Alfred Wallraff

(Vor- und Zuname)

Schützen-Regiment 394

(Truppenteil)

wurde das

Panzerkampfabzeichen

— Bronze —

verliehen.

Div.Gef.St., den 31. Jan. 1942

(Ort und Datum)

(Unterschrift)

Generalmajor und Div.-Kdeur.

(Dienstgrad und Dienststellung)

Above: Award document in the size DIN A5 for the Panzer Assault Badge in Bronze for *Gefreiter* Alfred Wallraff of the *Schützen-Regiment 394* (3. PzDiv), dated 31. January 1942. The document is signed by *Generalmajor* Hermann Breith (RK 3. June 1940, Oak-leaves on 31. January 1942 (#48) and Swords on 21. February 1944 (# 69).

BESITZZEUGNIS

DEM Leutnant
(DIENSTGRAD)

Erich Schmid
(VOR- UND FAMILIENNAME)

5./Pz.Rgt.Großdeutschland
(TRUPPENTEIL)

VERLEIHE ICH FÜR TAPFERE TEILNAHME
AN 25 EINSATZTAGEN

DIE II. STUFE ZUM PANZERKAMPFABZEICHEN IN SILBER

Rgt.Gef.Std., den 28.10.1944
(ORT UND DATUM)

(STEMPEL)

Kahl
(UNTERSCHRIFT)

Major und Regimentsführer
(DIENSTGRAD UND DIENSTSTELLUNG)

Above: Sample of an award document for a higher *Stufe* of the Panzer Assault Badge. It is for the Silver grade and made out to *Leutnant* Erich Schmid of the PzRgt "*Groß-deutschland*", dated 28. October 1944. It is signed by *Major* Bruno Kahl (Oakleaves # 270 on 8. August 1943). Kahl himself was an awardee of the Panzer Assault Badge *Stufe* III.

THE BADGE IN WEAR

The Panzer Assault Badge was worn on the left side of the tunic. If the Iron Cross First Class was present, it was to be attached below that higher award. If a higher *Stufe* was awarded, the previous one was to be discarded. However, it was allowed to wear the *Panzertruppenabzeichen* of the Legion Condor next to the current issue.

Left: *Hauptfeldwebel* Wilhelm Wendt (5. Kp/PzRgt 5, 21. PzDiv) wears the Panzer Assault Badge in Silver next to the Legion Condor *Panzertruppenabzeichen* and below the Iron Cross 1. Class.. He was awarded with the Knights Cross on 30. June 1941. On the right tunic side he wears the Spanish Cross in Bronze with Swords.

Right: *Hauptfeldwebel* Wilhelm Wendt in the year 1958 in *Bundeswehr* uniform. Note that he wears the Panzer Assault Badge in the 1957 version (no national eagle and swastika), but not his Legion Condor badge, which was not authorized for wear according to the law of 1957.

Above: *Oberfeldwebel* Theodor Hönniger, *Zugführer* of 3.Kp/PzRgt 27 (7. PzDiv) wears his Panzer Assault Badge in Silver below the Iron Cross 1. Class. He also wears the ribbon of the Iron Cross 2. Class and the East Medal in the button hole of his *Panzer* wrapper.

Above: The *Oberschütze* of the *InfRgt 1* (from 10. December 1942 on *PzGrenRgt 1*) of the *1. SS-PzDiv "Leibstandarte-SS-Adolf Hitler"* wears his Panzer Assault Badge in Bronze.

Above: *Oberleutnant* Jürgen Dultz wears his *Panzerkampfabzeichen in Silber, Stufe II* for 25 deployments. The award was made on 27. April 1944 while serving with the *Panzer-regiment "Großdeutschland."*

Above: This Knights Cross winner of the *Panzertruppe* wears his *Panzerkampfabzeichen in Silber* on the Panzer wrapper below the Iron Cross First Class.

STICKPINS

The Panzer Assault Badge was available for private purchase as a miniature in Silver and Bronze in the sizes 16 mm and 9 mm. Miniatures in the 16 mm size of the 25 and 50 deployment days are known in different styles. The badge for 75 and 100 deployment days does not seem to exist in the stickpin style.[5]

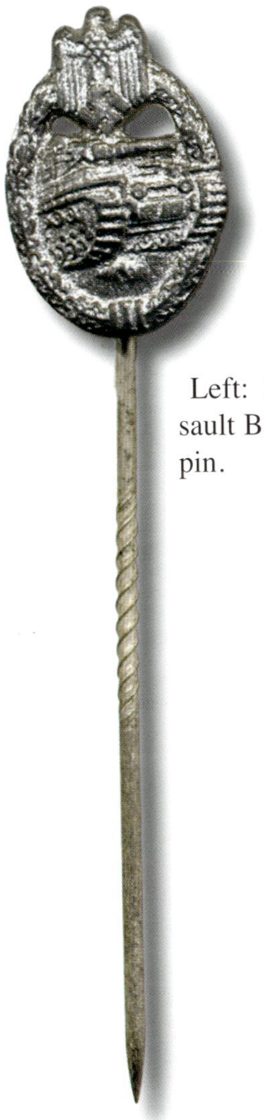

Left: 16 mm Panzer Assault Badge in Silver stickpin.

Right: 16 mm and 9 mm Panzer Assault Badge in Bronze stickpins.

Panzer Assault Badge stickpin in Silver (left) and Bronze (right) of the *Stufe* II (25 deployment days), size 16 mm.

Right: 16 mm Panzer Assault Badge in Silver stickpin of the *Stufe* III (50 deployment days).

Left: 16 mm Panzer Assault Badge in Bronze stickpin of the *Stufe* III (50 deployment days).

FAKES AND REPRODUCTIONS

Despite the fakes of the regular badge in Silver and Bronze in qualities ranging from ridiculously bad to convincingly good, the higher grades are the more dangerous ones. Most of the fakes are made creating a master die from an original badge and casting the fakes from it. Due to the shrinking process involved, these are smaller than the originals and also don't have the nice finish of the originals. Bad and sloppily formed rivets are also a giveaway.

It is imperative to study the originals and ask experienced collectors for help and a second opinion before buying one of the higher *Stufen* of the Panzer Assault Badge.[6]

THE 1957 VERSION OF THE BADGE

All versions of the *Panzerkampfabzeichen* were authorized for wear in the law of 1957. The required and prescribed de-nazification was easily done - the national eagle with the swastika was removed, everything else stayed the same.

Above: Panzer Assault Badge in Silver and Bronze in the 1957 version.

Right: Panzer Assault Badge in Bronze, *Stufe* III, in the version regarding the law of 1957.

Left: Picture of the *Stufe* IV (75 deployment days) as printed in the manufacturing instruction of the 1957 law.

Above: Ribbon devices of the Panzer Assault Badge in Silver and Bronze as authorized for the ribbon bar of the *Bundeswehr*.

FOOTNOTES

1 The initial name of the badge was *Panzerkampfwagen-Abzeichen* (tank combat car badge) in the style of the 1921 naming. The change to *Panzerkampfabzeichen* took place on 1. June 1940, together with the institution of the Bronze grade (HVBL B, page 379).

2 Nimmergut assumes that the production of the first samples as well as the acceptance must have already taken place in August 1939, meaning before the actual start of the war. Only by doing so, he argues, could it be possible to have the badge ready nine days after the institution (*Orden und Ehrenzeichen, Band IV*, page 2308).

3 The designation *Panzer-Grenadierregiment* was introduced in summer of 1942 (with the new color of the arms of "grass green"). Earlier the designation was *Schützenregiment der Panzerdivision* (color of arms "pink" with S on shoulder boards).

4 The makers are listed according to a common design type. This type of categorization was first introduced by Sascha Weber with his book *Das Infanterie Sturmabzeichen* (Selbstverlag 2008, Schönau) and was adopted by later authors as a fitting method to catalog similar die types. The listing in this book is taken from *The German Panzer Assault Badge of World War II* (Philippe De Bock, PapJay Publishing, 2009) and the listing also follows the design type categorization introduced by S. Weber. The Unknown Makers are summarized and are not design attributable.

5 Patzwall lists the miniatures of the *Stufe* "25" and "50" in his price catalog, but not the *Stufe* "75". Messing shows in his *Spezialkatalog* 1990/91 on page 43 a *Stufe* "75" and also lists a "100" as being in existence as a 16 mm miniature. It needs to be remarked that Messing also shows some miniatures which are extremely dubious and the grades "75" and "100" are extremely questionable as miniatures. Niemann ignores the miniatures of the higher *Stufen* completely in his price catalog.

6 DeBock shows a considerable number of fakes of all grades in his book in a dedicated chapter. Despite the fact that not even the best researcher can keep up with all the copies it is advisable to study the methods and typical errors encountered with nearly all fakes in order to raise the awareness level.

BIBLIOGRAPHY

DeBock, Philippe, *The German Panzer Assault Badge of World War II,* PapJay Publishing, 2009

Doehle, Dr. Heinrich, *Die Auszeichnungen des Grossdeutschen Reichs*, Berlin 1945

Dombrowski, Hanns, *Orden, Ehrenzeichen und Titel*, Franz Wahlen, 1940

Geeb, *Deutsche Orden und Ehrenzeichen*, Heymanns Verlag, 1985

Merkblatt 15/5, *Orden und Ehrenzeichen*, Biblio-Verlag, 1992

Messing, M., *Miniaturauszeichnungen des III. Reiches*, Eigenverlag, Nürnberg 1990

Nimmergut, Jörg, *Deutsche Orden und Ehrenzeichen*, Vol. IV, München, 2004

Patzwall, Klaus, *Katalog der Auszeichnungen Drittes Reich*, Paztwall Verlag, Norderstedt, 1992

Der Uniformen-Markt, Volumes 1939-1945

Schwert und Spaten, Volumes 1939-1942

Chapter
9
The General Assault Badge

Oberleutnant Alois Rampf received the Knights Cross on October 4, 1944 while serving with the *3./Pionier Battalion 88 (46. InfDiv)*. He wears his General Assault Badge next to the Wound Badge in Silver and below the Iron Cross 1. Class.

Table of Contents

THE GENERAL ASSAULT BADGE

HISTORY

The creation of the General Assault Badge (*Sturmabzeichen, allg.*) was a logical consequence of the earlier foundation of the Infantry Assault Badge and the Panzer Assault Badge on 20. December 1939. There was no provision for the troops which either accompanied the tanks or the pure infantry in an assault and despite having fulfilled the same requirements as the other troops were not entitled to either the Panzer Assault Badge or the Infantry Assault Badge.

That changed on 1. June 1940 when *Generaloberst* von Brauchitsch founded in his capacity as Supreme Commander of the *Wehrmacht* the General Assault Badge for:

> " *.. soldiers of all other arms, including the assault artillery, which are fighting together with the infantry or tanks or on their own fulfill the requirements of the Infantry Assault Badge, ..*"[1]

The 15. July 1940 issue of *Uniformen-Markt* (below) presented the badge to the public with the headline "Assault Badge for All Arms." The proper denomination *Sturmabzeichen, allg.* was not mentioned. It was stated that the requirements are the same as for the Infantry Assault Badge.

'Sturmabzeichen für alle Waffengattungen

Wie wir berichteten, hatte der Oberbefehlshaber des Heeres die Einführung eines Infanterie-Sturmabzeichens verfügt. Ein Ansporn zum persönlichen Einsatz und ein sichtbares Zeichen des im Sturmangriff bewährten Kämpfers wurde damit geschaffen. (Näheres siehe „UM" S. 14 und S. 54, Abbildung S. 29!) Die Verleihung dieses Abzeichens war zunächst auf die Schützenkompanien nichtmotorisierter Infanteriedivisionen und die Gebirgsjägerkompanien beschränkt. Im Verlauf der Westoffensive haben sich alle Teile des Heeres in zahllosen Sturmangriffen glänzend bewährt. Generaloberst von Brauchitsch hat daher in Würdigung dieser Tatsache neuerdings eine bedeutsame Erweiterung der Ver-Verleihungsbestimmungen befohlen. Mit Wirkung vom 1. Juni ab wird auch an Angehörige der motorisierten Infanterie-Regimenter das Infanterie-Sturmabzeichen verliehen. Die Farbe des Abzeichens (sonst ist das Abzeichen aus Neusilber) ist in diesem Falle Bronce. — Gleichzeitig mit dem Infanterie-Sturmabzeichen war vom Oberbefehlshaber ein Panzerkampfwagen-Abzeichen geschaffen worden. (Einzelheiten siehe „UM" S. 14, dort auch Abbildung.) Die Verleihung dieser in Panzerkampfabzeichen umbenannten Auszeichnung ist jetzt auch auf die Angehörigen der Schützenregimenter und der Kradschützenbataillone der Panzerdivisionen und der Panzerspäheinheiten ausgedehnt worden. Die Farbe des Panzerkampfabzeichens ist bei letzteren ebenfalls Bronze.

Aufnahme: Scherl (K)

Für die Soldaten aller anderen Waffengattungen einschließlich der Sturmartillerie, die mit der Infanterie oder den Panzern zusammen kämpfen oder im eigenen Verbande die Bedingungen des Infanterie-Sturmabzeichens erfüllen, ist ein besonderes Sturmabzeichen mit den Bestimmungen für das Infanterie-Sturmabzeichen eingeführt worden. (Siehe unsere heutige Abbildung!) Es besteht aus Stielhandgranate und Seitengewehr, gegeneinander gekreuzt, umgeben von einem ovalen Eichenkranz, der im oberen Teil das Hoheitsabzeichen der Wehrmacht trägt. Die Farbe ist Silber. — Höchste soldatische Leistung findet in den neuen ebenso wie in den bereits bestehenden Abzeichen eine ehrenvolle Würdigung. Jedermann im Volke soll wissen, daß die Träger dieses Abzeichens zu den Tapfersten des deutschen Heeres gehören.

REGULATIONS

The award regulations of the General Assault Badge were identical to the ones for the Infantry Assault Badge. Only the relevant troops to be awarded were defined differently. They were the troops of the regular army, the *Waffen-SS,* and police units which neither fell under the definitions of the Infantry Assault Badge nor under those of the Panzer Assault Badge. The definitions were:

- participation in three assaults
- on three different days
- in the first assault line
- with the weapon in hand, and
- broke into the enemy positions.

Forcible reconnaissance and counter-attacks were also valued as assaults, but only if close combat was involved.

More than three assaults were counted towards the award of the Close Combat Bar (see chapter C5).

Members of the assault artillery and self-propelled tank destroyer such as *Panzerjäger I, Marder I-III, Nashorn* and *Hornisse*, had to fulfill the conditions of the Panzer Assault Badge, namely:

- participation in three assaults
- on three different days
- with active participation in the fight

More than three assaults of these so-called "heavy weapons" were counted towards the higher grades of the General Assault Badge.

To award the General Assault Badge to members of the *Luftwaffe* and *Kriegsmarine* was generally not allowed, but there were exceptions.[2]

Just as was the case with the Panzer Assault Badge (but not with the Infantry Assault Badge where more deployment days only counted towards the Close Combat Clasp), higher *Stufen* of the General Assault Badge were introduced on 22.June 1943, two years after the beginning of the Russian campaign and on the same day as the higher grades of the Panzer Assault Badge.

The steps were the same as the ones of the Panzer Assault Badge, namely four with the numbers of deployment days "25", "50", "75", and "100". Also, as was the case with the Panzer Assault Badge, the design changed between the "50" and "75".

DESIGN

The design of the General Assault Badge came from the Berlin artist Ernst Wilhelm Peekhaus. It shows the national eagle with the swastika in its claws within an oval-shaped oak leaf wreath. Below the swastika a bayonet and German hand grenade are crossed over each other and laying on top of the wreath.

The design was revealed in a press release from the OKW, dated 29. June 1940 (picture left). Klietmann states that the first die was made by C.E. Juncker, Berlin.[3] This is contradicted by Nimmergut[4] who writes that the first die was made by Paul Meybauer, Berlin. (He also states that P. Meybauer was a supplier to C.E. Juncker, but does not give any more information to substantiate.) Paul Meybauer has not (yet) positively been identified as a maker of the General Assault Badge, but could very well be one of the six unknown makers. However, the pictured badge has most of the features of a typical C.E. Juncker made example and the first series was most likely made by that esteemed company.

The design for the higher *Stufen* of the General Assault Badge are similar to the ones of the Panzer Assault Badge. *Stufen* "25" and "50" have the same basic design as the entrance level but with a separately attached national eagle and weapons. The little number box at the bottom of the wreath shows the number of days.

The *Stufen* "75" and "100" are bigger with a flattened lower section of the wreath, which is gilded.

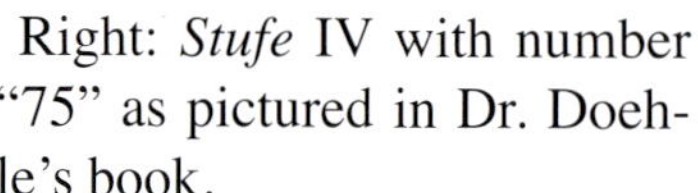

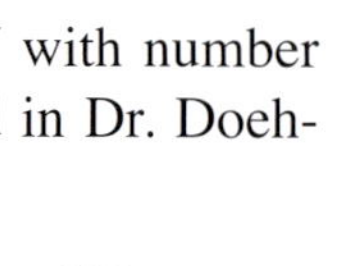

Right: *Stufe* IV with number "75" as pictured in Dr. Doehle's book.

THE BADGE

Right: Obverse of a typical General Assault Badge.

Left: Reverse of the same badge. It is a massive, zinc-made example.

Left: Obverse of *Stufe II*. The badge is made by Rudolf Karneth, Gablonz.

Right: Obverse of *Stufe III*. (Rudolf Karneth, Gablonz)

Right: Obverse of *Stufe IV,* for 75 deployment days. (Josef Feix Söhne, Gablonz)

Left: Obverse of *Stufe IV,* for 100 deployment days. (C.E. Juncker)

THE MAKERS OF THE GENERAL ASSAULT BADGE[5]

Grade I	Assmann & Söhne, Lüdenscheid	(3) known variations
	Berg & Nolte, Lüdenscheid	(3) known variations
	Gustav Brehmer, Markneukirchen	(2) known variations
	Förster & Barth, Pforzheim	(2) known variations
	Frank & Reif, Stuttgart	(4) known variations
	Gebrüder Wegerhoff, Lüdenscheid	(2) known variations
	Wilhelm Hobacher, Wien	(4) known variations
	Hymmen & Co., Lüdenscheid	(4) known variations
	Rudolf Karneth, Gablonz	(5) known variations
	Kerbach & Oesterheld, Dresden	(1) known variation
	Friedrich Linden, Lüdenscheid	(1) known variation
	B.H. Mayer, Pforzheim	(3) known variations
	Friedrich Orth, Wien	(2) known variations
	Rudolf Souval, Wien	(2) known variations
	Steinhauer & Lück, Lüdenscheid	(4) known variations
	Ferdinand Wiedmann, Frankfurt	(2) known variations
	Karl Wurster, Markneukirchen	(3) known variations
	Wilhelm Deumer, Lüdenscheid	(4) known variations
	Hermann Wernstein, Jena-Löbstedt	(8) known variations
	Franke & Co., Lüdenscheid	(1) known variation
	C.E. Juncker, Berlin	(4) known variations
	Schauerte & Höhfeld, Lüdenscheid	(5) known variations
	Biedermann & Co., Oberkassel	(3) known variations
	Carl Wild, Hamburg	(1) known variation
	Carl Poellath, Schrobenhausen	(1) known variation
	Paul Meybauer, Berlin	(1) known variation
	Petz & Lorenz, Unterreichenbach	(1) known variation
	Deschler & Sohn, München	(1) known variation
	(4) Unknown Maker	(10) known variations
Grade II (25)	Josef Feix & Söhne, Gablonz	(1) known variation
	Rudolf Karneth, Gablonz	(1) known variation
	C.E Juncker, Berlin	(1) known variation
Grade III (50)	Josef Feix & Söhne, Gablonz	(2) known variation
	Rudolf Karneth, Gablonz	(1) known variation
	C.E. Juncker, Berlin	(1) known variation
	(1) Unknown Maker	(1) known variation
Grade IV 75 & 100	Josef Feix & Söhne, Gablonz	(2) known variation
	C.E. Juncker, Berlin	(1) known variation
	(1) Unknown Maker	(1) known variation

Table might not show all variations known as of 2012 due to ongoing research.

PACKAGES

The General Assault Badge, just as was the case with most of the war badges of the German Army, was given out in non descriptive paper bags. Some had the content stamped on to the bag. Some had the content printed on, together with the company name on the reverse.

Right: Privately bought examples were sold in more elaborate cases without any descriptive marking.

AWARD DOCUMENTS

The General Assault Badge was awarded on the divisional level upon recommendation and record keeping of the required conditions. Therefore a lot of document variations do exist and it is nearly impossible (and also not necessary) to categorize them all. What follows is just a very small sample of what can be encountered as a collector or researcher.

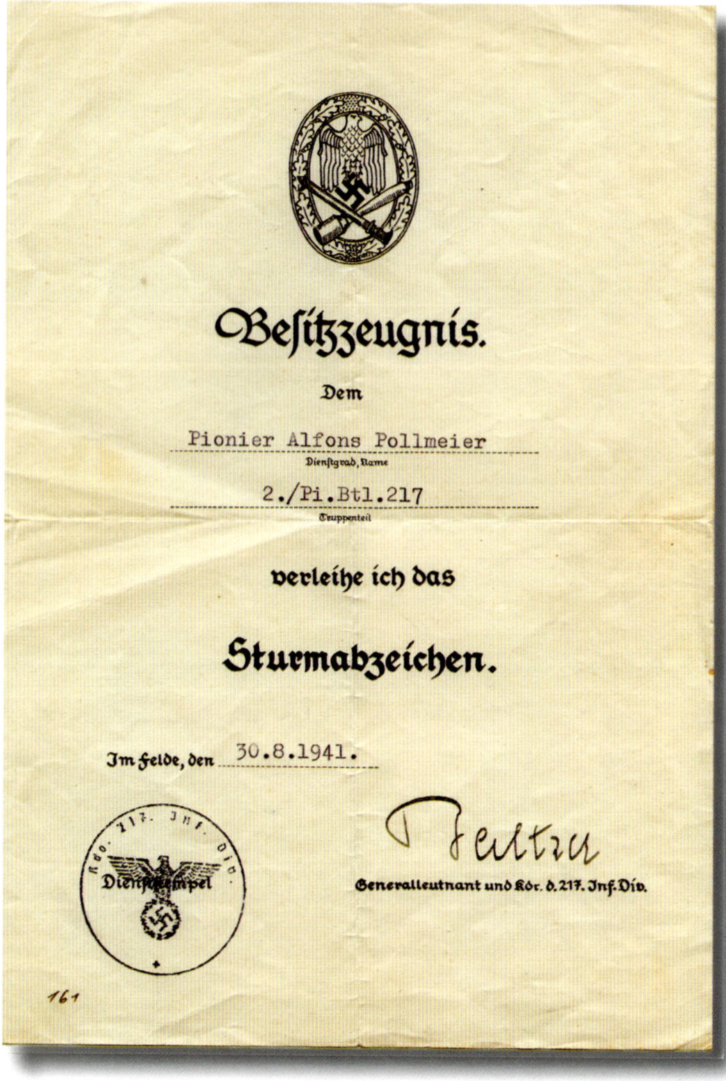

Besitzzeugnis.

Dem

Pionier Alfons Pollmeier

Dienstgrad, Name

2./Pi.Btl.217

Truppenteil

verleihe ich das

Sturmabzeichen.

Im Felde, den 30.8.1941.

Kdo. 217. Inf. Div.
Dienststempel

Generalleutnant und Kdr. d. 217. Inf.Div.

161

Above: Award document for a General Assault Badge in format DIN A5 to *Pionier* Alfons Pollmeier. The document is signed by the commander of the *217. InfDiv Generalleutnant* Richard Balzer.

Besitzzeugnis

Dem Obergefreiten
(Dienstgrad)

Paul Kuhn
(Vor- und Zuname)

2./Fla.Btl.59
(Truppenteil)

wurde das

Sturmabzeichen

verliehen.

O.U., 10.10.1941
(Ort und Datum)

Krüger
(Unterschrift)

Generalmajor und Kommandeur
der 1. Panzer-Division
(Dienstgrad und Dienststellung)

1. Panzer-Division

Above: This document style for the General Assault Badge in format DIN A5 is the most commonly encountered type. It is made out to *Obergefreiter* Paul Kuhn of the Flak battalion of the *1. Panzer Division*. The document is signed by the divisional commander Walter Krüger (Knights Cross 15. July 1941, Oakleaves 24. January 1944).

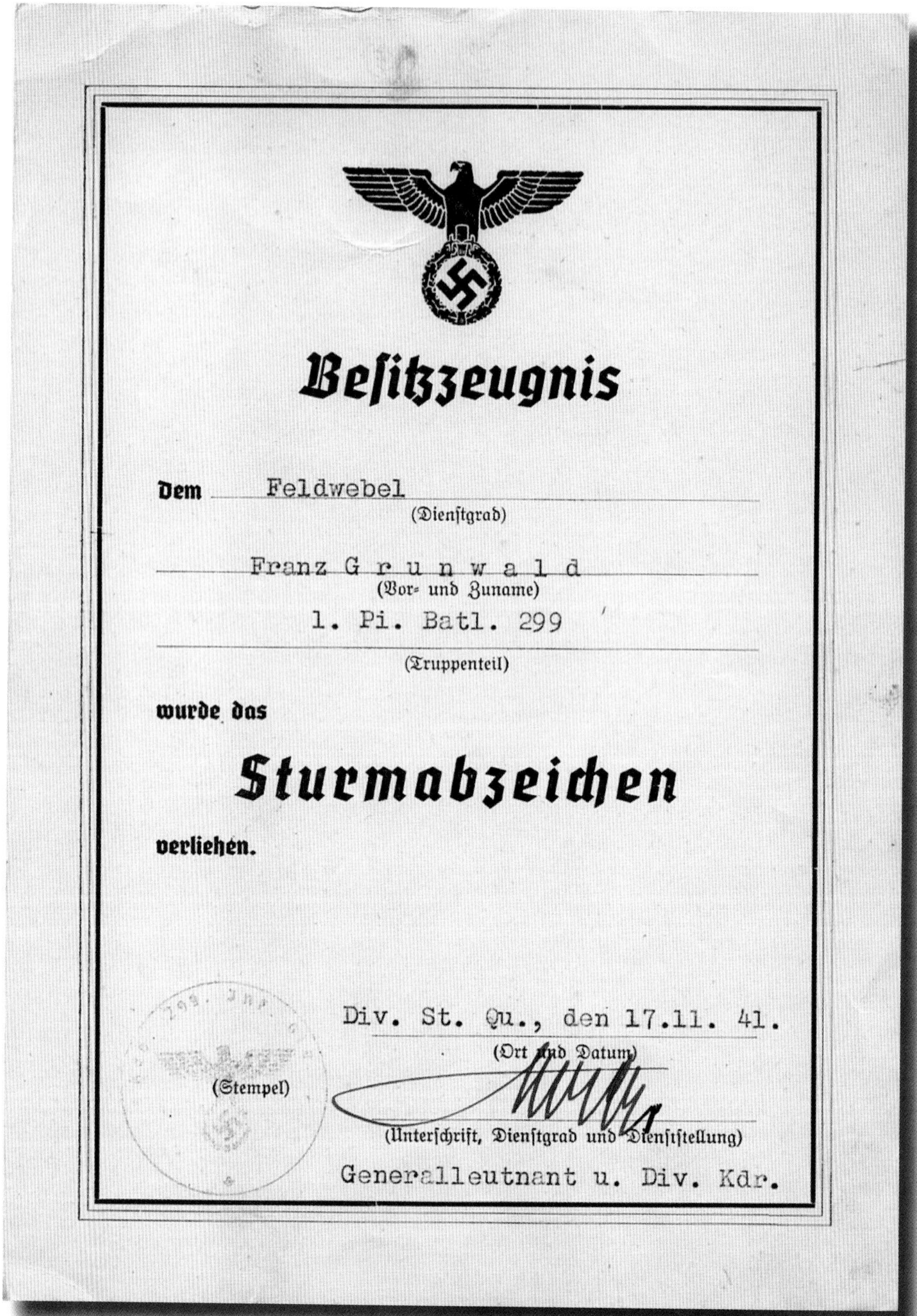

Besitzzeugnis

Dem Feldwebel

(Dienstgrad)

Franz G r u n w a l d

(Vor- und Zuname)

1. Pi. Batl. 299

(Truppenteil)

wurde das

Sturmabzeichen

verliehen.

(Stempel)

Div. St. Qu., den 17.11. 41.

(Ort und Datum)

(Unterschrift, Dienstgrad und Dienststellung)

Generalleutnant u. Div. Kdr.

Above: Award document in Format A 5, made out to *Feldweber* Franz Grunwald, signed by the commander of the *299. InfDiv Generalleutnant* Willi Moser. (Knights Cross on 26. October 1941).

BESITZZEUGNIS

DEM Unteroffizier
(DIENSTGRAD)

Heinz M o r a w i t z
(VOR- UND FAMILIENNAME)

3./Sturmgeschütz - Brigade 276
(TRUPPENTEIL)

VERLEIHE ICH FÜR TAPFERE TEILNAHME
AN 25 EINSATZTAGEN

DIE II. STUFE ZUM STURMABZEICHEN

O.U., den 3. 2. 1945
(ORT UND DATUM)

Sewera
(UNTERSCHRIFT)

(STEMPEL)

Hauptmann und Kommandeur der Brigade
(DIENSTGRAD UND DIENSTSTELLUNG)

Above: Award document for the *Stufe* II of the General Assault Badge to an *Unteroffizier* of the *Sturmgeschützbrigade 276*, signed by *Hauptmann* Sewera (GC 22. Sep.1944).

THE BADGE IN WEAR

The General Assault Badge was worn on the left side of the tunic. If the Iron Cross First Class was present, it was to be attached below that higher award. If a higher *Stufe* was awarded, the previous one was to be discarded.

Above: This *Funker-Unteroffizier* of the *s.H.Pz.Jg.Abt. 661* (towed 8.8 cm Pak 43/44) wears the General Assault Badge. The ribbon in the button hole is for the EK2.

Above: This *Obergefreiter der Pioniere* wears the General Assault Badge according to the regulations on the left breast pocket above the Wound Badge in Black. The ribbons in the button hole are for the Iron Cross 2. Class and the East Medal.

Above: This *Oberleutnant* of the *Nebeltruppe* wears the Iron Cross 1. Class above the General Assault Badge, the Sports Badge, and the Wound Badge in Black. The ribbons of the bar are of the Iron Cross 2. Class and the 4 Year Army Long Service Award.

Above: This *Rottenführer* of the *Waffen-SS* wears the Infantry Assault Badge and the General Assault Badge at the same time, which was against regulations. He also was awarded with the Close Combat Clasp in Bronze, the EK 2, and the East Medal.

STICKPINS

The General Assault Badge was available for private purchase as a miniature in the sizes 16 mm and 9 mm. Miniatures in the 16 mm size of the 25 and 50 deployment days are known in different styles. Stickpins and miniatures for the badges for 75 and 100 deployment days do not seem to exist.

Left: 16 mm and 9 mm stickpins of the General Assault Badge. Regarding to the sales list of mid-1943 the prices were 0.60 respectively 0.37 RM.

Right: 16 mm miniatures of the General Assault Badge *Stufen* II and III. Miniatures of the *Stufe* IV were most likely never produced. Even the time window for the *Stufe* II and III is very small - between the creation of the additional *Stufen* and the omission of 16 mm miniatures in favor of 9 mm ones is only one month.[6]

FAKES AND REPRODUCTIONS

The number of convincing fakes of the General Assault Badge is very high. (Frank Heukemes lists 18 in his book.) The detection of these fakes is no longer based on the make and material alone but also requires some basic understanding of the genuine makers and their markings and style. As is always the case, it is extremely important to study the originals and ask experienced collectors for help and a second opinion, especially when buying one of the higher *Stufen* of the General Assault Badge.

THE 1957 VERSION OF THE BADGE

All *Stufen* of the General Assault Badge were authorized for wear in the law of 1957. The required and prescribed de-nazification was easily done - only the swastika was removed. The prominent eagle remained, as did the *Karabiner 98k* and the potato masher hand grenade.

Right: Early production 1957 version of the General Assault Badge, made by Steinhauer & Lück.

Left: Proposed and executed design of the *Stufe* II General Assault Badge of the 1957 version.

Right: The *Stufe III* of the General Assault Badge as it was published by the Ministry of the Interior on 1. February 1959.[6]

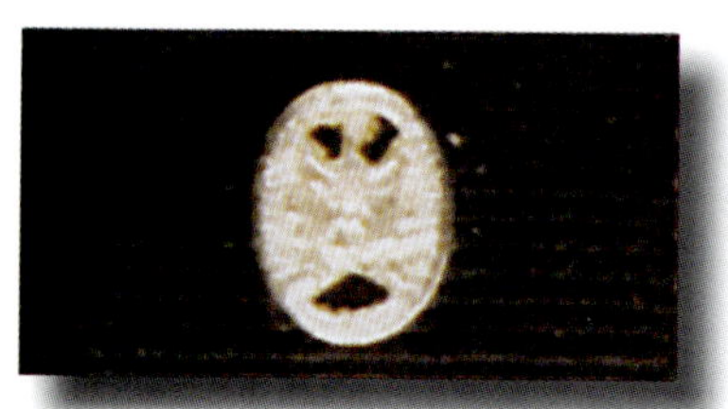

Left: Ribbon bar device of the General Assault Badge as it was authorized for the *Bundeswehr*.

FOOTNOTES

1 Daily Order of the Army, dated 1. June 1940, HVBL. B, page 379

2 As the war situation required more and more ground deployment of *Luftwaffen* troops, Göring founded the Luftwaffe Ground Combat Badge on 31. March 1942. For more information refer to *The Luftwaffe Ground Combat Badge* by Sascha Weber, B&D Publishing, Richmond, 2008.

3 Dr. Kurt-Gerhard Klietmann, *Deutsche Auszeichnungen,* page 170

4 Nimmergut, Jörg, *Deutsche Orden und Ehrenzeichen, Vol. IV,* page 2300

5 The listing is taken from *The General Assault Badge (*Frank Heukemes, Heukemes Publishing and the revised and amended edition *Das Sturmabzeichen (Allg.)* (B&D Publishing LLC, 2009). The Unknown Makers are summarized.

5 Patzwall lists the miniatures of the *Stufe* "25" and "50" in his price catalog, but not the *Stufe* "75". Messing shows in his *Spezialkatalog* 1990/91 on page 44 a *Stufe* "100" and also both "75" and "100" as being in existence as a 16 mm miniature. It needs to be remarked that Messing also shows some miniatures which are extremely dubious and the grades "75" and "100" are extremely questionable as miniatures. Niemann ignores the higher *Stufen* completely in his price catalog.

6 *Bekanntmachung des Bundesminister des Inneren*, I A 1-11 965 A - 65/58

Above: Assault Pioneers were amongst the troops decorated with the General Assault Badge (period drawing by Hans Liska).

BIBLIOGRAPHY

Doehle, Dr. Heinrich, *Die Auszeichnungen des Grossdeutschen Reichs*, Berlin 1945

Dombrowski, Hanns, *Orden, Ehrenzeichen und Titel*, Franz Wahlen, 1940

Geeb, *Deutsche Orden und Ehrenzeichen*, Heymanns Verlag, 1985

Heukemes, Frank, *The General Assault Badge*, Heukemes Publishing, 2005

Heukemes, Frank, *Das Sturmabzeichen (allg)*, B&D Publishiung, 2009

Klietmann, Dr. K.-G., *Deutsche Auszeichnungen*, Die Ordens-Sammlung Berlin, 1971

Merkblatt 15/5, *Orden und Ehrenzeichen*, Biblio-Verlag, 1992

Messing, M., *Miniaturauszeichnungen des III. Reiches*, Eigenverlag, Nürnberg 1990

Nimmergut, Jörg, *Deutsche Orden und Ehrenzeichen*, Vol. IV, München, 2004

Patzwall, Klaus, *Katalog der Auszeichnungen Drittes Reich*, Patzwall Verlag, Norderstedt, 1992

Der Uniformen-Markt, Volumes 1939-1945

Schwert und Spaten, Volumes 1939-1942

Chapter 10

The Anti-Partisan Badge

Oberst der Schutzpolizei Hans Griep displays quite a selection of awards, among them the Iron Cross First and Second Classes of the Great War and the two *Wiederholungsspangen* of 1939, the War Merit Cross 1. Class with Swords, and the Anti-Partisan Badge in Silver.

Table of Contents

THE ANTI-PARTISAN BADGE

HISTORY

The Anti-Partisan Badge (*Bandenkampfabzeichen* which literally means "gang fighting badge") was founded on 30. January 1944 in the grades Bronze, Silver, and Gold as a war badge of the *SS* and of the *Polizei*. The reason for the denomination "gang" instead of the usual word partisan, which is used for the English description, lies in an order by Adolf Hitler, dated 18. August 1942, in which he decreed that the up-to-now called partisans should be named "gangsters" (*Banditen*) which operated in gangs (*Banden*). The terminology "Partisan", despite not being protected by the Geneva Convention, sounded too official and recognized.

Consequently, the badge was not named *Partisanenkampfabzeichen* but rather *Bandenkampfabzeichen*.

The newly founded badge was shown in the 15. March 1944 issue of the *Uniformen-Markt* with the words:

Banden-Kampf-Abzeichen

Der Führer stiftete das Banden-Kampf-Abzeichen als Tapferkeits- und Leistungsabzeichen für die im Kampfe gegen die von Moskau organisierten Banden in Sumpf und Wald hinter der Ostfront sowie in den Schluchten und auf den Höhen der Gebirge des Südostens stehenden deutschen Soldaten oder die an ihrer Seite kämpfenden Waffengefährten der verbündeten europäischen Staaten zur Verleihung kommt. Das Abzeichen wird in drei Stufen Bronze, Silber und Gold — für jeweils 20, 50 und 100 Kampftage verliehen.

"The Führer has founded the Anti-Partisan Badge as a bravery and accomplishment badge for the soldiers who fight against the Moscow-organized gangs in the swamps and woods behind the Russian front lines as well as in the gorges and on the hill tops of the southeast mountains and also for their European comrades in arms who fight side by side with them. The badge will have the grades Bronze, Silver and Gold for 20, 50 and 100 deployment days."

REGULATIONS

The Anti-Partisan Badge was founded in three grades, Bronze, Silver, and Gold. The difference between the three grades was the amount of chargeable deployment days. Deployment days were counted as all days on which the members of infantry units had close combat contact with the enemy. This was true for an attack or a defensive operation, during reconnaissance operations, as a runner, or in the defense of an enemy reconnaissance operation.

For units with heavy weapons all days counted in which the members of such units (gun crews for example) were engaged in close combats with the partisans. The grade steps were as follows:

- for the first grade (bronze)	:	20 deployment days
- for the second grade (silver)	:	50 deployment days
- for the third grade (gold)	:	100 deployment days

Contrary to the award regulations for the other war badges of the army, where the divisional commanders had the right to award, the Anti-Partisan Badge was awarded by several offices and all of them very high up in the corresponding organization. Since multiple branches of the service were involved, multiple administrative offices were authorized:

- *Reichsführer* SS Heinrich Himmler
- the Commander of the Anti-Partisan troops for members of the individual staffs
- the *Höhere SS-and Polizeiführer* for all members of the SS and police
- the Supreme Command of the *Heer* for all members of the army
- the Supreme Command of the *Kriegsmarine* for all members of the navy
- the Supreme Command of the *Luftwaffe* for all members of the air force

The badge could also be awarded to foreign volunteers provided they took their oath to Adolf Hitler. On 5. October 1944 the regulations were expanded to include persons which were not part of the *Wehrmacht, Waffen-SS,* or police. This could be members of the national railroad or forestry service which were attacked by the partisans.

On 25. August 1944 *Reichsführer-SS* H. Himmler announced that he would award any Anti-Partisan Badges in Gold personally. The reported award numbers of this grade vary. K. Patzwall and R. Michaelis name ten awards.[1,2] Nimmergut mentions 23 awards[3] which seems to be wrong. Since there is no documented list, the numbers could very well be higher. The award numbers for the bronze grade are estimated at 3000 and the ones for the silver grade with approximately 800.[4]

DESIGN

The central design of the Anti-Partisan Badge is a nordic-looking sword in front of the so-called *Sonnenrad* (sun wheel), another form of the swastika. This symbolic design was most likely taken from the *Thule Gesellschaft,* a national and anti-semitic organization founded 1918 in Munich which also had some connection with the early days of the DAP, respectively NSDAP.

The depiction of the enemy as the multi-headed, snake-like Hydra of Greek mythology is fitting and the fight against them as a symbol of evil is a very old and commonly used allegory. The snake heads are inspired by Horned Viper (*vipera ammodytes*).[5] The inclusion of a death head in this case is most likely more a symbol for "death to come" rather than a symbol of the involved troops of the *Waffen-SS*.

The actual designer of the badge is not known.

Right: The Anti-Partisan Badge in Gold as shown in Dr. Doehle's book. Some allege that the depicted badge is the so-called "blue sword," meaning the darkening of the blade with paint.

THE BADGE

Right: Obverse of an Anti-Partisan Badge in Bronze.

Left: Hollow reverse of the same badge. Note the three cut-outs which correspond to the badge picture by Dr. Doehle in his 1945 issue of *Die Auszeichnungen des Grossdeutschen Reichs*.

Left: Obverse of the Anti-Partisan Badge in Silver.

Right: The reverse of this badge is also hollow stamped.

Right: Obverse of the Gold grade.

Left: The reverse of the Gold grade is also hollow and has two cut-outs. It is of the same type as the Silver grade. Note the two cut-outs which correspond to the badge pictured in the booklet *Der Lohn der Tat*.

The Gold grade was awarded to at least ten soldiers known by name.[6] All of them were *SS-Karstjäger* of the *24. Waffen-Gebirgs-(Kartsjäger-)Division der SS*. They were mainly deployed along the Adriatic coast line (*Operationszone Adriatisches Küstenland OZAK*). This list of names might be amended in time due to ongoing research.

Rank	Name	Date
SS-Obersturmführer	Erich Kühbandner	15. February 1945
SS-Obersturmführer	Helmut Pratsch	15. February 1945
SS-Hauptscharführer	Alfred Ludl	15. February 1945
SS-Sturmmann	Rudi Brauer	15. February 1945
SS-Sturmmann	Richard Armstark	9. March 1945
SS-Unterscharführer	Friedrich Fabel	9. March 1945
SS-Sturmmann	Michael Götzinger	9. March 1945
SS-Sturmmann	Johann Mootz	9. March 1945
SS-Unterscharführer	Kurt Sinemus	9. March 1945
SS-Oberscharführer	Oswald Walter	9. March 1945

This makes the Gold grade of the Anti-Partisan Badge one of the rarest awards of the Third Reich.

THE ANTI-PARTISAN BADGE IN GOLD WITH DIAMONDS

Regarding to Dr. Klietmann twenty Anti-Partisan Badges in Gold with Diamonds were made end of 1944 by the company of C.E. Juncker but were never awarded.[7] There is no document, no notice, and no other reference in the otherwise very fastidious files of H. Himmler, nor is there any mentioning in any other publication nor any note about possible award criteria. It has been theorized that the first awardee could or would have been *SS-Obergruppenführer* Erich von dem Bach-Zelewski, who led the troops against the Warsaw Uprising. However, von dem Bach-Zelewski was only holder of the Silver grade.

It has also been theorized that the Anti-Partisan Badge in Gold and with Diamonds was modeled after the Diamond Badges of the *Kriegsmarine* which were not an official award but rather a personal present from *Admiralsinspekteur der Kriegsmarine* Dr. h.c. Erich Raeder to recipients of the Oakleaves to the Knights Cross of the Iron Cross. None of the documented recipients of the Gold grade of the Anti-Partisan Badge were Knights Cross or Oakleaves awardees.

Despite the complete lack of any documentation, actual samples of the badge are documented in all relevant publications. The examples have four cut-outs (which is unique), are of the flatback style, and the broad pin is inscribed with C. E. Juncker, Berlin in cursive. Nimmergut reports two known examples which are allegedly samples made on Juncker's own initiative immediately after the foundation of the badge. He certified the authenticity of one of the two badges with no further evidence than the first reference by Klietmann in 1964.

This example is made of 800 silver and is gilded. The sun wheel of the obverse is studded with 25 small diamonds (below).

Left: Obverse of the Anti-Partisan Badge in Gold with Diamonds alleged by Nimmergut to be the one sample piece still in existence.

Right: Reverse of the badge with the peculiar script of C.E. Juncker, Berlin and the "800" incuse silver mark.

Another Anti-Partisan Badge in Gold with Diamonds, and one with a different design and arrangement of the diamonds, was auctioned off in the USA at the end of 2010.[8] This badge was kept by a former G.I who said he aquired it in 1945 when he was serving with the 80th Signal Co., 80th Infantry in Munich. It was only discovered in September 2010.

The badge shows traces of gilding and is made of silver and stamped as such with "800".

Left: Obverse of the Anti-Partisan Badge in Gold with Diamonds. This example has four diamonds set into the sun wheel and another four set into the grip of the sword.

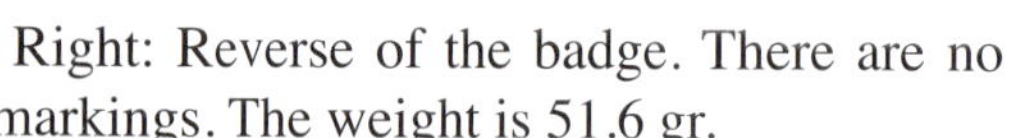

Right: Reverse of the badge. There are no markings. The weight is 51.6 gr.

Both badges are shown for reasons of completeness of the subject. There is no scientific way to prove that one or both of the shown examples are genuine and from the period nor is there any reasonable way to prove the opposite. Both badges are shown to inform the reader about their existence and to allow further research.

THE MAKERS OF THE ANTI-PARTISAN BADGE

The Anti-Partisan Badge is a late-war badge and is therefore always made of zinc. The amount of makers, however, and the style of the badges (hollow, semi-hollow, or flat backed) is a matter of continuous discussion. Earlier publications, such as the *Internationales Militaria-Magazin,* show five different maker variations[9], and Patzwall shows 15 different types in his 2003 publication and Nimmergut shows 13. The types range from hollow, semi-hollow, to flat-backed, they also vary in the amount of cut-outs (from none to three in different areas of the snakes) and in the pin system. None are marked.

Such a maker variation is astonishing and extremely hard to believe for a late war badge, especially in light of the possible number of recipients based on the troop numbers involved and requirements for the badge. Why would so many companies or so many variations be necessary for a time frame of about 15 months?

There is, however, an agreement about the first maker of the badge. Klietmann reports that the first series of badges (he calls them Type A) was made by C.E. Juncker, Berlin and that after the bombing of the company "another company" took over the production (Type B).[10]

Today, the collector community seems to accept only two styles with confidence. The hollow types shown on the previous page, a so-called semi-hollow style, and the "light" type. In addition, a variation called "blued sword" (which is a standard gold badge with a blue-colored sword) is testified by period photographs and it is assumed that only four were made. The so-called "flatbacks" are considered by many (but not all!) as post-war productions.

None of the above types has a definite maker assigned and no book with a solid categorization of the types and features exists as of the date of this volume.

Obverse and reverse of a genuine so-called "light Anti-Partisan Badge." The maker is not yet known.

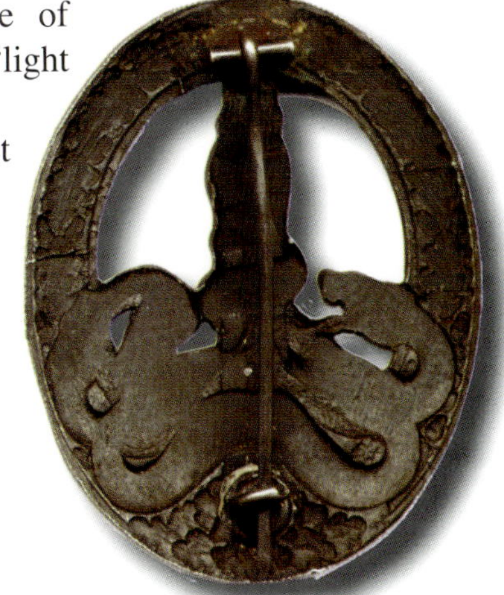

PACKAGES

There are no genuine and verified packages for the Anti-Partisan Badge of either grade that the authors are aware of. At this point in time it is advisable to be very cautious when acquiring any such bag or case if offered.

AWARD DOCUMENTS

Several styles of the award document for the grades of the Anti-Partisan Badge exist. They range from typewritten examples to fairly elaborate styles for members of the *Luftwaffe*.[11] The known example for the Gold grade to *SS-Obersturmführer* E. Kühnbandner is very plain but signed by *Reichsführer-SS* Heinrich Himmler.[12]

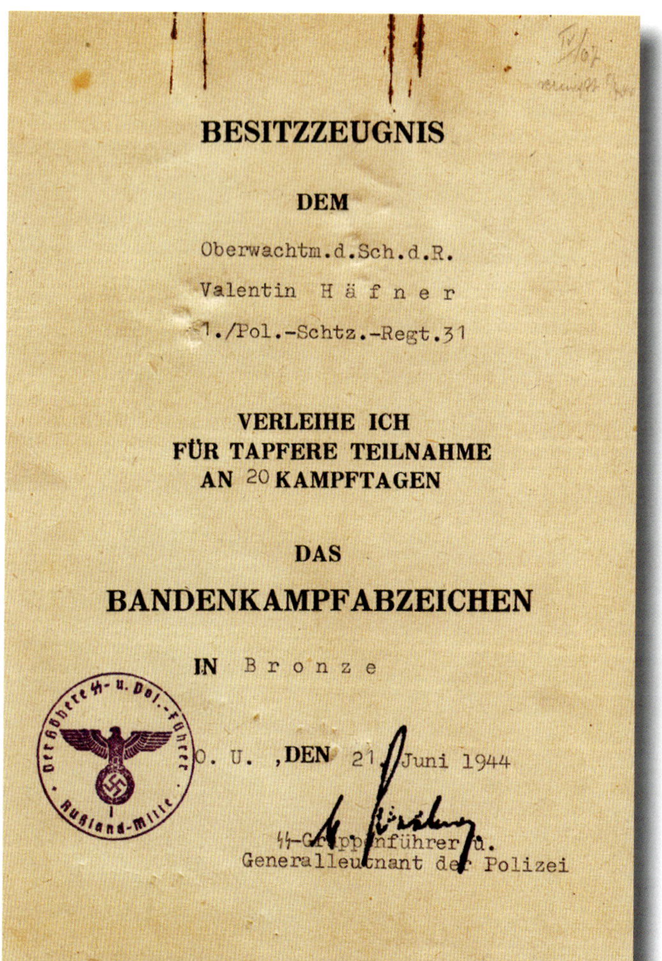

BESITZZEUGNIS

DEM

Oberwachtm.d.Sch.d.R.

Valentin H ä f n e r

1./Pol.-Schtz.-Regt.31

VERLEIHE ICH
FÜR TAPFERE TEILNAHME
AN 20 KAMPFTAGEN

DAS

BANDENKAMPFABZEICHEN

IN Bronze

Der Höhere SS- u. Pol.-Führer Russland-Mitte

O. U. ,DEN 21. Juni 1944

SS-Gruppenführer u.
Generalleutnant der Polizei

Left: Award document made out to *Oberwachtmeister der Schutzpolizei der Reserve* Valentin Häfner of the *SS-Pol. Rgt. 31* for the Anti-Partisan Badge in Bronze. The document is signed by *SS-Gruppenführer u. Generalleutnant der Polizei* Curt von Gottberg.

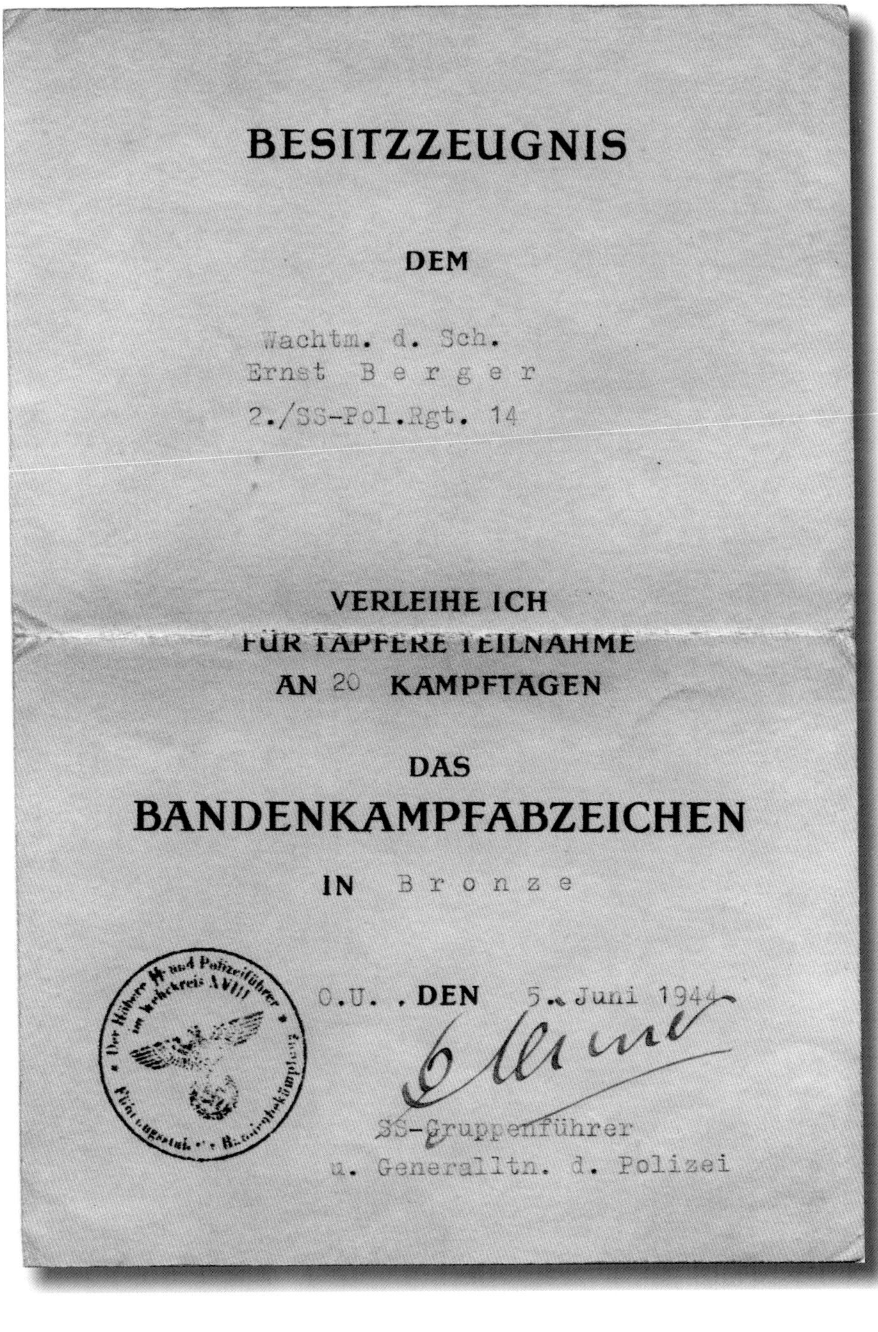

BESITZZEUGNIS

DEM

Wachtm. d. Sch.
Ernst B e r g e r
2./SS-Pol.Rgt. 14

VERLEIHE ICH
FÜR TAPFERE TEILNAHME
AN 20 KAMPFTAGEN

DAS

BANDENKAMPFABZEICHEN

IN B r o n z e

O.U. , DEN 5. Juni 1944

SS-Gruppenführer
u. Generalltn. d. Polizei

Above: Award document for the Anti-Partisan Badge in Bronze to *Wachtmeister der Schutzpolizei* Ernst Berger of the *SS-Pol.Rgt. 14* (size approx. DIN A5). The document is signed by *SS-Gruppenführer u. Generalleutnant der Polizei* Erwin Rösener.

THE BADGE IN WEAR

The Anti-Partisan Badge was worn on the left side of the tunic. If the Iron Cross First Class was present, it was to be attached below that higher award. If a higher grade was awarded, the previous one was to be discarded.

Above: The young *Oberwachtmeister der Schutzpolizei* wears an Anti-Partisan Badge in Bronze below the Infantry Assault Badge and at the same level as the Wound Badge in Black.

Above: Members of the *Waffen-SS* and Police in front of the Palace of Justice in Trieste/ Italy (Headquarters). The officer on the right side (as viewed) wears the Anti-Partisan Badge in Bronze against regulations above the War Merit Cross 1. Class (which was an order of the Third Reich and not a war badge).

Above: Compiled uniform of an *Oberfeldwebel der Jägertruppe* with the Anti-Partisan Badge in Silver, Iron Cross First Class, Infantry Assault Badge, and Wound Badge in Gold on the left breast side. The uniform also shows the German Cross in Gold and the Close Combat Clasp in Bronze. The ribbons are Iron Cross Second Class in the buttonhole and East Medal, Army Four Year Long Service Medal, and the West Wall Medal.

STICKPINS

If there are miniatures of the Anti-Partisan Badge in existence they can only be in the 9 mm size since the *Präsidialkanzlei* decreed on 5. July 1943 that from that date on all miniatures needed to be of the 9 mm size. The authors are of the opinion that there are no genuine miniatures of the Anti-Partisan Badge in existence.
M. Messing shows in his *Spezialkatalog 1990/91* all three grades in the size 16 mm, which is a fairly sure sign of them being fakes.

FAKES AND REPRODUCTIONS

The fact that all known ground-dug Anti-Partisan Badges are of the hollow or semi-hollow type on one side, and Nimmergut on the other side shows in his book *Deutsche Orden und Ehrenzeichen* 13 different versions (whereas seven are so-called flatbacks), is an indication that it might very well be that there is not only confusion about the originality of some of the badges but that there is an over-proportional amount of fakes of this badge on the market.

The problem with this badge is that there are not only the usual post-war creations by such well known companies as Steinhauer & Lück and R. Souval, but also cast copies from badges that are considered original.

Left: Fake Anti-Partisan Badge in Bronze. This example is marked "L/58" for Rudolf Souval, Wien. Souval made no Anti-Partisan Badges before May 1945 and there are no Anti-Partisan Badges with any LDO-number.

THE 1957 VERSION OF THE BADGE

In the initial decree and as well as in the the book by Dr. Doehle, the Anti-Partisan Badge was identified as a war badge of the *Waffen-SS* and the *Polizei*. That would have prevented it from being a permissible badge for the *Bundeswehr.* (The *Waffen-SS* was classified as a criminal organization by the Nuremberg trial of 1946, which recognized no difference between the *Allgemeine SS* and the *Waffen-SS*). However, since units of the regular *Heer*, the *Kriegsmarine*, and the *Luftwaffe* also were awarded with the Anti-Partisan Badge, it was deemed unobjectionable to include this war badge into those of the *Wehrmacht* as a whole.[13]

The design was changed insofar that the sun wheel swastika was removed and the circle was left blank. Also removed was the death head at the tip of the sword since that was thought to be an SS or National Socialist symbol.

Left: Anti-Partisan Badge in Silver in the version of the 1957 law. The maker is Steinhauer & Lück.

Righ: Anti-Partisan Badge in Bronze on the ribbon bar for the daily wear in the *Bundeswehr.*

FOOTNOTES

1 Klaus D. Patzwall, *Das Bandenkampfabzeichen*, page 48-49

2 Rolf Michaelis, *Die Träger des Bandenkampfabzeichens in Gold*, page 13

3 J. Nimmergut, *Deutsche Orden und Ehrenzeichen*, page 2344

4 Rolf Michaelis, *Die Träger des Bandenkampfabzeichens in Gold*, page 13

5 Sergio Corbatti/Marco Nava, *Karstjäger*, 2010, page 370

6 Names compiled from Michaelis, *Die Träger des Bandenkampfabzeichens in Gold*

7 Klietmann, *Deutsche Auszeichnungen*, page 227

8 Mohawk Arms Militaria Auction No. 64, Lot 336

9 Lefevre/de Lagarde, *Internationales Militaria-Magazin*, Vol. 6, No. 79, page 36-41

10 Klietmann, *Deutsche Auszeichnungen*, page 227

11 Patzwall, *Das Bandenkampfabzeichen*, page 44-47

12 ibit. page 50

13 Geeb/Kirchner/Thiemann, *Deutsche Orden und Ehrenzeichen*, page 198

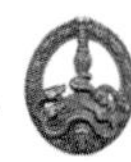

BIBLIOGRAPHY

Doehle, Dr. Heinrich, *Die Auszeichnungen des Grossdeutschen Reichs*, Berlin 1945

Dombrowski, Hanns, *Orden, Ehrenzeichen und Titel*, Franz Wahlen, 1940

Geeb, *Deutsche Orden und Ehrenzeichen*, Heymanns Verlag, 1985

Klietmann, Dr. K.-G., *Deutsche Auszeichnungen*, Die Ordens-Sammlung Berlin, 1971

Merkblatt 15/5, *Orden und Ehrenzeichen*, Biblio-Verlag, 1992

Michaelis, Rolf, *Die Träger des Bandenkampfabzeichens in Gold*, Michaelis,-Verlag, Berlin, 2011

Nimmergut, Jörg, *Deutsche Orden und Ehrenzeichen*, Vol. IV, München, 2004

Patzwall, Klaus, *Katalog der Auszeichnungen Drittes Reich*, Paztwall Verlag, Norderstedt, 1992

Patzwall, Klaus, *Das Bandenkampfabzeichen*, Patzwall, Norderstetd, 2003

S. Corbatti/M. Nava, *Karstjäger*, Editions Heimdal, 2010,

Der Uniformen-Markt, Volumes 1939-1945

Internationales Militaria-Magazin, Jhrg. 6, Nr. 79

Chapter
11
The Tank Destruction Badge

Oberleutnant Bodo Spranz (Knights Cross and Oakleaves [#308] on the same day, 3. October 1943) shows his four Tank Destruction Badges on the upper right arm sleeve.

Table of Contents

THE TANK DESTRUCTION BADGE

HISTORY

The heavy anti-tank weapons of the earlier war years were no longer sufficient to successfully fight and destroy the masses of enemy tanks. The troops were forced to use more and more other means of tank destruction, such as mines, rifle grenades, satchel charges, "Molotov cocktails," and *Hafthohlladungen* (adhesive hollow charges).

According to the directive of the OKH dated 23. October 1941 the destruction of an enemy tank was classified as an assault. In addition 14 days of special leave were granted for each destroyed enemy tank, a regulation which could not be held up due to the shortages within the fighting troops. Instead the Supreme Command decided to introduce a special award.

A decree dated 9. March 1942 was published by the OKH in the *Heeres-Verordnungsblatt* (army decree gazette) on 11. March 1942 with the following introduction:

> *"The Führer has authorized the implementation of a special badge for the overpowering of tanks and such by single fighters.*[1]*"*

Based on the repeated successes of some of the single fighters more and more strips were added to the sleeve and space became an issue.[2] On 7. January 1944 the *Allgemeine Heeresmitteilungen* printed the following decree of the Supreme Command of the Army:

> *The Führer has authorized the introduction of the special badge on a gold ribbon. The special badge on gold ribbon will be issued after the fifth overpowering of a tank or such instead of another special badge on silver ribbon. The previously awarded four special badges are to be discarded and stay with the soldier as a memento.*

Sonderabzeichen für das Niederkämpfen von Panzerkampfeinheiten durch Einzelkämpfer.
Beschrieben S. 50.
Aufnahme: Presse-Hoffmann (M).

Left: The badge was published for the first time in the 15. April 1942 issue of *Uniformen-Markt*.

REGULATIONS

The badge with the very long name of "Special Badge for the Overpowering of Armored Fighting Vehicles et cetera by Single Fighters" was awarded for each such vehicle which was destroyed by a single fighter with close combat means. Those means included anti-tank rifle, rifle grenades, satchel charges, and so on. Starting in late 1942/early 1943 the *Panzerfaust* and the *Panzerschreck* were introduced to the troops. These allowed the single fighter to "kill" a tank from greater ranges which no longer counted as close combat.

On 18. December 1943 it was decreed that any destruction of a tank by such means also counted as a requirement and the soldier was eligible for the Tank Destruction Badge. The Supreme Command of the Army issued in May 1944 a 24-page booklet with the title *Der Panzerknacker* (The Tank Cracker) in which detailed instructions for the destruction of enemy tanks were issued.

The Tank Destruction Badge was awarded by the battalion commander upon recommendation of the company commander. Only tank destructions after 22. June 1941 were eligible.

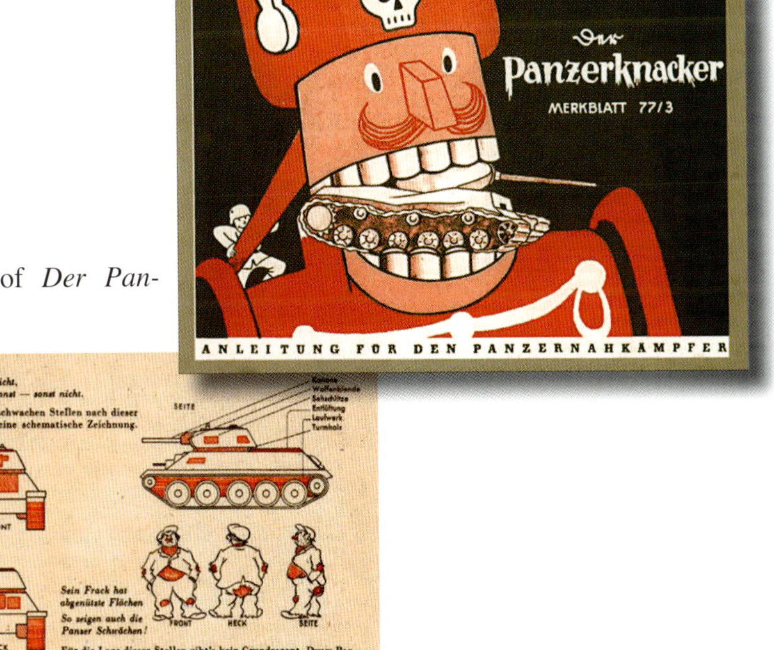

Right: Cover of *Der Panzerknacker.*

Left: One of the instruction pages inside.

DESIGN

The design of the badge is very simple and straightforward. The profile of a tank (the details of which are a mixture of the features of the *Panzer III* and *Panzer IV* tanks) made of either iron or *Tombak* is fixed to a ribbon of silver aluminum thread with black stripes on the upper and lower edges. The dimension of the Tank Destruction Badge is 90 mm wide and 32 mm high; the black stripes are to be 3 mm wide.

The tank is fixed to the ribbon with a rectangular plate and three prongs. The reverse is covered with glued-on cloth.

(One wonders why the depicted tank is clearly a German model and not the most sought after enemy tank for destruction: the Russian T-34.)

The Tank Destruction Badge in Gold was absolutely identical to the Silver version except that it had gold backing instead of silver.

Left: The Tank Destruction Badge as shown in Dr. Doehle's book.

Above: The *Panzerkampfwagen* IV (*Sd.Kfz. 161*) with the short 7.5 cm canon was the model for the Tank Destruction Badge.

THE BADGE

Above: Obverse of a Tank Destruction Badge in Silver, made by Moriz Hausch. Company Moriz Hausch AG, Pforzheim, is the only maker of the Tank Destruction Badge identified by name as of today[3]. The tank is non-magnetic.

Right: Reverse of the Tank Destruction Badge made by Moriz Hausch. The badge is covered with grey cloth. The impressions of the tank mounting prongs are hardly visible.

Left: Obverse of a Tank Destruction Badge in Silver, unknown maker.

Right: Reverse of the Tank Destruction Badge in Silver, unknown maker.

Above: Obverse of a Tank Destruction Badge in Gold of an unknown maker.

Right: The reverse of the Tank Destruction Badge is in this example covered with dark blue cloth.

Left: Obverse of a Tank Destruction Badge in Gold of an unknown maker. The ribbon is made of cellon thread and constitutes a rare example.

Right: Reverse of the Tank Destruction Badge in Gold of an unknown maker. The cloth backing is missing and the back plate and the prongs are visible.

Above: Detail photograph of the tank profile used by Moriz Hausch.

The actual state of the research acknowledges only three legitimate makers of the Tank Destruction Badge. One has been positively identified as Moriz Hausch, Pforzheim. Future investigation might turn up one or more other makers and their names.

Just as is the case with all other war badges of the Third Reich it is impossible to know how many Tank Destruction Badges were manufactured or awarded. The literature mentions that by mid-1944 already over 10,000 badges had been awarded.[4] On 27. May 1943 it was announced in the *Heeresmitteilungsblatt* that each recipient would be issued two badges at no cost and that officers would get three. Any replacement or additional badge should not be requested from the *Heeresbekleidungsamt* (official clothing store) but rather from the Army Personnel Office department PA 5 (b) against payment (right).

467. Kampfabzeichen usw.

1. In letzter Zeit mehren sich die Fälle, in denen Offiziere, Unteroffiziere und Mannschaften Kampfabzeichen aller Art und in beliebiger Menge kostenlos oder gegen Bezahlung beim H. Bkl. A Berlin I ohne Einhaltung des Dienstweges anfordern. Dies ist unzulässig. Kampfabzeichen, auch Ersatz für ohne Verschulden zu Verlust gegangene, sind grundsätzlich auf dem Dienstweg beim Heerespersonalamt P 5 (b) anzufordern, soweit der Bedarf aus Beständen der Truppe nicht gedeckt werden kann.

2. Ausstattungssoll.

	Kampfabzeichen, Verwundetenabzeichen (Ansteckabzeichen)	Kampfschilde (Narvik, Cholm, Krim)	Ärmelbänder (Kreta, Afrika)	Sonderabzeichen für Niederkämpfen von Panzerkampfwagen usw. durch Einzelkämpfer
		Stück	Stück	Stück
	Stück	insgesamt zu Feldbluse und Mantel		
a) Soldaten ausschließlich Selbsteinkleider	1	je 2	je 2	2 } für jeden Abschuß
b) Soldaten als Selbsteinkleider	1	je 5*)	je 5*)	3 } für jeden Abschuß

*) Nur für 1. Ausstattung.

O. K. H. (Ch H Rüst u. BdE), 27. 5. 43
— 64 c 32 — Abt Bkl (III a).

PACKAGES

There are only very few verified packages for the Tank Destruction Badge that the authors are aware of. At this point in time it is advisable to be very cautious when acquiring any such bag or case if offered.

AWARD DOCUMENTS

The regulatory statutes as printed in the *Merkblatt 15/5* indicate that no award document was intended for the Tank Destruction Badge. The regulation mentions only that the day of the award needed to be recorded into the *Wehrpass* and *Soldbuch* and a notarized copy of the battalion order should be given to the awardee.

B e s i t z z e u g n i s

Dem Leutnant Helmut W u l k o w , 1./Pi. Btl. 251 ist lt. Btl.Tagesbefehl Nr. 88/42 vom 12.7.42 auf Grund seiner Teilnahme an der Vernichtung eines Panzers am 8. Februar 1942

das

S o n d e r a b z e i c h e n

für das Niederkämpfen von Panzerkampfwagen durch Einzelkämpfer

verliehen worden.

Btl.Gef.St., den 11. Juli 1942

Hauptmann und Kommandeur des Pi.Btl. 251.

Above: The document is titled *Besitzzeugnis* but is rather an official copy of the daily battalion order No. 88/42, dated 12. July 1942, confirming the award of the Tank Destruction Badge to *Leutnant* Helmut Wulkow. The wording is interesting in such that it states that he was awarded the badge for his participation in the destruction of a tank some five months earlier.

This is in accordance to a clarification, dated 5. September 1942, that all soldiers taking part in the destruction of a tank will be eligible for the badge.

There are several types of award documents for the Tank Destruction Badge known and some are pictured in the literature. In most cases, however, the entrance in the *Soldbuch* was the only official documentation.

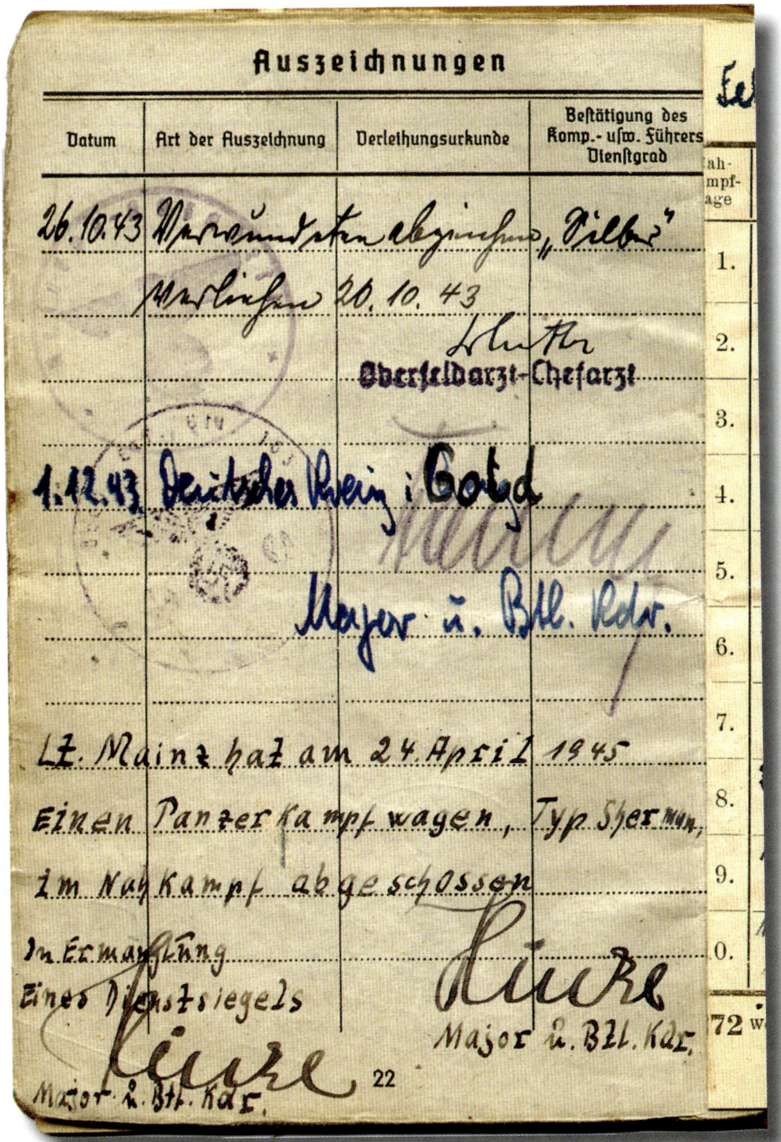
Auszeichnungen

Datum	Art der Auszeichnung	Verleihungsurkunde	Bestätigung des Komp.- usw. Führers Dienstgrad
26.10.43	Verwundetenabzeichen „Silber" verliehen 20.10.43		Oberfeldarzt-Chefarzt
1.12.43	Deutsches Kreuz i. Gold		Major u. Btl. Kdr.

Lt. Mainz hat am 24 April 1945
Einen Panzerkampfwagen, Typ Sherman,
im Nahkampf abgeschossen
In Ermangelung
Eines Dienstsiegels
Major u. Btl. Kdr.
Major u. Btl. Kdr.
22

Above: The entry for the Tank Destruction Badge in the *Soldbuch* of *Leutnant* Horst Mainz is dated 24. April 1945 and reads "Lt. Mainz has destroyed on 24. April 1945 an armored fighting vehicle, Type Sherman, in close combat."

Leutnant Mainz was also a recipient of the German Cross in Gold (1. December 1943).

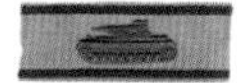

THE BADGE IN WEAR

The Tank Destruction Badge was to be worn on the right sleeve of the uniform (the left sleeve was reserved for campaign shields). The first badge was to be level with the top of the breast pocket.

Above: *Hauptmann* Bruno Karczewski wears two Tank Destruction Badges on his uniform. He was awarded with the Knights Cross on 12. March 1944 and was Oakleaves recipient number 767 (5. March 1945). He was also awarded with the Close Combat Clasp in Bronze, the Infantry Assault Badge in Silver, the East Medal, and the Wound Badge in Silver. He survived the war with the rank of *Oberstleutnant*.

Bundesarchiv

Above: This proud soldier of the *Panzer-Grenadier Division Großdeutschland* gets his first Tank Destruction Strip affixed to the upper sleeve. The tank in the background is a Russian T-34.

Above: *Major* Dr. Franz Bäke, *Kdr II./PzRgt 11(6.PzDiv)* in his tank shows three Tank Destruction Badges, He was awarded the Knights Cross 11. January 1943, followed by the Oakleaves (#262) on 1. August 1943 and the Swords (#49) on 21. February 1944.

Above: *Hauptmann* Gerhard Konopka of the *Großdeutschland* instructs the troops about destroying an enemy tank with the help of a board displaying a Russian T-34. He wears four Tank destruction Badges. He was also awarded with the German Cross in Gold, the Knights Cross (29. August 1943), and the Close Combat Clasp in Gold.

Right: After the introduction of the *Panzerfaust* this hand-held weapon was the most effective and deadliest instrument against any tank.

STICKPINS

M. Messing shows in his *Spezialkatalog 1990/91* the Silver and the Gold Tank Destruction Badge as a miniature with a ribbon. They are clearly the *Bundeswehr* device and it can be assumed with a very high degree of certainty that there was no 9 mm miniature stickpin of the Tank Destruction Badge in existence during the award period.

FAKES AND REPRODUCTIONS

The Tank Destruction Badge has been faked in both versions extensively. It is imperative to study the subject in depth before committing to buy. Some fakes are very easy to spot, some are very, very good. Only a detailed comparison with proven originals can determine what is real and what is not.

Above: Obverse and reverse of a fake Tank Destruction Badge. The tank is made of non-iron material, the backing is fieldgrey cloth over which a blue carton is glued. The tank is fixed correctly with a plate and three prongs.

THE 1957 VERSION OF THE BADGE

Since the Tank Destruction Badge did not show any of the forbidden symbols, such as the swastika or the SS-runes, there was no need to introduce a 1957 version of this award. It was only required to allow the display of the award in some form for the soldiers of the *Bundeswehr*. This was done as a ribbon bar device, whether in Silver or in Gold.

Right: *Bundeswehr Oberst* Wolfram Kertz (Knights Cross on 4. October 1944 during Operation Market Garden, see also page 232) shows his Tank Destruction Badge at the first place third row of his ribbon bar device. Other ribbons are for the Iron Cross First and Second Class, Close Combat Clasp in Bronze, Wound Badge in Silver, Infantry Assault Badge in Silver, Panzer Assault Badge in Bronze, and the *Bundeswehr* Sports Badge in Gold.

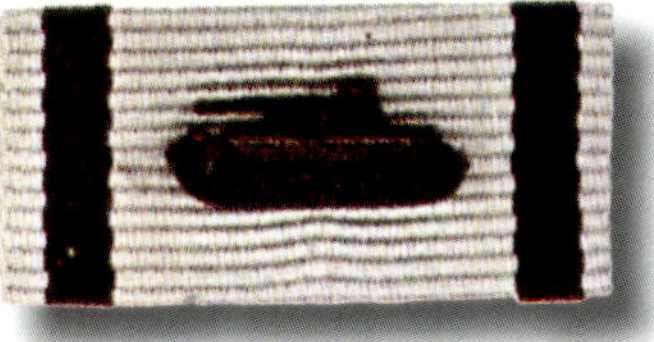

Above: Devices for the *Bundeswehr* ribbon bar of the Tank Destruction Badge in Silver and in Gold.

FOOTNOTES

1 *Heeres-Verordnungsblatt 1942, Teil B, 14. Ausg., Bl.5* , page 117, paragraph 190

2 Breyette/Bender (*Tank Killers, Bender Publishing, 2000*) shows a tunic with 8 strips on page 32

3 Schneider, Dirk, *Das Sonderabzeichen für das Niederkaempfen ...*"

4 Rudloff, Gerhard, *Das Abzeichen für die "Panzerknacker"*, INFO Sonderheft, Vol.1, Verlag Nickel, 1990, page 42. Unfortunately Rudloff gives no source at all for this number.

BIBLIOGRAPHY

Breyette, Thomas & Bender, Roger, *Tank Killers*, Bender Publishing, San Jose, 2000

Doehle, Dr. Heinrich, *Die Auszeichnungen des Grossdeutschen Reichs*, Berlin 1945

Dombrowski, Hanns, *Orden, Ehrenzeichen und Titel*, Franz Wahlen, 1940

Geeb, *Deutsche Orden und Ehrenzeichen*, Heymanns Verlag, 1985

Klietmann, Dr. K.-G., *Deutsche Auszeichnungen*, Die Ordens-Sammlung Berlin, 1971

Merkblatt 15/5, *Orden und Ehrenzeichen*, Biblio-Verlag, 1992

Nimmergut, Jörg, *Deutsche Orden und Ehrenzeichen*, Vol. IV, München, 2004

Schneider, Dirk, *Das Sonderabzeichen für das Niederkämpfen von Panzerkampfwagen durch Einzelkämpfer*, Verlag Sascha Weber, projected 2013

Der Uniformen-Markt, Volumes 1939-1945

Internationales Militaria-Magazin

Allgemeine Heeresmitteilungen 1939-1945

Chapter 12

The Aircraft Destruction Badge

Already in April 1944 the German *Luftwaffe* had lost air supremacy over France and parts of Germany. Attacks by low-flying Allied fighter planes became more and more frequent and dangerous.

Table of Contents

THE AIRCRAFT DESTRUCTION BADGE

HISTORY

The undisputed air supremacy of the Allied forces on all fronts placed an ever-growing burden on the regular army units to defend themselves against the low flying attack air craft.

The downing of an enemy aircraft with small caliber weapons was already acknowledged in the early days of the war by the issuing of a special recognition document to the soldier who brought the aircraft down. The document was instituted on 1. September 1941 and was named *Anerkennungsurkunde für Flugzeugabschüsse* (Certificate of Approval for Downing an Aircraft). The original size was DIN A5 and the documents were signed by *Generalfeldmarschall* von Brauchitsch. After Hitler took over the supreme command of the army, the size of the document was changed to A4 and issued from 19. December 1941 onwards. Until February 1945 a total of 535 such documents were issued.[1]

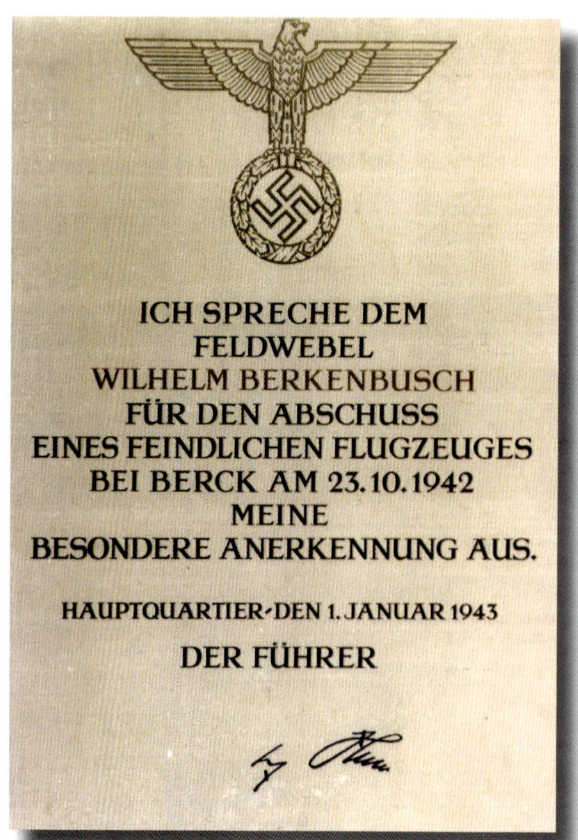

ICH SPRECHE DEM
FELDWEBEL
WILHELM BERKENBUSCH
FÜR DEN ABSCHUSS
EINES FEINDLICHEN FLUGZEUGES
BEI BERCK AM 23.10.1942
MEINE
BESONDERE ANERKENNUNG AUS.

HAUPTQUARTIER, DEN 1. JANUAR 1943

DER FÜHRER

Left: Document of the second type for the downing of an enemy aircraft with the facsimile signature of Hitler.

REGULATIONS

The Airplane Destruction Badge (*Tiefffliegervernichtungsabzeichen* or low flying aircraft destruction badge) was instituted by Adolf Hitler on 12. January 1945 as one of the very last war badges of the Third Reich.

The main reason was to create a visible award in addition to the certificate of approval. The institution was made with the following words:

> *"The downing of enemy air crafts with all means available is of outstanding importance. Therefore I order the institution of an Aircraft Destruction Badge for the shooting down of air crafts with hand-held or small caliber automatic weapons."*[2]

Any shooting down with dual-barrel or quadruple Flak guns did not count for this award but were credited for the Army Flak Badge.

For each downed aircraft the soldiers received one badge which was recorded into the personnel papers. The awarding was made upon the recommendation of the company leader by the brigade commander or higher. Every soldier who had already received the Certificate of Approval for Downing an Aircraft was entitled to receive the badge retro-actively.

The badge was instituted in Silver for one downed aircraft and in Gold for five.

— 19 —

Nur für den Dienstgebrauch! | Dies ist ein geheimer Gegenstand, Mißbrauch ist strafbar.

Allgemeine Heeresmitteilungen

Herausgegeben vom Oberkommando des Heeres

12. Jahrgang | Berlin, den 7. Februar 1945 | 3. Ausgabe

Führerbefehle.

48. Verordnung über die Stiftung des Tieffliegervernichtungsabzeichens vom 12. 1. 1945.

Der Abschuß feindlicher Tiefflieger mit allen zur Verfügung stehenden Mitteln ist von besonderer Wichtigkeit.

Ich ordne daher die Einführung eines Tieffliegervernichtungsabzeichens für den Abschuß von Flugzeugen durch Handwaffen oder kleinkalibrige Maschinenwaffen an.

Die Ausführungsbestimmungen erläßt der Chef des Oberkommandos der Wehrmacht.

Führerhauptquartier, den 12. Januar 1945

Der Führer
Adolf Hitler.

Durchführungsbestimmungen zur Verordnung über die Einführung des Tieffliegervernichtungsabzeichens vom 12. 1. 45

Auf Grund des letzten Absatzes der Verordnung über die Einführung des Tieffliegervernichtungsabzeichens wird auf Weisung des Führers bestimmt:

1. Das Sonderabzeichen wird an Soldaten verliehen, die in diesem Kriege mit Handwaffen (Gewehr, Maschinenpistole oder M. G. Ka. 1,2 cm und kleiner) einen feindlichen Tiefflieger abgeschossen haben. Für jedes abgeschossene Flugzeug wird an den entscheidend beteiligten Einzelschützen ein Sonderabzeichen verliehen.
2. Das Abzeichen besteht aus einem Band aus Aluminiumgespinst von 90 mm Länge und 32 mm Breite mit 2 eingewirkten schwarzen Streifen (3 mm breit), auf dem die aus Blech gestanzte Silhouette eines Flugzeuges in Schwarz angebracht ist.
3. Der Ärmelstreifen wird am rechten Oberärmel der Feldbluse getragen. Bei erneuter Verleihung wird ein weiterer Ärmelstreifen angelegt. An Stelle von 5 Abschüssen ist ein Abzeichen in Gold zu tragen.
4. Das Sonderabzeichen wird durch Truppenführer mindestens im Range eines selbständigen Brigade-Kommandeurs auf schriftlichen Vorschlag des Einheitsführers durch Tagesbefehl verliehen.
5. Tag der Verleihung ist in die Personalpapiere einzutragen. Beglaubigte Abschrift des Tagesbefehls ist den Beliehenen auszuhändigen.
6. Die Lieferung der Abzeichen wird dem Wehrmachtbeschaffungsamt (Bekleidung und Ausrüstung) übertragen.

Führerhauptquartier, den 13. Januar 1945.

Der Chef
des Oberkommandos der Wehrmacht
Keitel

Zusätze des Oberkommandos des Heeres zu den Durchführungsbestimmungen des O. K. W. zur Verordnung über die Stiftung des Tieffliegervernichtungsabzeichens.

I. Grundsätzliche Bestimmungen.

Zu 1. Einzelschützen, denen die bisherige Anerkennungsurkunde des Führers für den Abschuß feindlicher Flugzeuge mit Infanteriewaffen verliehen wurde, ist das Abzeichen nachträglich auszuhändigen. Ist nicht einwandfrei zu klären, wem der Abschuß zuzuschreiben ist, so muß von der Verleihung abgesehen werden.

Right: The institution of the new badge was announced in the *Allgemeine Heeresmitteilungen* issue 7. February 1945 together with the general regulations. It was the last issue printed.

DESIGN

The design of the badge is nearly identical to the one for the destruction of an enemy tank. On a silver or gold ribbon of 90 mm length and 32 mm height and with two black stripes a black aircraft, stamped from sheet metal, was to be affixed with prongs. The badge was to be sewn to the upper right arm sleeve.

Due to the very late institution of the badge, no contemporary depictions can be found in the Doehle book.

THE BADGE

It seems to be certain that no Aircraft Destruction Badges were manufactured or delivered and distributed to the troops. It also seems to be certain that no award documents were created nor issued to any recipient. Nimmergut shows one example in his book, but remarks that the actual piece was not on hand. He quotes Klietmann who stated in 1984 in regards to the pictured example that "it is, despite minor concerns, a period-made original of this rare war badge."[3] Strangely enough, in his 1989 book *Auszeichnungen des Deutschen Reichs 1936-1945* Klietmann does not mention this example and states that it is questionable that any awards were made or that any badges were handed out.[4]

The badge below is a post-war reconstruction and should only serve as a visual depiction of the intended award.

PACKAGES

No genuine packages for this war badge exist. Everything encountered can be safely assumed to be a post-war production.

AWARD DOCUMENTS

No genuine award documents for the Aircraft Destruction Badge are in existence.

THE BADGE IN WEAR

Since no badges were awarded before the war's end, no period pictures exist.

STICKPINS

No stickpins or ribbon devices of the badge were made before May 1945.

FAKES AND REPRODUCTIONS

All badges encountered, Silver or Gold, and any award documents can be safely assumed to be post war production (fakes).

THE 1957 VERSION OF THE BADGE

The Aircraft Destruction Badge was authorized for wear on the uniform of the *Bundeswehr* in the form of a ribbon bar device.

FOOTNOTES

1 Scherzer, Veit, *Die Inhaber der Anerkennungsurkunde des Oberbefehlshabers des Heeres für Flugzeugabschüsse 1941–1945,* Ranis-Jena, 1994

2 *Reichsgesetzblatt I*, 14. February 1945, page 23

3 Nimmergut, *Deutsche Orden und Ehrenzeichen*, Vol. IV, page 2329

4 Klietmann, Kurt-G., *Auszeichnungen des Deutschen Reichs 1936-1945*, page 120

BIBLIOGRAPHY

Dombrowski, Hanns, *Orden, Ehrenzeichen und Titel*, Franz Wahlen, 1940

Geeb, *Deutsche Orden und Ehrenzeichen*, Heymanns Verlag, 1985

Klietmann, Dr. K.-G., *Deutsche Auszeichnungen*, Die Ordens-Sammlung Berlin, 1971

Nimmergut, Jörg, *Deutsche Orden und Ehrenzeichen*, Vol. IV, München, 2004

Veit Scherzer, *Die Inhaber der Anerkennungsurkunde des Oberbefehlshabers des Heeres für Flugzeugabschüsse 1941–1945*. Scherzer's Militaer Verlag, Burgstadt Ranis 1994.

Allgemeine Heeresmitteilungen 1939-1945

Chapter 13

The Army Flak Badge

Above: This combat veteran wears his Army Flak Badge below the Iron Cross 1. Class and above the Wound Badge in Silver. He also was awarded with the Close Combat Clasp.

Table of Contents

THE ARMY FLAK BADGE

HISTORY

At the beginning of the Second World War the *Heer* units did not have any anti-aircraft units of their own. That task was either handled by the anti-aircraft troops of the infantry units (*Fliegerabwehr*) or by the units of the *Luftwaffe* (*Flugabwehr*). Only in 1940 the army flak units were introduced (color of arms was red) and by the war's end a total of 68 army flak units and 30 of the *Waffen-SS* had seen action.

After the *Luftwaffe* Flak Badge was instituted by Hermann Göring on 10. January 1941 in his capacity as Supreme Commander of the *Luftwaffe, Generalfeldmarschall* von Brauchitsch followed suit about six months later with the foundation of the Army Flak Badge.

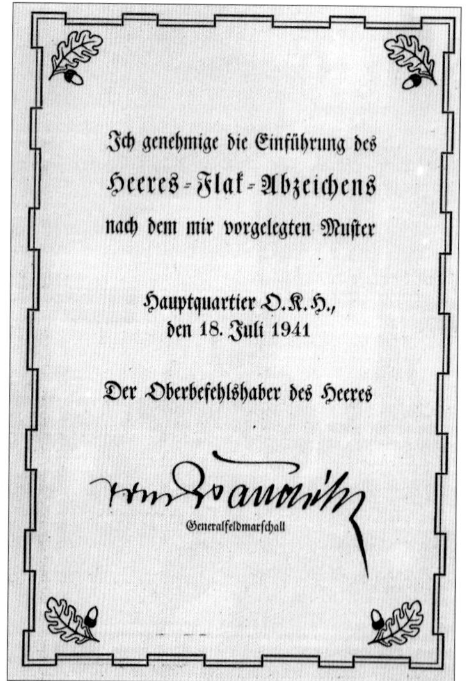

Ich genehmige die Einführung des

Heeres-Flak-Abzeichens

nach dem mir vorgelegten Muster

Hauptquartier O.K.H.,
den 18. Juli 1941

Der Oberbefehlshaber des Heeres

Generalfeldmarschall

Left: Announcement about the foundation of the Army Flak Badge by the Supreme Commander of the Army *Generalfeld-marschall* von Brauchitsch.

Right: First picture of the badge in the *Uniformen-Markt*, issue 15. September 1941.

REGULATIONS

The regulations for the Army Flak Badge were complicated and the tracking effort was cumbersome, the reason being the attribution of downed air crafts and the central handling by the Supreme Command of the Army (OKH).[1]

Starting in June 1941 any awarding had to fulfill the following conditions to receive the badge:

1. For flak companies and light batteries of the flak artillery with at least 5 kills with the guns of the same platoon to the platoon leader, the gun leader, and the gun operators, as far as those batteries were directly involved in the kills.

2. For heavy batteries of the flak artillery for at least 5 kills to the troops of the attacking battery, as far as those batteries were directly involved in the kills.

3. To the immediate superiors of the involved units even if they did not direct the shooting personally:
   - to company and battery leaders, if half of their batteries already received the Army Flak Badge and if said superiors were in charge of the units while those units performed the attacks.
   - to commanders, if at least half of the companies' battery leaders had already been awarded the Army Flak Badge and if said superiors were in charge of the units while they performed the attacks.

Contrary to the award regulations of the *Luftwaffe*, the Army Flak Badge was considered mainly an award of group achievement instead of a badge for individual achievement.

On 4. September, 1942, the Supreme Army Commander changed the award regulations in order to harmonize with the ones for the *Luftwaffe* Flak Badge. The badge was from that point on awarded only to individuals based on a point system. From then on, 16 points were necessary to receive the award, and the *Heer, Waffen-SS*, and *Luftwaffe* basically followed the same rules. Each member of the unit credited with some aspect of destroying an enemy aircraft received:

4 points:	For the unaided destruction of an aircraft.
2 points:	For cooperating in the shooting down of an enemy aircraft.
1 point:	For first detection of an enemy aircraft by a searchlight or sound-locator.

If the shooting down was credited to several cooperating units, each unit received the points regarding the table. Participation was defined as a direct involvement with the action which led to the successful outcome.

This meant that not only the troops handling the anti-aircraft gun but also other soldiers in other functions, such as radio operators, messengers, and such could qualify.

The downing of an aircraft had to be acknowledged by the Supreme Command of the Army (OKH) in order to be counted towards the award of the Army Flak Badge. This required a clear report from the requesting unit together with at least one neutral witness and a sketch which had to encompass:

- the location of the shooting
- the location of the shooting unit
- the line of fire
- the crash location
- the location of the witness

The document had to be submitted through the official channels together with a statement from the relevant regiment or the division. The report had also to include any other units which were involved in the downing of the aircraft.

Heeres-Flak-Abzeichen

Das Heeres-Flak-Abzeichen wurde am 18. 7. 1941 gestiftet und wird an die Angehörigen von Heeres-Fla-Truppen und Heeres-Flak-Einheiten verliehen, und zwar für erfolgreiche Beteiligung an Abschüssen feindlicher Flieger. Dieses Abzeichen kommt nur in einer Ausführung, nämlich Altsilber, zur Verleihung und wird auf der linken Brustseite getragen.

8

KAMPFABZEICHEN DES HEERES

When the downing was acknowledged by the OKH, the unit received an acknowledgement document together with a unique acknowledgement number. Each unit had to keep a record of each soldier and his point standing.

Relatively few soldiers of the army were awarded with the Army Flak Badge because the ever-growing deficiency of heavy weapons required the use of the Flak guns in a ground combat role. However, for this deployment not the Army Flak Badge was awarded but rather the General Assault Badge. Therefore it was permissible to award and to wear the Army Flak Badge next to the General Assault Badge.

DESIGN

The Army Flak Badge was introduced seven months after the *Luftwaffe* Flak Badge. It was therefore obvious to use the same basic design and adapt it to the Army. The *Luftwaffe* eagle was replaced by the one used by the Army and the central motif of the anti-aircraft gun remained unchanged.

Both designs were produced by Ernst Wilhelm Peekhaus of Berlin.[2]

Above: *Luftwaffe* Flak Badge (left) and Army Flak Badge, both by the maker Steinhauer & Lück.

THE BADGE

Most all known Army Flak Badges are solid die cast of zinc. They differ regarding to make in minor details and in the style of the pin system and its mounting to the reverse of the badge.

Left: Obverse of an Army Flak Badge made by Hermann Aurich, Dresden.

Right: Reverse of the badge. The pin system is crimped to the badge.

Right: Obverse of an Army Flak Badge made by Rudolf Souval, Wien.

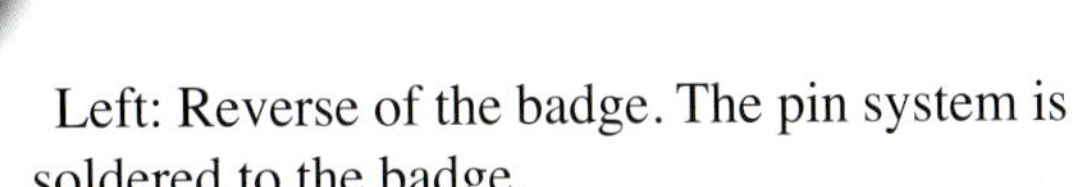

Left: Reverse of the badge. The pin system is soldered to the badge.

THE MAKERS OF THE ARMY FLAK BADGE[3]

Hermann Aurich, Dresden	(1) known variation
Förster & Barth, Pforzheim	(2) known variations
Funke & Brüninghaus, Lüdenscheid	(1) known variation
Wilhelm Hobacher, Wien[4]	(1) known variation
C.E. Juncker, Berlin	(5) known variations
Rudolf Souval, Wien	(2) known variations
Steinhauer & Lück, Lüdenscheid	(1) known variation
Friedrich Linden, Lüdenscheid	(1) known variation
Lind & Meyrer, Idar-Oberstein	(1) known variation
(Possibly) Paul Meybauer, Berlin	(2) known variations
Unknown Maker	(2) known variations
Unknown Maker "Flatback"[4]	(1) known variation
Unknown Maker "Pillow Crimp"	(1) known variation
Unknown Maker "Grayback"[4]	(1) known variation

PACKAGES

The Army Flak Badge was given out in either a non-descriptive paper bag or a simple carton box. Some had the content printed on; some of the paper bags had the company name on the reverse.

Above: Typical paper bag which most likely was used most of the time for this war badge. The maker, Wilhelm Hobacher, is printed on the reverse.

Left and below: A more elaborate carton box with the imprint *Heeres-Flakabzeichen*.

Left: A very rare combination is the Flak Badge in a cellophane LDO-bag. LDO-marked Flak Badges are extremely rare and only two are known as of today: "L/13" and "L/56".

AWARD DOCUMENTS

The Army Flak Badge was always awarded by the Supreme Headquarters and over the award period only three types of documents were used.

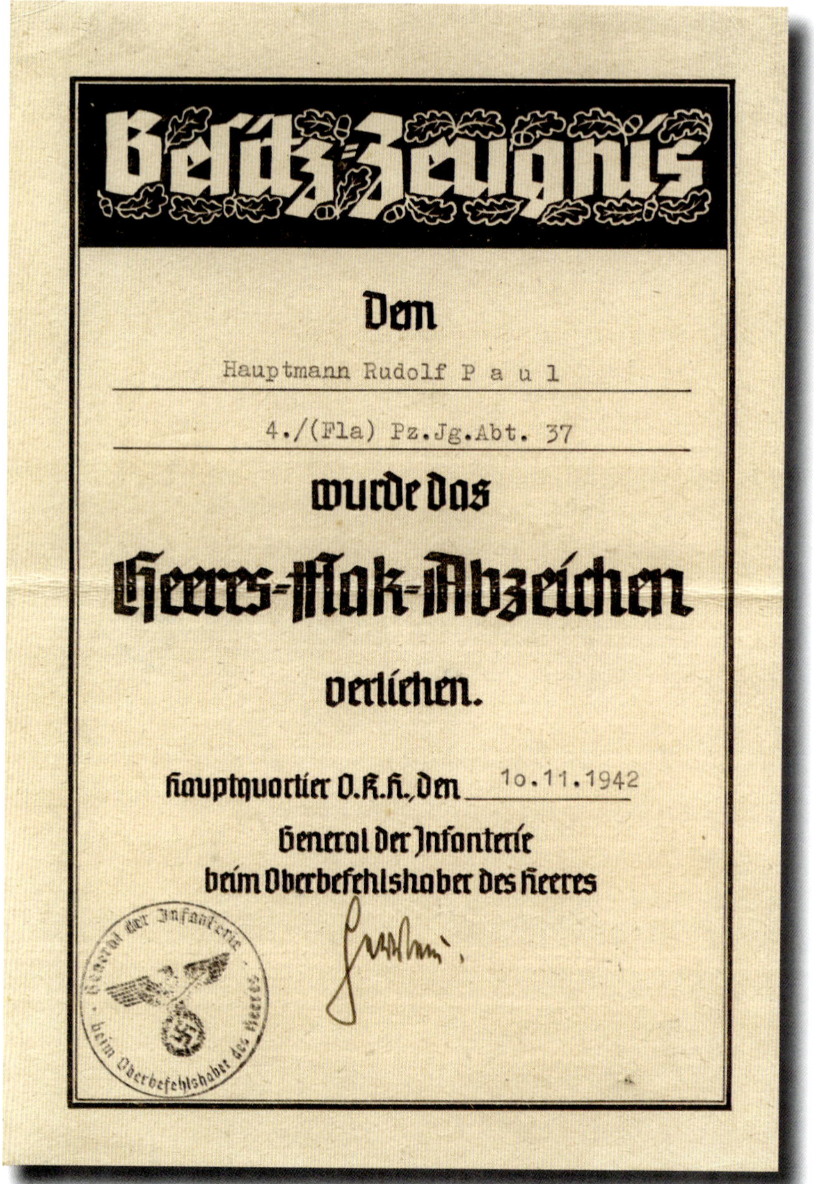

Besitzzeugnis

Dem

Hauptmann Rudolf P a u l

4./(Fla) Pz.Jg.Abt. 37

wurde das

Heeres-Flak-Abzeichen

verliehen.

Hauptquartier O.K.H., den 10.11.1942

General der Infanterie
beim Oberbefehlshaber des Heeres

General der Infanterie beim Oberbefehlshaber des Heeres

Above: Early document in DIN A5 size, made out to *Hauptmann* Rudolf Paul of *4./(Fla) PzJgAbt 37 (1. PzDiv).*

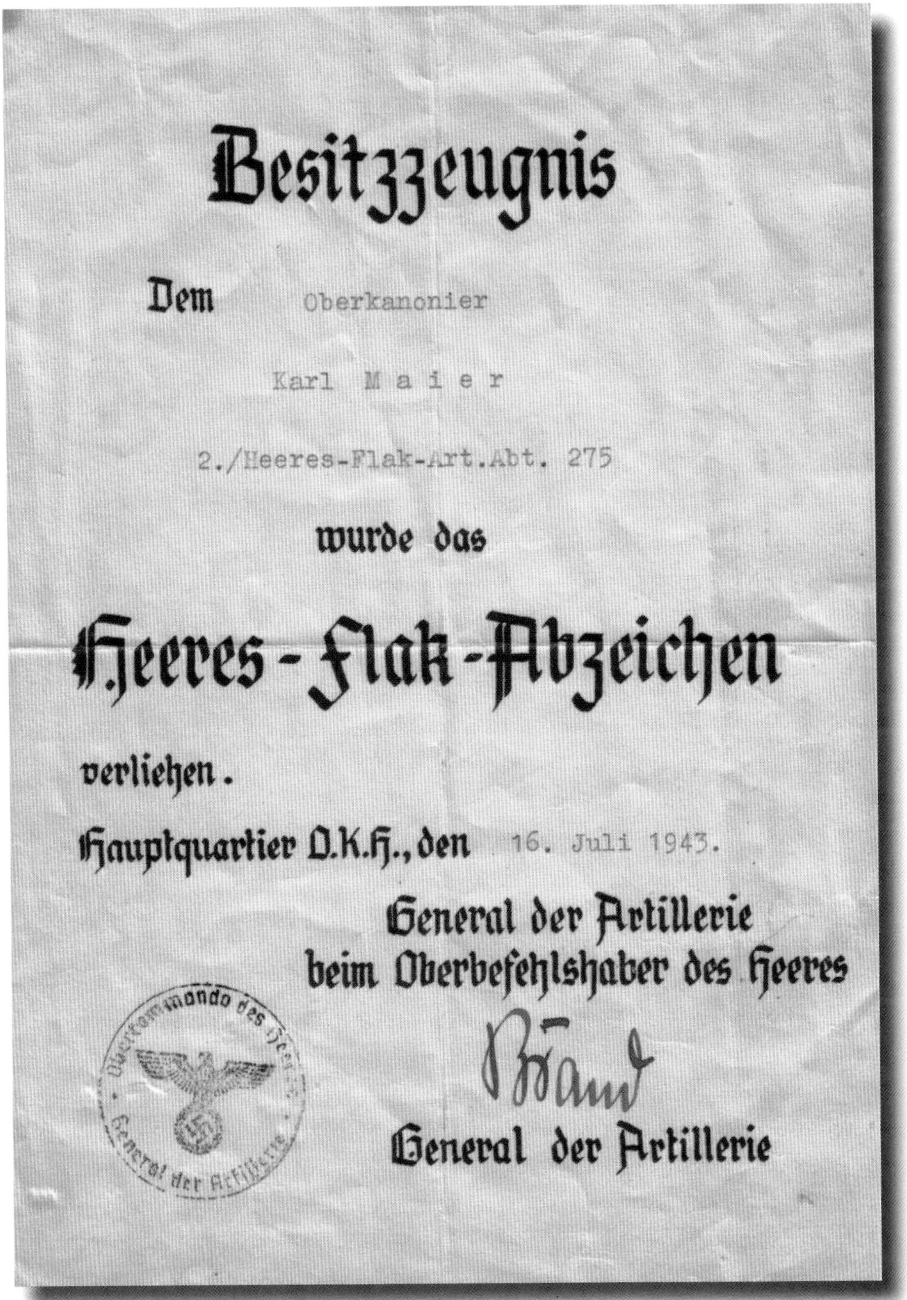

Besitzzeugnis

Dem Oberkanonier

Karl M a i e r

2./Heeres-Flak-Art.Abt. 275

wurde das

Heeres-Flak-Abzeichen

verliehen.

Hauptquartier O.K.H., den 16. Juli 1943.

General der Artillerie
beim Oberbefehlshaber des Heeres

Oberkommando des Heeres
General der Artillerie

Brand

General der Artillerie

Above: Mid-war document made out to *Oberkanonier* Karl Maier of *2./Heeres-Flak-Art. Abt. 275*. The document is signed by *General der Artillerie* Fritz Brand (German Cross in Silver 23. September 1943, Knights Cross of the War Merit Cross with Swords 24. December 1944).

DEM

Gefreiten

Hermann K o l l e r

16.(Fla)/Pz.-Füs.-Rgt. G.D.

WURDE DAS

HEERES-FLAK-ABZEICHEN

VERLIEHEN

HAUPTQUARTIER O.K.H., DEN 18. Dezember 1944

GENERAL DER HEERES-FLAKTRUPPEN

Wößner

GENERALLEUTNANT

Above: Late-war document made out to *Gefreiter* Hermann Koller of the *PzFüsilier-Rgt der Panzergrenadier-Division Großdeutschland*, signed by *Generalleutnant* Eugen Wößner, who signed all documents for the Army Flak Badge from 25. June 1944 until the end of the war.

THE BADGE IN WEAR

The Army Flak Badge was worn on the left side of the tunic. If the Iron Cross First Class was present, it was to be attached below the higher award. Just as was the case with the Anti-Partisan Badge, the Army Flak Badge could be worn together with the General Assault Badge.

Above: This *Unterscharführer der Waffen-SS* (NCO) wears both the Army Flak Badge and the General Assault Badge below the Iron Cross 1. Class.

Above: This soldier of the *Großdeutschland Division* wears the Iron Cross 1. Class above the General Assault Badge, the Wound Badge in Silver, and the Army Flak Badge on his assault gun wrapper.

STICKPINS

The Army Flak Badge was produced as a miniature in 16 mm size as well as in 9 mm.

Left: 16 mm size miniature of the Army Flak Badge.

Right: 9 mm size miniature of the Army Flak Badge.

FAKES AND REPRODUCTIONS

The number of fakes of the Army Flak Badge is high. In the book by Marc Garlasco, *The Flak Badges of the Luftwaffe and Heer,* 18 different fakes are listed and one can assume the list is ever-growing. As has been said earlier, it is extremely important to study the originals and ask experienced collectors for help and a second opinion, especially when buying any Third Reich war badges or orders.

Left: Obverse of a very convincing fake of an Army Flak Badge of the original maker Wilhelm Hobacher, Wien.

Right: Reverse of the "Hobacher" fake.

THE 1957 VERSION OF THE BADGE

The 1957 version of an Army Flak Badge had the national eagle removed and stayed unchanged otherwise.

Right: Obverse of an early 1957 Army Flak Badge, made by Steinhauer & Lück.

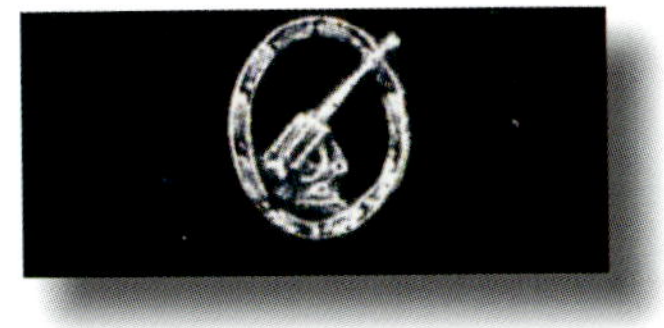

Left: Ribbon bar device for the *Bundeswehr* uniform.

FOOTNOTES

1 *Merkblatt 15/5*, pages 158 - 174

2 Nimmergut, *Deutsche Orden und Ehrenzeichen*, page 2321

3 List compiled from Garlasco, *The Flak Badges of the Luftwaffe and Heer*, pages 260-328

4 *International Medal Collector*, Vol. 1, No. 3, page 35-40

BIBLIOGRAPHY

Doehle, Dr. Heinrich, *Die Auszeichnungen des Grossdeutschen Reichs*, Berlin 1945

Dombrowski, Hanns, *Orden, Ehrenzeichen und Titel*, Franz Wahlen, 1940

Garlasco, Marc, *The Flak Badges of the Luftwaffe and Heer*, B&D Publishing 2008

Geeb, *Deutsche Orden und Ehrenzeichen*, Heymanns Verlag, 1985

Klietmann, Dr. K.-G., *Deutsche Auszeichnungen*, Die Ordens-Sammlung Berlin, 1971

Merkblatt 15/5, *Orden und Ehrenzeichen*, Biblio-Verlag, 1992

Nimmergut, Jörg, *Deutsche Orden und Ehrenzeichen*, Vol. IV, München, 2004

***Allgemeine Heeresmitteilungen*,** Volumes 1939 - 1945

International Medal Collector, Vol. 1, Number 3

Der Uniformen-Markt, Volumes 1939-1945

Schwert und Spaten, Volumes 1939-1945

Chapter 14

The Sniper Badge

Above: A German sniper in a concealed position. The picture is taken from a propaganda film.

Table of Contents

THE SNIPER BADGE

HISTORY

The *Reichsheer* of the Weimar Republic already instituted in 1920 an insignia for sharpshooters. Regarding the publication[1] it was worn as a braid next to the sleeve cuff. However, when the *Wehrmacht* introduced the shooting lanyard in 1936 it was decreed that the sharpshooter insignia was to be omitted.[2]

On 20. July 1943 the following request was issued by the Supreme Command of the Army to all military districts:

> *"It is intended to institute a special badge for sharp shooters to be worn on the uniform. Regarding shape and carrying method proposals made by the troops are very welcome.*
> *The size should not exceed 6 x 4 cm, but deviations for otherwise usable proposals are possible. It can be made from cloth or metal and will be awarded to all privates and NCOs who have fulfilled the requirements for a sharp shooter. Proposals including a simple colored sketch have to be submitted until 15. August 1943 to the Stellv. Gen.Kdo A.A.K. Abt. IIaO."*

The reason to introduce a sniper badge was due on one side to the prominent impact Russian sharp shooters had on the troops which needed to be countered, and on the other hand the fact that only the Iron Crosses Second and First Class were a visible decoration for the German snipers.

The submitted proposals did not satisfy the authorities and an earlier design by Paul Casberg, Berlin, was also rejected. However, out of that design the later accepted one evolved and after a long time of deliberation - mostly about the discrepancy of naming the enemy snipers "bounty hunters" and then awarding the own soldiers for basically the same deed.

Left: Rejected proposal for the Sniper Badge

REGULATIONS

The Sniper Badge was instituted on 20. August 1944 by order of the *Führer.*

> *"In recognition of the full dedication of the single soldier with his rifle as a sniper and in appreciation of the achieved successes I institute for the Army and the SS-Verfügungstruppe*[3] *the Sniper Badge. The Sniper Badge will be awarded in three grades"*

The specific regulations were published by the OKH under the name of the *General der Infanterie* on the same date. The Sniper Badge was to be awarded by the superior officer of at least regimental level to soldiers which were trained and deployed in the role of a sharp-shooter and upon recommendation of the unit leader. The award was accompanied by an award document and was entered into the personnel papers.

Führerbefehle.

168. Scharfschützenabzeichen.

Der Führer
und Oberbefehlshaber der Wehrmacht

F. H. Qu., den 20. 8. 1944

1. In Anerkennung des hohen Einsatzes des Einzelschützen mit Gewehr als Scharfschütze und zur Würdigung der hierbei erzielten Erfolge führe ich für das Heer und die ss-Verfügungstruppe das

Scharfschützenabzeichen

ein.

Das Scharfschützenabzeichen wird in 3 Stufen verliehen.

2. Die Durchführungsbestimmungen erläßt der Gen d Inf b Chef Gen St d H.

The Sniper Badge had three grades. Grade 1 was awarded for at least 20 kills (achieved after 1. September 1944), the 2. Grade was for at least 40 kills and the 3. Grade was to be awarded for at least 60 kills. Any kills during close combat did not count. The enemy needed to be shot in such a way that he remained motionless and should not have been in the process of defection or surrendering.

Abzeichen der Scharfschützen

In Anerkennung des hohen Einsatzes des Einzelschützen mit Gewehr als Scharfschütze und zur Würdigung der hierbei erzielten Erfolge hat der Führer für das Heer und die Waffen-ss das Scharfschützen-Abzeichen eingeführt.

Das Abzeichen ist ein Oval mit Adlerkopf und Eichenlaub und wird auf dem rechten Unterarm getragen. Die Umrandung — ohne, mit silberfarbiger oder goldfarbiger Kordel — kennzeichnet die drei Stufen, in denen das Abzeichen an planmäßig ausgebildete und als Scharfschützen eingesetzte Soldaten verliehen wird.

Right: First picture in the *Uniformen-Markt*, issue September 1944 shows the rejected design but has already the correction from *SS-Verfügungstruppen* to *Waffen-SS.*

DESIGN

Scharfschützenabzeichen
Amtliches Muster – veröffentlicht:
AHM., 21. Ausg., 7. IX. 1944, S. 272
Lw.V.Bl., 3. Ausg., 15. I. 1945, S. 29

The central design of the Sniper Badge is the head of an eagle and two oak leaves. The badge is machine embroidered.

Dr. Doehle, who also prints only a black and white sketch of the badge (not an actual sample) describes the color as:

eagle: black-white
background: grey
oak leaves: dark vermilion green
veining and border: may green
beak and eye: ochre

Left: Design of the Sniper Badge as it was published in the *Heer* and *Luftwaffe* gazettes as "official sample."

Scharfschützenabzeichen
Amtliches Muster – veröffentlicht:
Marine-V.Bl., Heft 2, 15. I. 1945, S. 23

Right: the "official sample" as it was published in the *Marine-Verordnungsblatt* on 15. January 1945.

THE BADGE

The lack of any actual period photograph of the Sniper Badge gave and still gives grounds for intensive discussions about the details and characteristics of genuine examples. All that is known is that genuine examples exist and were given out to the troops. This is also testified to by the fact that all three grades of the badge are shown in the *Handbook of German Military Forces*, issued by the US War Department on 15. March 1945 (left)[4].

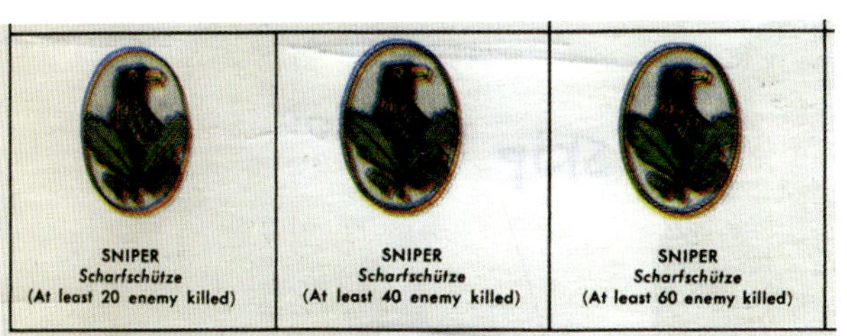

SNIPER *Scharfschütze* (At least 20 enemy killed)	SNIPER *Scharfschütze* (At least 40 enemy killed)	SNIPER *Scharfschütze* (At least 60 enemy killed)

Left: Obverse of a Grade 1 (*1. Stufe*) Sniper Badge believed to be genuine.

Right: Reverse of the same badge.

Left: Obverse of a Grade 2 (*2. Stufe*) Sniper Badge believed to be genuine. The only difference to the Grade 1 is the silver cord surrounding the otherwise unchanged badge.

Right: Obverse of a Grade 3 (*3. Stufe*) Sniper Badge believed to be genuine. The silver cord is replaced by a golden one.

PACKAGES

No known genuine packages for this war badge exist. Everything encountered can be safely assumed to be a post-war production.

AWARD DOCUMENTS

No genuine award documents for the Sniper Badge are known to the authors. Niemann lists in his price guide formal documents as well as typewritten ones on plain paper. At any rate, any documents should be viewed with caution.

THE BADGE IN WEAR

Unfortunately, no pictures of the badge in wear exist.

STICKPINS

No stickpins or ribbon devices of the badge were made before May 1945.

FAKES AND REPRODUCTIONS

All three grades of the badge are faked and are very dangerous since no real comparison fingerprints of the originals have been established as of today.

THE 1957 VERSION OF THE BADGE

The Sniper Badge was authorized for wear on the uniform of the *Bundeswehr* in the form of a ribbon bar device. Instead of the different border cords, the badge was shown in bronze, silver, and gold.

FOOTNOTES

1 *Heeres-Verordnungsblatt, 2. Jhrg, Nr. 77,* 24. Dec. 1920, pages 1013 and 1018

2 OKH - V5 (IIa), 14. September 1936

3 The use of *SS-Verfügungstruppe* was a mistake and was corrected on 28. Sept. to *Waffen-SS*.

4 War Department TM-E 30-451, plate VII

BIBLIOGRAPHY

Doehle, Dr. Heinrich, *Die Auszeichnungen des Grossdeutschen Reichs*, Berlin 1945

Dombrowski, Hanns, *Orden, Ehrenzeichen und Titel*, Franz Wahlen, 1940

Geeb, *Deutsche Orden und Ehrenzeichen*, Heymanns Verlag, 1985

Nimmergut, Jörg, *Deutsche Orden und Ehrenzeichen*, Vol. IV, München, 2004

Der Uniformen-Markt, Volumes 1939-1945

Allgemeine Heeresmitteilungen, Volumes 1934-1945

Handbook of German Military Forces, War Department, Washington, 1945

Chapter 15

The Balloon Observer Badge

Above: Deployment of a German captive balloon on the Eastern Front.

Table of Contents

THE BALLOON OBSERVER BADGE

HISTORY

The observers of the artillery were not only deployed in the trenches at the front line but also served in balloon units. The captive balloon went up to a height of 300 - 1000 meters (900 - 3300 ft). From that position the rear area of the enemy line was to be observed and the friendly artillery fire was to be guided into possible targets.
To perform that task in a small, shaky gondola together with two to three comrades was certainly a very difficult and dangerous task.

On 7. August 1944 the *Allgemeine Heeresmitteilungen* announced that the *Führer* had authorized in recognition of the services of the balloon observers the institution of a Balloon Observer Badge (below).[1]

419. Ballonbeobachterabzeichen.

Verordnung über die Einführung des Ballonbeobachterabzeichens.

1. Der Führer hat in Anerkennung des Einsatzes der Ballonbeobachter die Einführung des Ballonbeobachterabzeichens genehmigt.
2. Das Ballonbeobachterabzeichen ist ein Leistungsabzeichen.
3. Das Ballonbeobachterabzeichen wird an der linken Brustseite getragen.
4. Die zuständigen Vorgesetzten sind für die Einhaltung der Bestimmungen verantwortlich.
5. Die Durchführungsbestimmungen erläßt der Gen d Art b. Chef Gen St d H.

Im Auftrage
Schmundt.

O. K. H., 8. 7. 44
PA/P 5 (f).

REGULATIONS

The Balloon Observer Badge was a "proficiency badge for front line time-tested observers in a captive balloon" and was to be awarded to privates, NCOs, and officers in three grades:

1. Grade - Bronze : for 20 accumulated points
2. Grade - Silver : for 45 accumulated points
3. Grade - Gold : for 75 accumulated points

The point system was defined as follows[2]:

- reconnaissance of important tactical targets, which are especially important, such as troop concentrations, movements, per target (1) point
- fire control of the artillery, per target .... (1) point
- unsuccessfully shot at by enemy artillery or airplane .... (1) point
- front deployment, for four hours each .... (1) point
- damage to the balloon due to enemy fire .... (3) points
- first time parachute jump from the gondola .... (10) points
- each additional jump with a parachute from the gondola .... (5) points

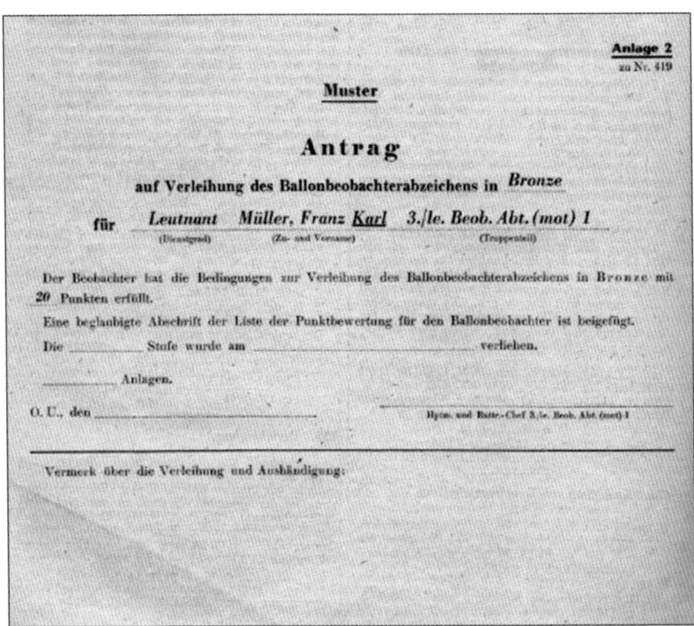

Anlage 2
zu Nr. 419

Muster

Antrag

auf Verleihung des Ballonbeobachterabzeichens in *Bronze*

für *Leutnant* *Müller, Franz Karl* *3./le. Beob. Abt. (mot) 1*
(Dienstgrad) (Zu- und Vorname) (Truppenteil)

Der Beobachter hat die Bedingungen zur Verleihung des Ballonbeobachterabzeichens in Bronze mit *20* Punkten erfüllt.

Eine beglaubigte Abschrift der Liste der Punktbewertung für den Ballonbeobachter ist beigefügt.

Die ________ Stufe wurde am ________________ verliehen.

________ Anlagen.

O. U., den ________________

Hptm. und Battr.-Chef 3./le. Beob. Abt. (mot) 1

Vermerk über die Verleihung und Aushändigung:

Above: The *Heeresmitteilungen* supplied the troops with a sample of the request form for the awarding of the Balloon Observer Badge.

DESIGN

No period sketches nor photographs of the badge are in existence. There was no publication or announcement in the *Uniformen-Markt* nor does Dr. Doehle show the badge in his early 1945 book. He cites the regulations in the amendment of the 5th edition but remarks that an image of the badge was not available at the date of the press time (most likely November 1944).

The late American collector W.C. Stump reports in his exhaustive essay about the Balloon Observer Badge[3] that he was shown an alleged original photograph of the original sample of the badge. The photograph came from the designer of the badge, Ellmar Lang. Klietmann further reported that the badge never made it to the production stage and only one example was made. Mr. Stump comes to the conclusion, based on intensive research, that it was not possible to bring the badge to production and that all examples in existence are post-war fantasy pieces. However, one can find in nearly all publications and price guides the Balloon Observer Badge in all three grades.[4]

Courtesy W.C. Stump

Left: Photograph of the sample regarding to Dr. Klietmann.

THE BADGE

Due to the most likely fact that only one or two pre-production samples of the badge were in existence (even that is disputable), no pictures of the badges can be shown. The example on the cover of this chapter is an artistic rendering of the Bronze grade.

The collector is advised that any badge encountered, no matter how high or low the price, or how good and solid the provenance might allegedly be, can never be positively determined to be an original piece.

PACKAGES

No genuine packages for this war badge exist. Everything encountered can be safely assumed to be a post-war production.

AWARD DOCUMENTS

Nimmergut shows a printed but not named award document for the 1. Grade, complete with signature and stamp.[5] Klietmann shows the exact same document (same stamp, same signature) in his book, but this time awarded to a Willibald Sellner.[6] One or both documents are a fake. The authors doubt the existence of genuine documents.

THE BADGE IN WEAR

Logically, no pictures of the badge in wear exist.

STICKPINS

No stickpins or ribbon devices of the badge were made before May 1945.

FAKES AND REPRODUCTIONS

All three grades of the badge are faked and are very dangerous as no real comparison to a genuine wartime example can be made.

Above and below: Observer balloons are readied for deployment. Note the equipment and manpower necessary to do so.

THE 1957 VERSION OF THE BADGE

The Balloon Observer Badge was authorized for wear on the uniform of the *Bundeswehr* in the form of a ribbon bar device. The regular sized version was also made available in all three grades despite the fact that it was highly unlikely that either the 2. or the 3. Grade was ever awarded, considering the time and the requirements.

Right: Balloon Observer Badge in Gold in the 1957 version.

Left: Balloon Observer Badge in Bronze for the *Bundeswehr* ribbon bar.

FOOTNOTES

1 *Heeres-Verordnungsblatt, 11. Jhrg, Nr. 18*, 7. August 1944, page 236

2 ibid. page 237

3 W.C. Stump/K. Patzwall, *"Das Ballonbeobachterabzeichen des Heeres - existieren zeignössische Originale?" Militaria Magazin, 29. Jhrg.*, Mai/Juni 2006, Heft 3, page 88ff. An Internet version in English also exists on www. wehrmacht-awards.com

4 Nimmergut lists the Silver and Bronze grade, Forman lists Bronze, Silver, and Gold in his 2012 price guide. Niemann also lists all three grades in his price guide.

5 Nimmergut, *Deutsche Orden und Ehrenzeichen*, Vol. IV, page 2330

6 Klietmann, *Auszeichnungen des Deutschen Reichs 1936-1945*, page 122

BIBLIOGRAPHY

Doehle, Dr. Heinrich, *Die Auszeichnungen des Grossdeutschen Reichs*, Berlin 1945

Geeb, *Deutsche Orden und Ehrenzeichen*, Heymanns Verlag, 1985

Klietmann, Kurt, *Auszeichnungen des Deutschen Reichs 1936-1945*, Motorbuch-Verlag, 1989

Niemann, Detlev, *Bewertungskatalog Deutschland 1871-1945*, Niemann-Verlag, 2009

Nimmergut, Jörg, *Deutsche Orden und Ehrenzeichen*, Vol. IV, München, 2004

Der Uniformen-Markt, Volumes 1939-1945

***Allgemeine Heeresmitteilungen*,** Volumes 1934-1945

***Militaria Magazin*,** Patzwall Verlag, Jhrg. 29

Chapter 16

The Army Paratrooper Badge

FALLSCHIRMJÄGER

MELDUNGEN BEI ALLEN WEHRBEZIRKSKOMMANDOS

Above: Period recruitment poster for the *Fallschirmjäger* troops.

Table of Contents

THE ARMY PARATROOPER BADGE

HISTORY

On 20. February 1937 the *Allgemeine Heeresamt* of the Supreme Command of the *Heer* directed the formation of a Paratrooper company with an initial strength of 160 men. The company was to be ready for training on 1. April 1937 in the *Luftwaffe* Parachute School in Stendal/Saxony-Anhalt.

The Supreme Commander of the Army at that time, *Generaloberst* Freiherr von Fritsch instituted for the newly founded troops the Army Paratrooper Badge on 1. September 1937 as a proficiency badge.

The initial paratrooper company grew from 1. June 1938 onwards up to the size of a battalion with its commander *Major* Richard Heidrich (later *General der Fallschirmtruppe*, Knights Cross on 14. June 1941, Oakleaves #382 on 5. February 1944 and Swords # 55 on 25. March 1944) and a strength of about 600 soldiers. The battalion was transferred from Stendal to Braunschweig in November 1938.

On 1. January 1939 the Paratrooper Battalion of the Army was transferred into the *Luftwaffe* as II. Battalion of the Paratrooper Regiment 1.

That ended the awarding of the Paratrooper Badge of the Army temporarily. However, former members of the army paratroopers were allowed to wear the Army Paratrooper Badge instead of the Paratrooper Badge of the *Luftwaffe*.

In the summer of 1943 the *SS-Fallschirmjägerbataillon 500* was formed in Chulm (protectorate Bohemia and Moravia) from volunteers of the *Waffen-SS* divisions and from members of the SS-Punishment Battalions. After costly deployments against partisans in the Balkans the unit was renamed to *SS-Fallschirmjägerbataillon 600* and was deployed in the Baltic, Pomerania, in the Ardennes and in Mecklenburg.

Das Leistungsabzeichen der Fallschirm - Infanterie

Für die Fallschirm-Infanterie ist dieses neue Leistungsabzeichen geschaffen worden, das bei mindestens sechsmaligem Absprung verliehen wird. Aufnahme: Presse-Hoffmann (K)

Left: Announcement of the Army Paratrooper Badge in *Schwert und Spaten*, September 1939.

On 11. March another paratrooper unit of the army was formed in Stendal. This was the paratrooper battalion of the division "Brandenburg." This unit was mainly deployed in the Balkans.

Based on the new formations the *Heerespersonalamt* (HPA, personnel office of the army) saw it fit to reinstitute the Paratrooper Badge of the Army. This was announced on 1. June 1943.[1]

REGULATIONS

In order to be awarded the Army Paratrooper Badge the soldier had to pass the airborne qualification course and successfully complete six jumps ranging in height from 150 to 250 meters.[2]

The amount of jumps as well as the height were recorded in a so-called *Sprungkarte* (jump index card). After successful completion of the training course the soldier was issued a parachute license (*Fallschirmschützenschein*) and the request for the awarding of the Paratrooper Badge was made and issued together with an award document and an entrance into the *Soldbuch*.

Right: The Army Paratrooper Badge as depicted in Dr. Doehle's book.

DESIGN

The Army Paratrooper Badge was instituted about three months after the introduction of the Paratrooper Badge of the Luftwaffe and just as was the case with the Army Flak Badge the design of the new badge was similar to the earlier one already established. The *Luftwaffe* eagle has a swastika in its talons. That was removed and instead the army eagle and the swastika were located on top of the wreath. The wreath with the small eagle was gilded. The larger, diving eagle affixed to it was silvered.

Above: Army Paratrooper Badge (left) and *Luftwaffe* Paratrooper Badge, both by the maker C.E. Juncker, Berlin.

THE BADGE

The early Army Paratrooper Badges were all made of aluminum by C.E. Juncker. Later badges were made of zinc and another maker, Friedrich Linden of Lüdenscheid, joined C.E. Juncker in the manufacture of this very rare badge.

Right: Obverse of a so-called "2nd Pattern" Army paratrooper Badge by C.E. Juncker. The material is aluminum.

Left: Reverse of the badge. The pin system is typical for C.E. Juncker.

Left: Obverse of a 3rd Pattern C.E. Juncker badge. The material is zinc.

Right: Reverse of the badge.

Right: C.E. Juncker also made Army Paratrooper Badges from silver "800". They were available for private purchase.

Left: The reverse of this example is engraved with the name of the recipient. Note the "800" stamp.

Left: The Army Paratrooper Badge was also produced in two cloth versions. This is the 1937/38 version.

Right: The Army Paratrooper Badge in Cloth of the 1943 version.

THE MAKERS OF THE ARMY PARATROOPER BADGE[3]

C.E. Juncker, Berlin	Aluminum	(3) known variations
C.E. Juncker, Berlin	Zinc/Alu	(1) known variation
C.E. Juncker, Berlin	Zinc	(3) known variations
C.E. Juncker, Berlin	Silver	(1) known variation
Friedrich Linden, Lüdenscheid	Zinc	(2) known variations

PACKAGES

The Army Paratrooper Badge was given out in the typical *Luftwaffe*-blue case. The inscription on top reads *Fallschirmschützen-Abzeichen*.

Left: Case for the Army Paratrooper Badge.

Right: The same case open. Note the impression of the Army Paratrooper Badge.

AWARD DOCUMENTS

There are basically two types of documents. The earlier ones from the time frame 1937/38 and the later ones from 1943 onwards.

VERLEIHUNGSURKUNDE

Ich verleihe dem

Oberschützen Reinhold B e l g e r

Dienstgrad, Vor- und Zuname

Fallschirm - Jnfanterie - Kompanie

Truppenteil

das

Fallschirmschützenabzeichen

Oberkommando des Heeres – Inspektion der Infanterie

Dienst-stempel

Der Oberbefehlshaber des Heeres

Im Auftrage

Generalleutnant und Inspekteur der Infanterie

Nr. der Urkunde

Berlin, den 18.12.37

Above: Early document dated 18. December 1937. The early documents had a serial number in the lower left corner.

Das

Fallschirmschützen-Abzeichen des Heeres

ist dem

Gefreiten

Heinz B i e l i g

4./Fallschirmjäger-Bataillon
B r a n d e n b u r g

verliehen worden

Btl.Gef.Stand, am 9.August 1944

Im Auftrage:

Dienstsiegel

№ 00672

Hauptmann u.Btl.Kdr.

8476 Sonderdruck. Gustav Kühn, Neuruppin

Above: Late-war award document to Gefreiter Heinz Bielig *4./Fallschirmjäger-Bataillon "Brandenburg"*.

THE BADGE IN WEAR

Above: *Oberleutnant* Alfred Schwarzmann, *Fallschirmjäger-Regiment 1*, (left, Knights Cross 29. May 1940) together with a comrade of the *Luftwaffe*. Both wear the Army Paratrooper Badge. Alfred Schwarzmann won three team Gold Medals (equestrian) and two individual Bronze Medals (gymnastics) at the 1936 Olympic Games in Berlin.

Above: The *Oberfeldwebel* of the *Luftwaffe* wears the Army Paratrooper Badge above the Sports Badge. The button hole holds the ribbon for the Iron Cross 2nd Class. The ribbon bar shows a *Luftwaffe* Long Service award and another unidentifiable ribbon.

STICKPINS

It might very well be that there are Army Paratrooper stickpins in existence, both in the size of 16 mm and 9 mm. However, none which could be considered genuine have surfaced so far.[4]

FAKES AND REPRODUCTIONS

There are a number of fakes of the Army Parachute Badge on the market. They usually can be spotted by comparing to the very well made originals. So far, none of the reproductions has reached the quality and level of detail which can be found in original badges by Juncker and Linden, the only two genuine makers of this badge.

Left: Fake Army Paratrooper Badge trying to imitate a Juncker model.

THE 1957 VERSION OF THE BADGE

The 1957 version of the Army Paratrooper Badge had the national eagle and the swastika removed. Since the *Luftwaffe* Paratrooper Badge had an eagle with the swastika in its talons, this newly created 1957 version of the Paratrooper Badge was used for both services, *Heer* and *Luftwaffe*.

Right: Obverse of an early 1957 Army Paratrooper Badge.

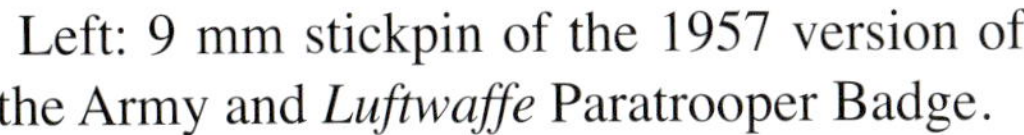

Left: 9 mm stickpin of the 1957 version of the Army and *Luftwaffe* Paratrooper Badge.

Left: Ribbon bar device for the *Bundeswehr* uniform.

FOOTNOTES

1 *Merkblatt 15/5*, page 183, OKH 1.6.43-29e-PA/P5(f)

2 Durante, *The German Luftwaffe and Heer Paratrooper Badge*, page 24

3 List compiled from Durante, *The German Luftwaffe and Heer Paratrooper Badge*, page 435

4 Not even M. Messing, who shows otherwise the most exotic miniatures in his booklet, could produce one. Niemann doesn't show it in his price guide either.

BIBLIOGRAPHY

Doehle, Dr. Heinrich, *Die Auszeichnungen des Grossdeutschen Reichs*, Berlin 1945

Dombrowski, Hanns, *Orden, Ehrenzeichen und Titel*, Franz Wahlen, 1940

Durante, Thomas, *The German Luftwaffe and Heer Paratrooper Badges*, CEJ Books, 2010

Geeb, *Deutsche Orden und Ehrenzeichen*, Heymanns Verlag, 1985

Klietmann, Dr. K.-G., *Deutsche Auszeichnungen*, Die Ordens-Sammlung Berlin, 1971

Merkblatt 15/5, *Orden und Ehrenzeichen*, Biblio-Verlag, 1992

Nimmergut, Jörg, *Deutsche Orden und Ehrenzeichen*, Vol. IV, München, 2004

Queen, Eric, *Red Shines the Sun*, Bender Publishing, San Jose, 2002

Allgemeine Heeresmitteilungen, Volumes 1939 - 1945

Der Uniformen-Markt, Volumes 1939-1945

Schwert und Spaten, Volumes 1939-1945

Chapter 17

The East Medal

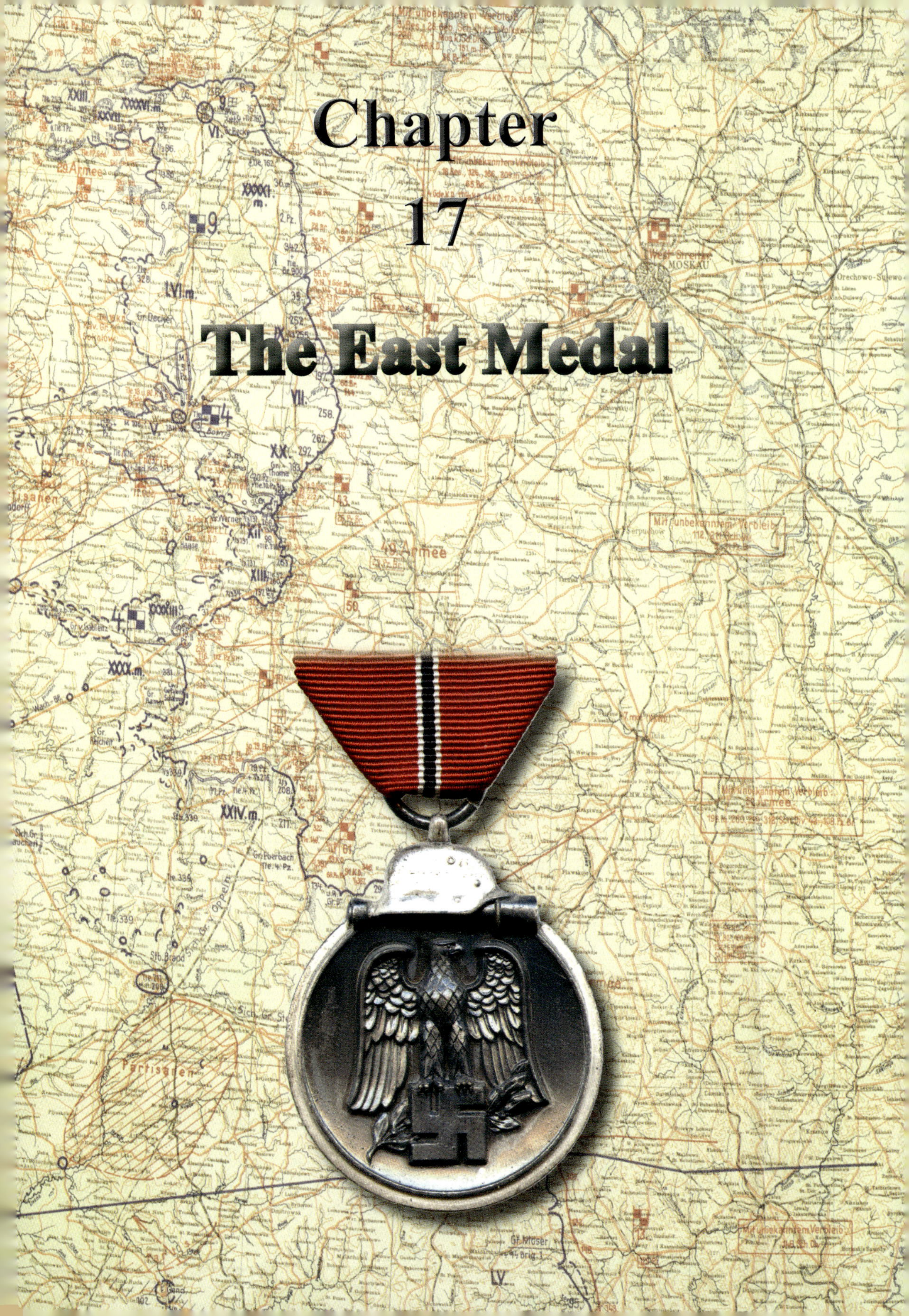

Above: Two German soldiers on watch duty during the winter 1941/1942 in Russia.

Table of Contents

THE EAST MEDAL

HISTORY

The front line in Russia at the beginning of December 1941 was running from Leningrad - west of Moscow - Rostov/Don. The German soldiers were exposed to a winter which was even for Russian proportions a harsh one. The troops had no proper winter clothes. The supply organization, the weapons, the vehicles, and the general equipment was no match for such a brutal winter war.

Starting on the 5./6. December 1941 the Red Army launched a counter offensive with newly arrived troops which were exceptionally well equipped for the winter. Subsequently the German Army Group North lost ground south of Leningrad and German forces were encircled in the areas of Demjansk and Cholm. The German armies of the Army Group Center which were close to Moscow were thrown back to a line Orel-Rshew and the Red Army broke through in the area of Wjasma but failed to cut off the vitally important runway to Smolensk. The Army Group South lost the peninsula of Kertsch and the Red Army gained some ground south of Charkow and in the area of Rostow.

Many of the responsible leaders were convinced that an orderly retreat to better defensive positions was indispensable. Hitler, however, banned any non-authorized retreat and this lead to considerable arguments between him and the Supreme Commander of the Army, Generalfeldmarschall von Brauchitsch. As a direct result von Brauchitsch was removed from his post on 19. December 1941 and Hitler himself resumed the Supreme Command of the Army and issued orders to hold positions at all costs and unconditionally. His decisions were met by many troop leaders with incomprehension, since they saw the desperate struggle and the distress of their troops.

In tactical situations which were previously considered absolutely impossible, and under the harshest conditions and with unspeakable strains on bodies and minds of the troops, it was possible for the Germans to maintain some kind of cohesion on the Eastern Front until March 1942, when the enemy forces were also almost completely exhausted. The spring mud restricted all operations and was a very welcomed reprieve, which was used to stabilize the front line.

The German Army had survived a very hard ordeal and the Russian Army had not succeeded in its strategic goal to encircle and destroy the Army Group Center and therefore bring the whole central part of the front to a total collapse.

The price that was paid by the German army was very high: one quarter of the personnel of the eastern Front and about half of the material was lost during the winter period.

On 22. June 1942 - one year after the start of *Operation Barbarossa* - the following announcement was made in the *Allgemeine Heeresmitteilungen:*

To honor the heroic dedication against the Bolshevik enemy during the winter 1941/1942 I institute the Medal for the 'Winter Battle in the East 1941/42' (East Medal).[1]

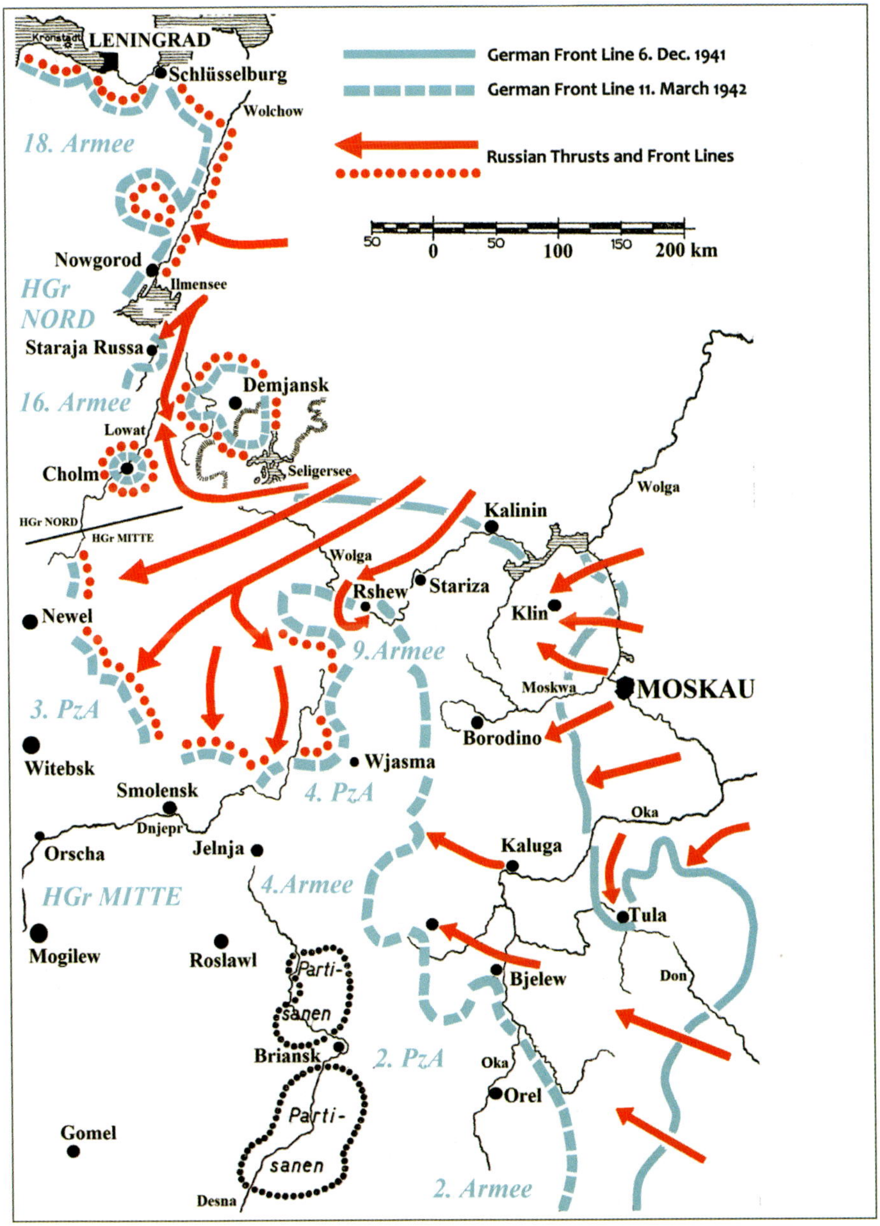

Above: The Russian Winter Offensive 5./6. Dec. 1941 - March 1942 - Army Group North and Army Group Center.

REGULATIONS

The East Medal could be awarded:

- to all members of the *Wehrmacht* and also to non-members of the *Wehrmacht* and to women and to those killed in action.
- to members of allied forces which were subordinated to the *Wehrmacht*.
- to all foreign volunteers fighting within the *Wehrmacht*.
- to volunteers of the Eastern People from the occupied regions of the Soviet Union fighting under the command of the German *Wehrmacht*.

All members of the *Heer* eligible for the East Medal had to be in the area east of Minsk or in the operational area of Finland during the time between 15. November 1941 and 15. April 1942 and had to fulfill the following conditions:

- at least 14 days of active fighting, or
- a wound or a freeze for which a Wound Badge was issued, or
- to prove oneself in another uninterrupted deployment of at least 60 days.

If there was a substantial case of hardship due to the strict adherence to the borderline "east of Minsk" a request for an exception could be made with the Supreme Command of the *Wehrmacht* (OKW).

The troops invented a multitude of nicknames for the East Medal. The most popular was of course the "Frozen Meat Order." Also popular were "Snowman with Steel Helmet," "Runway Medal," "Winter Sport Medal," and "Vacation Substitute."

The distribution of the medal ended officially on 15. October 1944. At that point in time the number of awarded medals was most likely between 2.5 - 3.0 Million. To this one has to add the medals in storage and production. This most likely makes the East Medal one of the most produced medals of the Third Reich. This is also reflected in the amount of makers.

——— = Verleihungsgrenze für die Ostmedaille

Anmerkung:
Die Städte Kiew und Dnjepropetrowsk liegen in ihrer Gesamtheit westlich der Verleihungsgrenze

Above: The official map of the border line for the award area.[2]

DESIGN

The East Medal was designed by the war reporter of the *SS-Leibstandarte Adolf Hitler*, Ernst Krause[2]. The medal is round with a white border, crowned by a white German steel helmet and a German hand grenade. The obverse shows the the German national eagle with a swastika in its talons. The reverse holds the inscription "*Winterschlacht im Osten 1941/42*" with a laurel branch crossed by a sword.

The medal came with a red ribbon with a central white-black-white strip. The ribbon was worn in the second button hole of the tunic, the medal itself was only worn on the medal bar.

Ostmedaille

Above: The East Medal as depicted in Dr. Doehle's book. Even the meaning of the ribbon was subjected to some typical soldier humor. It was described as "Street in the middle, snow, and the Red Army left and right."

THE MEDAL

All genuine examples of the East Medal are made of zinc. The ribbon ring is usually made of iron and holds the maker's mark, if present. A large number of makers produced the East Medal and most of their medals are marked with the *Präsidialkanzlei* number, but some also have the LDO code stamped into the ring.

Left: Obverse of an East Medal. The ring is marked with "14" which stands for Christian Lauer, Nürnberg.

Right: Reverse of the medal.

Right: Obverse of an East Medal which has retained the silver border and the silver steel helmet.

Left: Reverse of the medal. The ring is stamped "65" for Klein & Quenzer, Idar-Oberstein.

THE MAKERS OF THE EAST MEDAL[4]

PKZ	Company	Town
1	Deschler & Sohn	München
3	Wilhelm Deumer	Lüdenscheid
4	Steinhauer & Lück	Lüdenscheid
5	Hermann Wernstein	Jena-Lobstedt
6	Fritz Zimmermann	Stuttgart
7	Paul Meybauer	Berlin
8	Ferdinand Hoffstätter	Bonn
10	Förster & Barth	Pforzheim
11	Grossmann & Co.	Wien
13	Gustav Brehmer	Markneukirchen
14	Christian Lauer	Nürnberg
15	Friedrich Orth	Wien
16	Alois Rettenmayer	Schwäbisch-Gmünd
18	Karl Wurster KG	Markneukirchen
19	E. Ferd. Wiedmann	Frankfurt/Main
20	C.F. Zimmermann	Pforzheim
21	Gebrüder Godet & Co.	Berlin
22	Boerger & Co	Berlin
23	Arbeitsgemeinschaft f. Heeresbedarf ...	Berlin
25	Arbeitsgemeinschaft der Graveure, ..	Hanau
26	B.H. Mayer Kunstprägeanstalt	Pforzheim
28	Eugen Schmidhäussler	Pforzheim
29	Hauptmünzamt Berlin	Berlin
30	Hauptmünzamt Wien	Wien
35	F.W. Assmann und Söhne	Lüdenschied
39	Rudolf Berge	Gablonz a.d. Neiße
41	Gebrüder Bender	Gablonz a.d. Neiße
43	Julias Bauer &Söhne	Zella-Mehlis
50	Karl Gschiermeister	Wien
51	Eduard Görlach & Söhne	Gablonz a.d. Neiße
53	Glaser & Söhne	Dresden
55	J.E. Hammer & Söhne	Geringswald
57	Karl Henzler	Pforzheim
58	Artur Jöckel & Co.	Gablonz a.d. Neiße

PKZ	Company	Town
60	Katz & Deyhle	Pforzheim
61	Rudolf A. Karneth	Gablonz a.d. Neiße
63	Franz Klast & Söhne	Gablonz a.d. Neiße
65	Klein & Quenzer	Idar-Oberstein
66	Friedrich Keller	Oberstein
71	Rudolf Leukert,	Gablonz a.d. Neiße
73	Franz Manert	Gablonz a.d. Neiße
74	Carl Maurer & Sohn	Oberstein
76	Ernst L. Müller	Pforzheim
77	Hauptmünzamt München	München
80	G.H. Osang	Dresden
83	Emil Peukert	Gablonz a.d. Neiße
85	Julius Pietsch	Gablonz a.d. Neiße
88	Werner Redo	Saarlautern
92	Josef Rückert & Sohn	Gablonz a.d. Neiße
93	Richard Simm & Söhne	Gablonz a.d. Neiße
98	Rudolf Souval	Wien
100	Rudolf Wächtler & Lange	Mittweida
107	Carl Wild	Hamburg
108	Arno Wallpach	Salzburg
110	Otto Zappe	Gablonz a.d. Neiße
112	Argentorwerke Rust & Hetzel	Wien
117	Hugo Lang	Wiesenthal
127	Moriz Hausch AG	Pforzheim
138	Julius Maurer	Oberstein
n/a	Metallwarenfabrik Posen	Posen

Table might not show all makers due to ongoing research.

LDO	Company	Town
L/55	Rudolf Wächtlere & Lange	Mittweida
L/57	Boerger & Co.	Berlin
L/58	Rudolf Souval	Wien

THE SPANISH VERSION OF THE EAST MEDAL

The Spanish Blue Division fought in the Army Group North in the area of Leningrad during the Winter of 1941/42. The members of the division were sworn to Hitler and therefore eligible for the award of the East Medal.

Left: Obverse of a Spanish-made East Medal with the typical ribbon device.

Right: Reverse of the same East Medal.

PACKAGES

The East Medal was distributed in the normal *Zellstoffbeutel*. The paper bags had the imprint *Medaille "Winterschlacht im Osten 1941/42" (Ostmedaille)*. The reverse of the bags had in most cases the name of the maker imprinted.

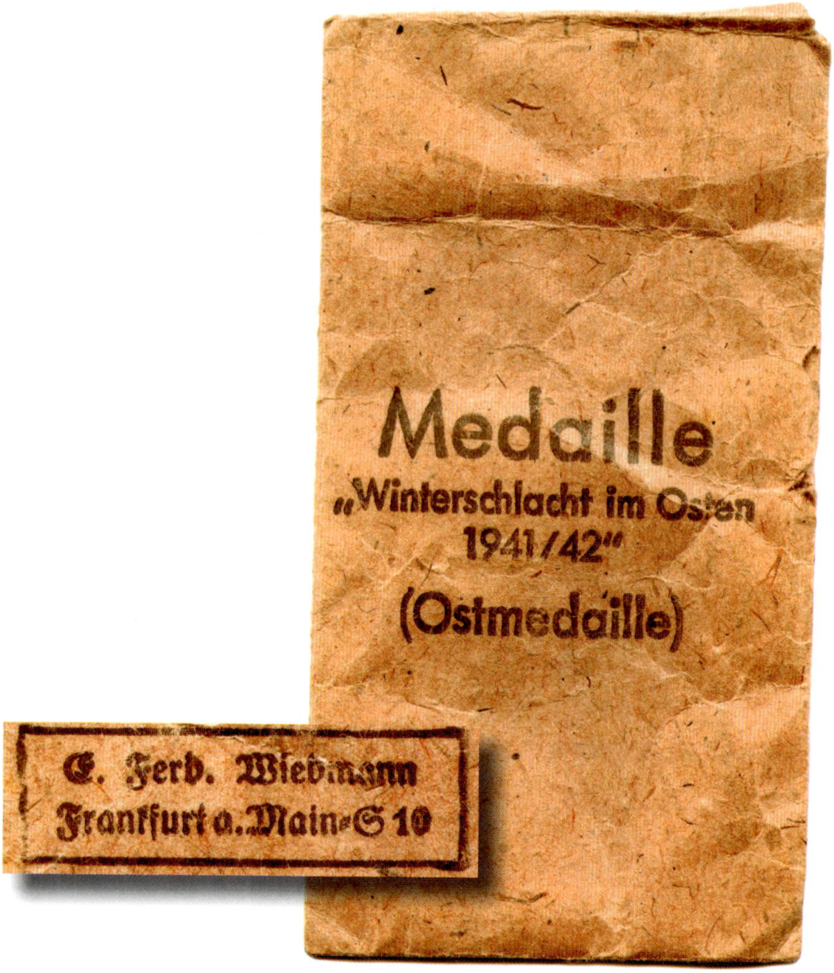

Above: Typical paper bag for the East Medal with the imprint of the maker on the reverse.

AWARD DOCUMENTS

The great majority of all award documents of the East Medal used the predetermined sample, but also multiple decorative versions exist.

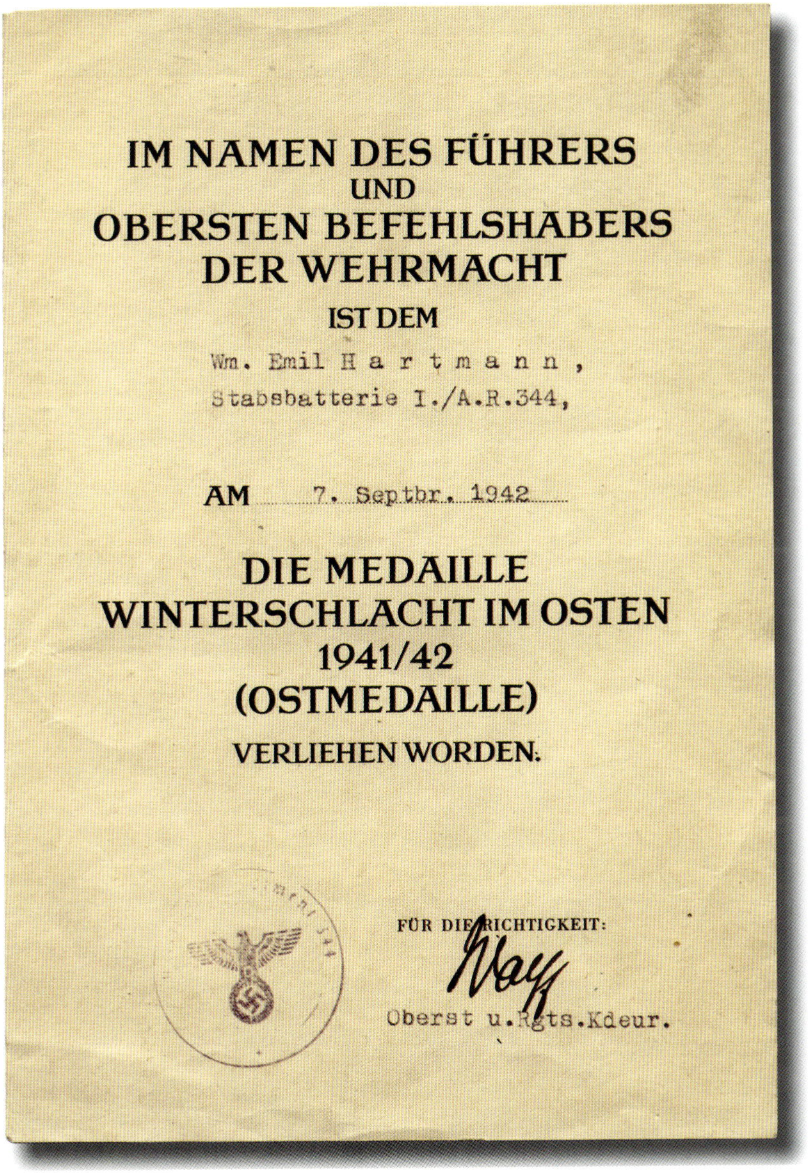

IM NAMEN DES FÜHRERS
UND
OBERSTEN BEFEHLSHABERS
DER WEHRMACHT
IST DEM
Wm. Emil H a r t m a n n ,
Stabsbatterie I./A.R.344,

AM 7. Septbr. 1942

DIE MEDAILLE
WINTERSCHLACHT IM OSTEN
1941/42
(OSTMEDAILLE)
VERLIEHEN WORDEN.

FÜR DIE RICHTIGKEIT:
Oberst u.Rgts.Kdeur.

Above: Standard document for the East Medal, signed by the commander of the *Artillerierregiment 344*.

IM NAMEN DES FÜHRERS
UND
OBERSTEN BEFEHLSHABERS
DER WEHRMACHT
IST DEM

Obergefreiten Karl S c h a i b

AM 13. 8. 1942

DIE MEDAILLE
WINTERSCHLACHT IM OSTEN
1941/42
(OSTMEDAILLE)

VERLIEHEN WORDEN.

FÜR DIE RICHTIGKEIT:

Major ~~im Stabe des~~
~~Stellv.Gen.Kdo.XII.A.K.~~

Lfde. Nr. ....

Above: Another standard document for the East Medal for *Obergefreiter* Karl Schaib. He was a member of the *2./Fla-Btl (mot) 602* of the *Heeresflak*.

IM NAMEN DES
FUEHRERS UND
OBERSTEN
BEFEHLSHABERS
DER WEHRMACHT
VERLEIHE ICH DEM

Gefreiten Kurt Müller
5./Grenadier-Regiment 487

DIE MEDAILLE
„WINTERSCHLACHT
IM OSTEN 1941/42"

Im Felde, den 11. Nov. 1942

Oberstleutnant u. Rgt.Kommandeur

Above: Unusual document for the East Medal, made out to *Gefreiter* Kurt Müller in the *Grenadier-Regiment 487* (*267. Infanterie-Division*, part of the *LVI. Panzerkorps*). Part of that *Korps* was the *Korpskartenstelle (mot) 456*, which produced this unusual documents.

THE MEDAL IN WEAR

The East Medal could only be worn on the parade medal bar. On the regular uniform either the ribbon alone was worn in the second button hole or as a ribbon bar above the right breast pocket.

Above: *General der Panzertruppe* Walther Kurt Nehring wears the ribbon of the East Medal in the second button hole.

Above: *Major d.R.* Dr. Hans Gidion (Knights Cross 7. August 1942) wears the East Medal on the ribbon bar in the second position.

Above: Parade medal bar with the East Medal at third place behind the Iron Cross 2nd Class and the War Merit Cross 2nd Class with Swords.

Above: *Luftwaffe* member parade medal bar with the East Medal at fourth place, behind the Medal for the Commemoration of the 1. October 1938. This arrangement is wrong, that medal should be at the last place because the East Medal was a war decoration.

MINIATURES AND STICKPINS

The East Medal was produced in 16 mm size as a miniature with a ribbon and also as a 9 mm stickpin.

Right: 9 mm size miniature of the East Medal.

Left: 16 mm size miniature of the East Medal with the ribbon.

Right: 9 mm size stickpin combination with the East Medal at fourth place. Only the East Medal is marked "L/16" for Steinhauer & Lück.

FAKES AND REPRODUCTIONS

Even such a low priced high production award as the East Medal is faked. It seems that even a market price of $ 40.- (2012) makes the faking a profitable venture. Comparison with known and verified period examples is extremely advisable.

Left: Obverse of a very convincing fake, only disguised by some minor production flaws (rims) and the stamp “585”.

Right: Reverse of the same fake.

THE 1957 VERSION OF THE MEDAL

The 1957 version of the East Medal had the swastika on the obverse replaced with a laurel wreath. The reverse stayed unchanged.

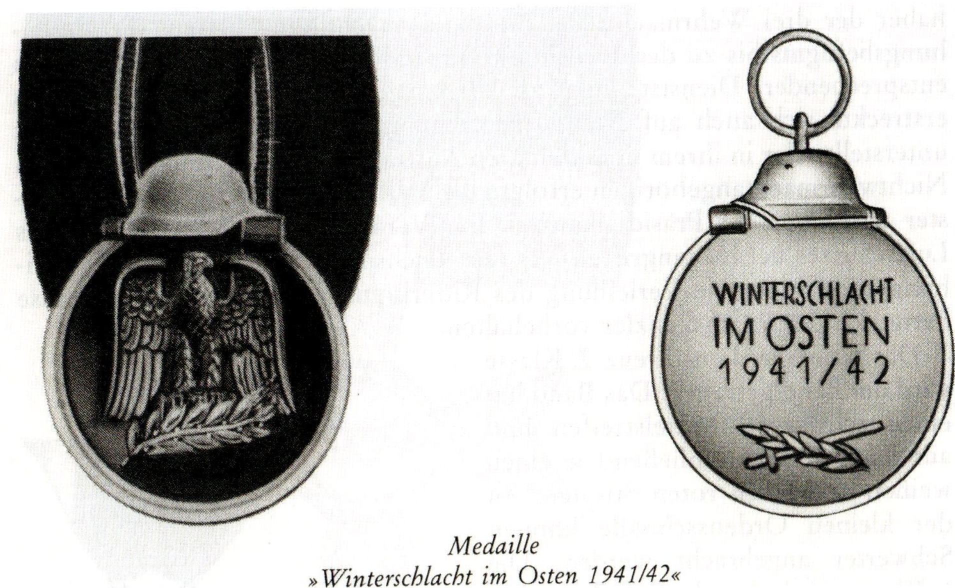

Medaille
»Winterschlacht im Osten 1941/42«

Left: The ribbon device was left unchanged.

FOOTNOTES

1 *Allgemeine Heeresmitteilungen, 9. Jhrg., 15. Ausgabe,* 22. June 1942

2 *Merkblatt 15/5*, Appendix

3 Nimmergut, *Deutsche Orden und Ehrenzeichen*, page 2233

4 List compiled with the help of members of the collector community, as of June 2012.

BIBLIOGRAPHY

Doehle, Dr. Heinrich, *Die Auszeichnungen des Grossdeutschen Reichs*, Berlin 1945

Dombrowski, Hanns, *Orden, Ehrenzeichen und Titel*, Franz Wahlen, 1940

Geeb, *Deutsche Orden und Ehrenzeichen*, Heymanns Verlag, 1985

Klietmann, Dr. K.-G., *Deutsche Auszeichnungen*, Die Ordens-Sammlung Berlin, 1971

Merkblatt 15/5, *Orden und Ehrenzeichen*, Biblio-Verlag, 1992

Nimmergut, Jörg, *Deutsche Orden und Ehrenzeichen*, Vol. IV, München, 2004

Allgemeine Heeresmitteilungen, Volumes 1939 - 1945

Der Uniformen-Markt, Volumes 1939-1945

Schwert und Spaten, Volumes 1939-1945

Appendix

Neuester Stand der Genehmigungen der Präsidialkanzlei

zur Herstellung von Orden, Ehrenzeichen, Ordenbändern und Ordendekorationen für den privaten Handel

Die häufigen Anfragen bei unserer Schriftleitung über das neueste Verzeichnis der von der Präsidialkanzlei erteilten Genehmigungen zur Herstellung von Orden, Ehrenzeichen, Ordenbändern und Ordendekorationen für den privaten Handel veranlassen uns, nachstehend eine vollständige Aufstellung (Stand vom 15. Februar 1944) zu veröffentlichen. [illegible] sich, das Verzeichnis sorgfältig auf[illegible] Ergänzungen zweckmäßig eingefügt werden können.

Die Schriftleitung.

A. Herstellerfirmen für Orden und Ehrenzeichen

Boerger & Co., Berlin SO 16, Adalbertstr. 42
Brehmer, Gustav, Markneukirchen i. Sa.
Deschler & Sohn, München 9, Wirtstr. 9
Deumer, Wilhelm, Lüdenscheid, Postfach 151
Förster & Barth, Pforzheim, Tunnelstr. 71
Funcke & Brüninghaus, Lüdenscheid, Postschließfach
Gebr. Godet & Co., Berlin W 8, Charlottenstr. 55
Hoffstätter, Ferdinand, Bonn a. Rh., Postfach 321
Hymmen & Co., Lüdenscheid, Karlstraße
Juncker, C. E., Berlin SW 68, Alte Jakobstr. 13
Koechert, A. E., Wien I, Neuer Markt 15
Lauer, L. Chr., Nürnberg-W.
Maurer, Julius, Oberstein a. d. Nahe
B. H. Mayer's Hof-Kunstprägeanstalt, Pforzheim
Orth, Friedrich, Wien 56, Schmalzhofgasse 18
Rettenmaier, A., Schwäb. Gmünd, Parlerstr. 27
Schauerte & Höhfeld, Lüdenscheid
Souval, Rudolf, Wien, Straße der Julikämpfer 23
Steinhauer & Lück, Lüdenscheid
Wächtler & Lange, Rudolf, Mittweida (Sa.)
Wernstein, Hermann, Jena-Löbstedt
Wiedmann, E. Ferd., Frankfurt a. M., S. 10, Schifferstraße 52—54
Zimmermann, C. F., Pforzheim, Luisenstr. 55
Zimmermann, Fritz, Stuttgart-W, Silberburgstr. 58.

B. Herstellerfirmen für Ordenbänder

Botschen, Joh. Carl, Böhm.-Leipa (Sudetengau)
Dittrich, Albrecht, Leipzig C 1, Blücherstr. 11
Feldhoff & Co., Langenberg (Rheinland)
Freyberger, Lohmann & Co., W.-Oberbarmen, Postfach 658
Harpke & Sohn, Anton, Pilnikau, Kreis Trautenau (Sudetengau)
Keßler, W. & G., Berlin SO 36, Hoffmanndamm 31
Knoblauch, Carl, Berlin C 2, Poststr. 23
Koppold, Josef, München 2, Tegernseer Str. 2
Langensiepen & Müller, W.-Ronsdorf
Löwer, Rudolf, W.-Ronsdorf
Loy, Carl, München 5, Westermühlstr. 28
[illegible], Heinrich, Kettwig (Ruhr)
[illegible]önig, Remscheid-Lüttringhausen.

C. Herstellerfirmen für Ordendekorationen

Acker, Hugo, Stuttgart-N., Königsbaupassage
Bender, Albrecht, Weißenburg i. Bay.
Bertsch, L., Karlsruhe, Kaiserstr. 165
Buckstöver, Bruno, Kiel, Gerhardstr. 85
Cramer, Käthe, Köln, Hahnenstr. 52
Engelhardt, Georg, Darmstadt, Bismarckstr. 54
Esser & Co., Köln, Auf dem Hunnenrücken 32
Fahnen-Winkler, Fürth i. Bay., Königsplatz 8
Fleck & Sohn, Hamburg 11, Rödingsmarkt 1
Gante, Erich & Ida, Berlin SW 68, Dresdner Str. 71
Geißler, Wilhelm, Leipzig C 1, Michaelstr. 7
Gutenkunst, Erich, Berlin-Schöneberg, Hauptstr. 136
Harbrecht-Baun, Stuttgart, Arnimstr. 19
Hecker, Chr. Gottlob, Leipzig C 1, Thomasgasse 4
Herbeck jun., Rudolf, W.-Elberfeld, Kolk 13
Hoegen, Emma, Köln-Ehrenfeld, Venloer Str. 251
vom Hofe, Albert, Lüdenscheid, Loher Straße
Jüngermann, Carl, Lüdenscheid
Kottke, Max, Berlin O 112, Frankfurter Allee 323
Küst, Max, Berlin, Niederwallstr. 32
Küst, Paul, Berlin SW 68, Seydelstr. 19a
Liepe, Wolfgang, Berlin NW 87, Flensburger Str. 9
Meyer, Friedrich, A. H., Berlin-Friedenau, Moselstr. 13
Müncheberg, Richard, Berlin SW 68, Wilhelmstr. 22
Muthig, Heinrich Alex, Bernburg a. d. Saale
Pfeiffer, E. C., W.-Barmen, Freiheitstr. 42
Puttlitz & Söhne, Gustav, Stettin, Schulzenstr. 20
Reich, Max, Breslau 1, Ring 55
Reifferscheidt, F., Leipzig C 1, Nordstr. 19
Reisener, Carl, Berlin SW 68, Ritterstr. 64
Schiffer, Eduard, Bielefeld
Schulz, Theodor, Schalksmühle i. Westf., Adolf-Hitler-Platz 4
Schwerdt, Ad., Stuttgart-S., Tübinger Str. 31
Timm, Heinrich, Berlin C 2, Wallstr. 9
Weber-Liel & Co., A. M., Hamburg 11, Gr. Burstah

List of *Präsidialkanzlei* Numbers

1 Deschler und Sohn, München
2 C. E. Juncker, Berlin
3 Wilhelm Deumer, Lüdenscheid
4 Steinhauer und Lück, Lüdenscheid
5 Hermann Wernstein, Jena-Lobstedt
6 Fritz Zimmermann, Stuttgart
7 Paul Meybauer, Berlin
8 Ferdinand Hoffstätter, Bonn/Rhein
9 Liefergemeinschaft Pforzheimer Schmuckhandwerker, Pforzheim
10 Förster und Barth, Pforzheim
11 Grossmann und Co., Wien
12 Frank und Reif, Stuttgart
13 Gustav Brehmer, Markneukirchen
14 Lauer, Nürnberg
15 Friedrich Orth, Wien
16 Alois Rettenmaier, Schwäbisch Gmünd
17 unknown
18 Karl Wurster KG, Markneukirchen
19 E. Ferd. Wiedmann, Frankfurt am Main
20 C. F. Zimmermann, Pforzheim
21 Gebr. Godet & Co., Berlin
22 Boerger & Co., Berlin
23 Arbeitsgemeinschaft für Heeresbedarf in der Graveur- und Ziselier-innung, Berlin
24 Arbeitsgemeinschaft der Hanauer Plakettenhersteller, Hanau
25 Arbeitsgemeinschaft der Gravur-, Gold- und Silberschmiedinnungen, Hanau
26 B.H. Mayer, Pforzheim
27 Anton Schenkl, Wien
28 Eugen Schmiedehäussler, Pforzheim
29 Hauptmünzamt, Berlin
30 Hauptmünzamt, Wien
31 Hans Gnad, Wien
32 W. Hobacher, Wien
33 Friedrich Linden, Lüdenscheid
34 Willy Annetsberger, München
35 F.W. Assmann und Söhne, Lüdenscheid
36 Bury & Leonhard, Hanau
37 Adolf Baumeister, Lüdenscheid
38 Josef Bergs, Gablonz

39 Rudolf Berge, Gablonz
40 Berg & Nolte, Lüdenscheid
41 Gebrüder Bender, Oberstein
42 Biedermann & Co., Oberkassel bei Bonn
43 Julius Bauer & Söhne, Zella-Mehlis
44 Jakob Bengel, Idar-Oberstein
45 Franz Jungwirth, Wien
46 Hans Doppler, Wela Oberdonau
47 Erhard & Söhne A.G., Schwäbisch Gmünd
48 Richard Feix, Gablonz
49 Josef Feix & Söhne, Gablonz
50 Karl Gschiermeister, Wien
51 Eduard Görlach & Söhne, Gablonz
52 Gottlieb & Wagner, Idar Oberstein
53 Glaser & Sohn, Dresden
54 unknown
55 J.E. Hammer & Söhne, Geringswald
56 Robert Hauschild, Pforzheim
57 Karl Hensler, Pforzheim
58 Artur Jäkel & Co., Gablonz
59 Louis Keller, Oberstein
60 Katz & Deyle, Pforzheim
61 Rudolf A. Karneth & Sohn, Gablonz
62 Kerbach & Österhelt, Dresden
63 Franz J. Klast & Söhne, Gablonz
64 Gottlieb Friedrich Keck & Sohn, Pforzheim
65 Klein & Quenzer, Idar Oberstein
66 Friedrich Keller, Oberstein
67 Robert H. Kreisel, Gablonz
68 Alfred Knobloch, Gablonz
69 Alois Klammer, Innsbruck
70 Lind & Meyrer, Oberstein
71 Rudolf Leukert, Gablonz
72 Franz Lipp, Pforzheim
73 Franz Mänert, Gablonz
74 Carl Maurer & Sohn, Oberstein
75 unknown
76 Ernst L. Müller, Pforzheim
77 Hauptmünzamt, München
78 Gustav Miksch, Gablonz
79 unknown

80 G.H. Osang, Dresden
81 Overhoff & Cie, Lüdenscheid
82 Augustin Prager, Gablonz
83 Emil Peukert, Gablonz
84 Carl Pellath, Schrobenhausen
85 Julius Pietsch, Gablonz
86 Paulmann & Crone, Lüdenscheid
87 Roman Palme, Gablonz
88 Werner Redo, Saarlautern
89 Rudolf Richter, Schlag bei Gablonz
90 August F. Richter KG, Hamburg
91 Josef Rössler & Sohn, Gablonz
92 Josef Rücker & Sohn, Gablonz
93 Richard Simm & Söhne, Gablonz
94 unknown
95 Adolf Scholze, Grünwald
96 unknown
97 unknown
98 Rudolf Souval, Wien
99 Schwertner & Cie, Granz-Eggenberg
100 Rudolf Wächtler & Lange, Mittweida
101 Rudolf Tham, Gablonz
102 Philipp Türk, Wien
103 August G. Tam, Gablonz
104 Heinrich Ulbrichts, Kaufing
105 Heinrich Vogt, Pforzheim
106 Gebrüder Schneider, Wien
107 Karl Wild, Hamburg
108 Arno Wallpach, Salzburg
109 Walter & Henlein, Gablonz
110 Otto Zappe, Gablonz
111 Ziemer & Söhne, Oberstein
112 Argentor-Werke Rust & Hetzel, Wien
113 Herman Aurich, Dresden
114 Ludwig Bertsch, Karlsruhe
115 unknown
116 Funcke & Brüninghaus, Lüdenscheid
117 Hugo Lang, Wiesenthal
118 August Menz & Sohn, Wien
119 unknown

120 Franz Petzl, Wien
121 unknown
122 J. J. Stahl, Straßburg
123 Beck, Hassinger & Co., Straßburg
124 Rudolf Schanes, Wien
125 Eugen Gauss, Pforzheim
126 Eduard Hann, Oberstein
127 Moriz Hausch AG, Pforzheim
128 S. Jablonski GmbH, Posen
129 Fritz Kohm, Pforzheim
130 Wilhelm Schröder & Co., Lüdenscheid
131 Heinrich Wander, Gablonz
132 Franz Reischauer, Idar Oberstein
133 unknown
134 Otto Klein & Co., Hanau
135 Julius Moser sen., Oberstein
136 J. Wagner & Sohn, Berlin
137 J. H. Werner, Berlin
138 Julius Maurer, Oberstein
139 Hymmen & Co., Lüdenscheid
140 Schauerte & Hohfeld, Lüdenscheid
141 Sohni, Heubach & Co., Oberstein
142 A. D. Schwerdt, Stuttgart

List of LDO numbers

L/10 Deschler & Sohn, München
L/11 Wilhelm Deumer, Lüdenscheid
L/12 C. E Juncker, Berlin
L/13 Paul Meybauer, Berlin
L/14 Friedrich Orth, Wien
L/15 Otto Schickle, Pforzheim
L/16 Steinhauer & Lück, Lüdenscheid
L/17 Hermann Wernstein, Jena-Lobstedt
L/18 B. H. Mayer, Pforzheim
L/19 Ferdinand Hoffstätter, Bonn
L/21 Förster & Barth, Pforzheim
L/22 Glaser & Sohn, Dresden
L/23 Julius Maurer, Oberstein
L/24 Fritz Zimmermann, Stuttgart
L/25 A. E. Köchert, Wien
L/26 Klein & Quenzer, Idar-Oberstein
L/50 Gebr. Godet, Berlin
L/51 E. Ferd. Wiedmann, Frankfurt am Main
L/52 C. F. Zimmermann, Pforzheim
L/53 Hymmen & Co., Lüdenscheid
L/54 Schauerte & Höhfeld, Lüdenscheid
L/55 Wächtler & Lange, Mittweida
L/56 Funcke & Brüninghaus, Lüdenscheid
L/57 Boerger & Co., Berlin
L/58 Rudolf Souval, Wien
L/59 Alois Rettenmaier, Schwäbisch Gmünd
L/60 Gustav Brehmer, Markneukirchen
L/61 Friedrich Linden, Lüdenscheid
L/62 Werner Redo, Saarlautern
L/63 G. H. Osang, Dresden
L/64 F. W. Assmann & Söhne, Lüdenscheid
L/65 Franke & Co., Lüdenscheid
L/66 A. D. Schwerdt, Stuttgart

GENERAL BIBLIOGRAPHY

Angolia, John R., *For Führer and Fatherland,* Bender Publishing, San Jose, 1976

Brinkmann, Jürgen, *Orden und Ehrenzeichen des Dritten Reiches,* J. Brinkmann, Minden 1977

Dotti, Giorgio, *Tapferkeits- und Verdienstauszeichnungen der deutschen Wehrmacht 1933-1945*, Ermanno Albertelli Verlag, Castelbolognese, 1991

Dörr, Manfred, *Die Inhaber der Anerkennungsurkunde des Oberbefehlshaber des Heeres 1941-1945,* Biblio-Verlag, Osnabrück, 1993

Nenning/Herfurth, *Orden & Ehrenzeichen - Handbuch der Phaleristik*, Böhlau-Verlag, 2010

Hettler, Eberhard, *Uniformen der Deutschen Wehrmacht*, reprint of the edition 1939/45, Militariaarchiv Patzwall, Hamburg 1979

Hormann, Jörg-M., *Uniformen der Panzertruppe 1917 bis heute*, Podzun-Pallas Verlag, Friedberg 1989

Keilig, Wolf, *Die Generale des Heeres*, Podzun-Pallas Verlag, Friedberg 1993

Lenfeld, Erwin & Thomas, Franz, *Die Eichenlaubträger 1940-1945*, Weilburg Verlag, Wiener Neustadt 1983

Michaelis, Rolf, *Deutsche Kriegsauszeichnungen 1939-1945*, Michaelis-Verlag, Berlin 2003

Nimmergut, Jörg, *Bibliographie zur Deutschen Phaleristik*, Battenberg-Verlag, 2010

Range, Clemens & Düfel, Andreas, *Die Ritterkreuzträger in der Bundeswehr*, Selbstverlag Range/Düfel, Berlin/Suderburg 2000

Scharfenberg/Thiede, *Lexikon der Ordenskunde*, Battenberg-Verlag, 2010

Schlicht, Adolf/Angolia, John R., *Die Deutsche Wehrmacht 1933-1945, Band 1, Das Heer,* Motorbuchverlag, Stuttgart 1992

Waffen-Revue, miscellaneous issues

TABLE OF CONTENTS
VOLUME II